# Trout Rigs & Methods

# Trout Rigs & Methods

All you need to know to construct rigs
that work for all types of trout flies
& the most effective fishing methods
for catching more & larger trout

# Dave Hughes

STACKPOLE
BOOKS

Copyright © 2007 by Dave Hughes

Published by
STACKPOLE BOOKS
5067 Ritter Road
Mechanicsburg, PA 17055
www.stackpolebooks.com

Printed in the United States

First edition

10  9  8  7  6  5  4  3  2  1

*Illustrations by Dave Hall*
*Cover design by Caroline Stover*

**Library of Congress Cataloging-in-Publication Data**

Hughes, Dave, 1945–
    Trout rigs and methods : all you need to know to construct rigs that work for all types of trout flies and the most effective fishing methods for catching more and larger trout / Dave Hughes. — 1st ed.
        p. cm.
    ISBN-13: 978-0-8117-3354-0 (alk. paper)
    ISBN-10: 0-8117-3354-8 (alk. paper)
    1. Fishing rigs. 2. Trout fishing. I. Title.

SH452.9.R5H84 2007
799.17'57—dc22
                                                2006025046

# CONTENTS

**PART 3.   LAKES AND PONDS**                                **253**

# INTRODUCTION

# The Full Range of Rigs and Methods

The more versatile you become as a trout fisherman, the more often you'll catch trout, the fewer times you'll get skunked, and the more and inevitably larger trout you'll catch. The wider the range of ways you learn to rig your fly-fishing tackle and the greater the number of methods with which you're able to apply each given rig against trout, the more trout fishing situations you're going to be able to solve, and the more often you're going to go home happy because that day, building into days upon days, you caught fish.

A *rig* is the way your terminal tackle is set up: The type of fly line, the length and taper of your leader, the length and strength of the tippet at the end of the leader, the fly tied to the tippet, and any trinkets fixed to the leader and tippet—split shot, putty weight, strike indicators, dropper flies, point flies, and indicator flies— all constitute a rig. It might be as simple as a 10-foot knotless tapered leader and a single dry fly or as complex as a hand-tied tapered leader with a couple of indicators a foot apart and three flies of ascending or descending size with putty weight or tiny split shot pinched to each short section of tippet between the flies.

I was reminded about the value of knowing a wide array of rigs on a recent fishing trip. After driving across Oregon's Cascade Range with physician Curt Marr to a small cattail-lined pond in flat wheat country, I expected to encounter the normal morning and evening midge hatches that happen nearly every spring day on almost all such stillwaters. We arrived long after dark, set up our backpacking tents not far from the water, had a last look at a sky that was more black with clouds than shining with masses of stars, and put the night to bed. While we slept, a wind crept up and blew the front of a storm toward us. In the morning, huddled in the lee of our tents to escape the cold wind and drink our coffee, we watched water that was covered with whitecaps rather than hatching midges. At least it wasn't raining.

The only calm water we could find was a 40-foot strip in the lee of the slight dike that backed up a gully seep to form the pond. No midges were hatching even in that bit of flat water, but at least we could cast our lines out of the wind. Any backcast high enough to loft above the dike got knocked down by the wind, so we were forced to roll cast. Fortunately a tailwind allows even duffers to deliver 40-foot roll casts. It just so happened that the deepest water in the pond, in this case something short of 10 feet, was butted up against that dike, and every angler knows that when nothing is happening on top of the water, trout tend to bunch up in the deepest part of a shallow stillwater.

I rigged with a combination that had a long history of being dependable for me on that pond and many other stillwaters, both large and small: a clear intermediate sinking line, a 10-foot leader tapered to a 4X tippet, to which I tied a size 12 beadhead Black Woolly Bugger trailed by a size 16 black midge pupa pattern on a 12-inch tippet. I began rolling this rig out and counting it down ten seconds, then twenty, and finally thirty before retrieving the flies slowly back toward me. They returned weeded up on the thirty-second count, so I went back to twenty. Within a few casts, I felt a strong pull, raised the rod to set the hook, and not long later landed a 2-pound rainbow that was so reluctant to surrender that I had to get my hands wet and cold to land and release it.

I dried off my hands, put them into my pockets to warm a bit and then went back to casting, pretty sure I had life solved. I even advised Curt to rig the way I was. Fortunately for him he didn't have an intermediate line in his vest. He'd rigged with a floating line, yarn strike indicator, 8- to 9-foot leader, and a brace of small midge pupa patterns, which were in my nose-tilted opinion a pair of pretty nondescript flies. One of them had a tungsten beadhead, enough weight to tug both of them slowly down to the extent that the leader allowed.

I'd been casting, counting, and retrieving without any action for a few minutes when I heard Curt say something sharp. I looked over and saw him bringing in his outfit to discover the point fly missing, snapped off when his indicator dipped and he reacted with a quick hookset. He replaced it, cast again, and drew in just enough slack to keep in close touch with his indicator. I found myself watching it as well, attending to his fishing more closely than I attended my own. When his indicator again disappeared abruptly, he lifted the rod, which bent and then straightened, and I heard that same sharp expression. He brought in the rig and stoutened the tippet to his point fly from 5X to 4X. Apparently, some large, strong trout were cruising around in those minor depths.

Curt landed the next two trout, while I continued casting fruitlessly. I hated to abandon a rig that has a long history of success behind it and that also caught the first trout of the day. But the next time Curt's indicator dipped down and he raised his rod hollering, I went over and got my hands wet and cold unpinning and releasing his fish for him. I pretended to be helpful, but I was really snooping out precisely how he was rigged.

Within minutes I had respooled with a floating line and rerigged with a yarn indicator, hinged 8-foot leader, and two quite attractive midge pupa patterns with a pinch of putty weight on the tippet between them. We then went about even on a dozen or more fat trout through the remainder of that morning and caught as many if not more after warming up with hot soup in the early afternoon. The wind never did die, and the trout never made a move toward the surface. Both of our indicators continued their occasional dipping as those foolish trout never did wise up and become selective to my prettier flies. It was the rig that suspended those flies in the zone where the trout were cruising, rather than the tidiness of the flies dangled there, that conned the fish that day.

A *method* is the way you present a given rig to the trout. For each rig, there are from as few as a couple to as many as a couple dozen methods that can be used to solve different situations. Ironically, the simplest rig, the standard tapered leader and dry fly, can be fished with the most methods, while more complicated rigs, such as the deadly split shot and strike indicator nymphing rig, are used in fewer different ways, though each method can in itself become somewhat complex. Just casting a rig with an indicator, some form of added weight, and one or two nymphs on the leader without getting into a fearful tangle can require adjustment to your casting stroke.

Within each rig and for each method, there are almost always ways to adjust the setup to suit the precise situation you're trying to solve. If, for example, you're fishing a standard Adams or Elk Hair Caddis dry fly and a hatch of small insects suddenly causes trout to narrow their focus, then you might need to extend your leader with 2 or 3 feet of fine tippet and tie on a fly that matches the natural. Or you might be successfully fishing a riffle or run with the shot-and-indicator rig, when your success drops off because the water you've fished your way into has become a foot or two deeper. If you adjust your indicator higher up the leader and add an extra small split shot, it's surprising how often you'll be right back into the brisk business of catching trout.

Over time, given experience and some of the success that comes with it, you'll learn to choose the right rig for a given set of circumstances. You'll also learn to assess the situation and choose the correct method to use with the rig, given the conditions that exist at that moment. You'll know when to adjust a rig that isn't working or when to use the same rig but with a different method—say, switching from the upstream dry fly in a riffle to the cross-stream dry when you move up onto a smooth flat—or when to cease the unsuccessful casting with one rig and rerig entirely. For example, let's say you are enjoying good nymphing and suddenly find yourself surrounded by trout rising to a hatch. Some fisherman would continue nymphing as long as they continue catching trout, but most smart folks quickly strip the nymphs, indicators, and split shot off their leaders, refresh their tippets, and fish with a dry fly to catch some of those visible rising trout.

I'll end with an admonition: Don't rig up as soon as you arrive at the water, without any more than a glance at the conditions on the creek, stream, river, or still-water you're about to fish. Instead, insert yourself into your waders, shrug into your vest, pick up your rod and reel, and step down to the waterside. Take a close look at what might be happening before you begin to assemble your terminal tackle. Choose your rig based on your observations about conditions on the water.

First, take into account the season and, within the season, the weather. If it's winter and it's cold, you're more likely to succeed with nymphs than you are with drys. If it's spring and the air is warm, then a dry fly is clearly an option. After observing conditions in the air, take a close look at the water. If it's high and off color, restrict your options to a nymph or streamer tumbled on or near the bottom. If the water is low and clear, a nymph or streamer still might be appropriate, but consider other methods, plus wet flies and drys. Observe what the trout might be doing. Look carefully, and don't overlook the trout that might be feeding with delicate sipping rises tight along the edges or in slightly wrinkled water. If trout are up and feeding, you'll need to figure out what they're taking, so that you select the right rig and correct method, and even a matching fly pattern, to fool them.

Once you've observed all the conditions of the air and the water and know what the trout are doing, then it's time to choose a rig and a method suitable to precisely those conditions. Only after you've chosen the rig, method, and fly or flies most likely to provide some success is it time to launch yourself and go fishing.

You'll find some combinations of rigs and methods so useful that you'll come back to them time and time again to solve the widest range of trout-fishing situations. Examples include the standard tapered leader rig and upstream dry-fly method and the shot-and-indicator nymphing rig and shotgun method. Throughout the book, the most versatile, commonly successful rigs and methods are highlighted

with this key. These are the ones you'll turn to most often. But don't forget that the more rigs you learn to construct and the more methods you learn to apply with them, the more situations you'll solve and the more trout you'll catch.

# PART 1

# Getting Ready

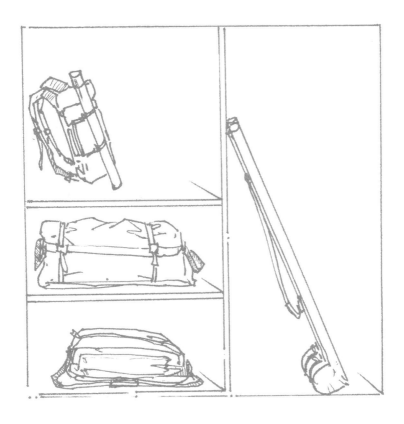

# CHAPTER 1

# Gearing Up

Although the waters that hold trout come in different shapes and sizes, many of the same rigs and methods can be used to fish all the various types. The tackle you use for one type of water, however, will not always be best suited to the others. If you plan to fish all types of water, then you'll eventually want to arm yourself with separate outfits appropriate to each type. If you plan to fish mostly a single type, then select your tackle for that. It's possible, with some minor restrictions, to buy a single outfit that will fish well on one type of water and still be suitable on others. If you are interested in such a compromise outfit, then buy what is best suited to the kind of water you want to fish most often but is still useable, if perhaps less well suited, to those you will fish less often.

For the purpose of selecting tackle, moving waters are broken down here into *rivers,* which vary from modest size to very large, *streams,* which are average-size trout waters, and *creeks,* often referred to as small streams. These are somewhat arbitrary trout-fishing definitions. According to Webster, a river is *a natural flow of water larger than a creek,* a stream is *any flow of liquid, specifically a small river,* and a creek is *a small stream, somewhat larger than a brook.* The definition of a brook as *a small stream, usually not so large as a river,* means nothing in fishing terms, so the term is not used in this book. Because of its first definition as any flow of liquid, I use the term *stream* in blanket fashion to cover rivers, streams, and creeks. After a look at Webster, you can see why I define moving trout waters in fly-fishing terms.

A workable definition of a creek might be a water small enough that you can easily cover its holding lies, side to side, with fairly short casts from a single position. A stream might be defined as a water you must wade from position to position in order to cover all its lies, from side to side, with casts of more normal length. A river might be a water so wide that you must approach it riffle by riffle, run by run, pool by

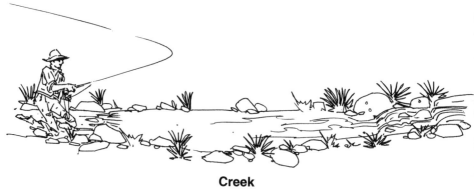

**Creek**

**Stream**

**River**

pool, covering each piece from a succession of positions. Note that fishing a big river successfully encourages movement but does not necessarily require long casts.

Within the three size categories, a moving water can also be defined by its source, whether it's freestone, spring fed, or tailwater. A *freestone water*, whether creek, stream, or river, gathers runoff and groundwater and flows over a normal bed of sand, gravel, cobble, and boulders. A *spring-fed stream,* almost always called a spring creek no matter its size, arises from steady sources and typically flows over a stable streambed with stone bottoms in some places and rooted vegetation in others. A *tailwater* trout fishery is formed by releases from dams and, depending on the nature of the releases, might have stable flows or abrupt surges of high water.

Many freestone streams have meadow reaches that are similar to spring creeks, and spring creeks, tipped into a steep enough gradient, often take on the rushing features of freestone streams. Some tailwaters are like freestone streams; others are more like spring creeks. Although the definitions of moving water are not as arbitrary as those for stream size, only by observing the water flowing in front of you will you know how best to rig and fish it.

Stillwaters are divided into lakes, ponds, and reservoirs. A *lake* is a modest to immense body of stillwater, a *pond* is a small lake—defined as seven acres or smaller in one of my dictionaries—and a *reservoir* is formed by a dam on a creek, stream, or river. When fishing stillwaters, tackle is less varied than what is required for moving waters. That's because not only will you rarely have to deal with obstructions when casting in stillwaters, but you'll almost always want to maximize your casting distance. Your major challenge will be selecting the right line to reach the correct depth on any stillwater, no matter its size.

## GEAR:     CREEKS AND SMALL STREAMS

**Shape of the water.** Creeks can vary from mountain torrents to foothill feeders to lowland meanders. Headwaters tend to be steep with successions of plunges, deep pools, and runs along and above protruding and submerged boulders. Trout hold where obstructions—boulders, logs, rootwads—break the current and where depth protects them from predators. You'll find most trout close enough to the main current to dash into it and take whatever food trots past them.

Foothill creeks have the more normal riffle-to-run-to-pool structure. Most riffles are too shallow and fast to hold trout, but you might find holding pockets of slower, deeper water formed by boulders, ledges, or trenches. Foothill runs are fishable if they have obstructions and enough depth—1$^1$/$_2$ to 3 feet—to provide protection from predators. Most trout will be found in the pools, close to the main central or side current that carves out the greatest depths and delivers the most food to them.

Lowland creeks slow down and meander in serpentine curves. Again, trout will almost always be found in the deepest water in or near the main current. Most lowland creeks form their deepest slots against the outside banks of bend pools. A deep pool just downstream from a riffle will usually hold a pod of trout. If the current slides along an undercut grassy bank, trout will be lined up, spaced every few feet down the length of it.

**Nature of the challenges.** The key to catching trout on creeks is moving and covering lots of water. You'll spend most of each day either wading up the small stream or bushwhacking alongside it. Brush on both sides of the creek might constrict your rod movement and get in the way of your backcast area. Often branches dangling from trees overhead will force you to keep your backcast low; sometimes their limbs will sweep protectively over the water where you'd like to place your fly. You need the kind of equipment that lets you move briskly and stop to place flies accurately on those small holding lies.

**Basic outfit.** Strip your gear to the honest essentials and carry it in a belt, shoulder, or chest pack, or a short and light vest. Small-stream experts often pare their gear to what fits in shirt pockets. Wear felt-soled hip boots or breathable waders, and dress in colors that blend with the vegetation. Tuck a windbreaker shirt or rain jacket into a pocket or tie it to your fishing bag, and carry a water bottle on your belt. Condense your flies to a single box of attractor drys, nymphs, and soft-hackled wet flies, such as the Royal Wulf, Elk Hair Caddis, Beadhead Hare's Ear, and March Brown Spider.

Your rod for average creek fishing should be 7 to 7$^1$/$_2$ feet long, 8 at most. It should toss tight loops with maximum control and accuracy and should roll cast well. A dry-fly or fast-action rod is perfect. Never buy a stiff rod that fails to load with 10 to 20 feet of line in the air. Because small-stream dry flies are usually hackled for flotation, you will need at least a 3-weight line to boss them around. A 4-weight is better, and a 5-weight is maximum. The line can be a double-taper or weight-forward, as long as it loads the rod properly on a short cast. The last thing you want on a small stream is the often-prescribed soft, sweet 2- or 3-weight rod. Your open loop will catch more trees than trout.

On lowland creeks, where tall grasses and brush behind you are more common obstacles than trees hemming you in, a 9-foot rod will work fine.

**Creek/small-stream situation.** In a typical small-stream scenario, you will be crouched or kneeling at the tailout of a small pool, with brush behind you limiting your backcast area and tree limbs drooping over the water restricting your forecast. You must read the water to locate the main current line, which will usually also define the deepest slot. Most trout will be holding to the sides and beneath this current, but they'll also be found on the tailout, hiding around rootwads and any other cover, and at the corners where the riffle above plunges into the pool you're about to fish. Show your dry fly, nymph, soft-hackled wet fly, or dry fly and dropper rig on two to three casts to each of those likely lies, and give extra effort at both sides and down the center of the current tongue.

**Contents of belt, shoulder, chest bag, or vest.** Fly box; 3, 4, 5, and 6X tippet spools; leader nippers; hemostat; fly drying patch; dry-fly floatant; strike indicator yarn; putty weight or split shot; line cleaner; spare $7^1/_2$-foot, 3X base leader; mosquito repellant; sunscreen; emergency cigarette lighter and fire starter tablets; wader repair tape; and toilet paper.

**Shape of the water.** Most medium streams have the full range of water types: riffles, runs, pools, flats, pocket water, and bank water. Many riffles will be deep enough to hold trout around obstructions or sprinkled randomly, and most runs provide productive fishing. Pools take on their own anatomies, with a head, deep center, and tailout. You'll encounter hatches on flats, and bank water holds trout wherever they can find a current to deliver food and enough depth to protect them from overhead predators.

Mountain streams, which will be bounding and difficult to wade, contain strong riffles, runs, and pocket water. You can try nibbling at its edges and pockets, but you'll find the best fishing in places where the gradient levels off, however briefly. Where a stream descends in drops and benches, trout can be found in current tongues that course between drops.

Foothill streams, the classic forested trout streams of American fly fishing, move through a succession of riffles and runs and pools, repeated at intervals. All of their water types hold trout, but their gorgeous pools are best known for containing trout.

As lowland streams meander, they form more flats, pools, and bank water. Because their riffles produce large quantities of aquatic insects, trout will hang in the nearest runs and pools downstream. Grassy banks will provide falls of terrestrial insects such as grasshoppers, ants, and beetles, and trout will tuck against undercuts to feed on them.

**Nature of the challenges.** A good fly fisherman is prepared to fish all of the different water types of a typical trout stream and is equipped with the fullest range of rigs and methods so that he or she can fish all levels in the water column, from top to bottom. Because trout will feed on a wide array of natural food forms, sometimes selectively, from aquatic and terrestrial insects to aquatic worms and baitfish, your fly boxes should reflect that variety.

Brush and trees will not restrict your casting as often on medium streams, and you'll more often want long casts and control of your line once it's on the water. Therefore, a long rod is a good choice on average trout streams.

**Basic outfit.** Wear chest-high felt-soled waders, preferably breathables as they are by far the most comfortable. Layer your clothes appropriate to the season and water temperature. Unless the water is peaceful, carry a folding wading staff on your belt. Wear a vest with abundant pockets, and since you'll often wade deep, make it a midlength or shortie, not full-length, so that your fly boxes don't get wet. If that happens, your hooks will rust.

Your rod should be $8^{1}/_{2}$- to 9-foot fast action, neither too stiff nor a soft noodle. It should be able to handle both short and long casts, roll casts, wiggle casts, and reach casts, and mend and tend line well once it's on the water. A floating line, either double-taper or weight-forward, will be all you need. A 3-weight will work if your streams are windless, but a 4- or 5-weight is better. A 6-weight is a bit heavy. My favorite medium-stream rod is a 9-foot, 4-weight that loads best with a 5-weight line. Leaders will range from the length of the rod to 14 or 15 feet; you'll need 9- or 10-foot base leaders and tippet spools from 2 to 6X in order to rebuild the tapers and fine the tippet down when necessary.

Your fly boxes should contain a broad selection of searching dry flies, nymphs, wet flies, and streamers. At least two or three additional boxes should hold imitations of the most abundant hatches—mayflies, stoneflies, and caddisflies, plus the dominant terrestrials—in their immature and mature stages.

**Trout stream situation.** Most likely, you'll move along a trout stream and fish the various water types as you come to them. Start at the tailout of a pool, fishing any holding lies formed by boulders there. Next fish through the body of the pool, being sure to cast to any peripheral bank lies, and then fish up the run of water that feeds the pool. You'll often find the most trout in the current tongues and riffle corners at the heads of pools and runs, because that's where food is delivered. If the riffle feeding the pool is not too swift and shallow, fish it, or any pockets in it, on your way upstream to the next pool.

Streams often hold fish more so in one water type. Explore the stream until you discover what water type is most productive; then focus on that type.

**Contents of vest.** Three to five boxes of searching and imitative flies; base leaders and 2 to 6X tippet spools; dry-fly floatant; fly drying patch; split shot and putty weight; yarn and hard strike indicators; line cleaner; leader nippers on retriever; hemostat with scissors; insect repellant; sunscreen; stream thermometer; rain jacket; fingerless wool gloves; water filter bottle; toilet paper; emergency flashlight; cigarette lighter and fire starter cubes; and small aquarium net for capturing bugs on which trout are feeding.

**Shape of the water.** Large and small rivers have the same water types as creeks and trout streams—riffles, runs, pools, pockets, flats, and banks—but each is naturally bigger, and you'll spend more time fishing one piece of water. It's common to spend an hour or two nymphing a productive riffle or half a day pestering trout on a single flat if they are rising to feed on insects.

Movements on rivers tend to be both more restricted—you fish one piece of water as long as it's productive—and bigger. Once you've worn out a riffle, flat, pool, or stretch of bank, pick up and hike if you're on foot, or float if you're boating, to the next piece of water that looks similar to the one where you just caught a lot of trout.

Rivers vary widely in structure according to the ruggedness or flatness of the country through which they flow and how long they've had to erode their watercourses. A young river—a few thousand to a few million years old—tends to be higher in the foothills, faster, and rougher, with more riffles, runs, and pocket water lies than pools and flats. An older river—several to many millions of years old—will, as a result of its own erosion, tend to be in flat country and will contain long pools, runs, and flats. Some old rivers are unfeatured and difficult to read.

**Nature of the challenges.** The biggest problem on rivers is finding productive water instead of fishing water that is unlikely to supply any action. It's easy to spend most of the day fishing water that is almost absent of trout. To avoid this, focus on shallow water, riffles and riffle corners, featured water, bouldered runs, and well-shaped banks.

It can also be difficult locating trout in water that can be productively fished with flies. Some deep, unfeatured runs can be mineswept with spinners or bait, but it might be tedious to try to fish them with nymphs or streamers. So the main challenge on rivers becomes finding trout concentrated in fishable water and learning to pass by the dead water.

**Basic outfit.** Not surprisingly, your basic big river outfit is precisely the one you assembled to fish average trout streams. You want to make short to long casts and maintain maximum control after the cast has been made. The flies you use will be largely the same as the ones chosen for an average stream. Most of your fishing on big water will require a 9-foot, 4- to 5-weight rod, floating line, and leader 10 to 14 feet long. This "presentation" outfit is ideal for fishing hatches, something you'll do even more on big water than you do on creeks and streams. Carry the same gear in the same vest you outfitted for medium trout streams, but add a sinking-tip line for fishing occasional wet flies and streamers.

If your fishing will be focused on big rivers, then select a basic outfit at the upper end of the spectrum: a 9-foot, 5- to 6-weight rod. If you will be drifting rivers in a boat or pontoon craft, then add an extra outfit that you will keep rigged for nymphing or pounding the banks with streamers as you move from one piece of water to the next. This outfit should be a 9- to 9$^{1}/_{2}$-foot rod balanced with a 6- to 8-

weight line. The first line should be a weight-forward floater for distance; keep a sinking-tip and perhaps wet-head line on spare spools for probing deep runs and pools. If you'll be boating often, you'll appreciate a boat bag to hold extra fly boxes and backup clothing. If the rivers you fish are slippery, you might prefer wading brogues with studded felt soles.

**River situation.** When you fish a small to large river, most likely you'll be focused on a single piece of water, usually a broad riffle, a stretch of bank water, or a flat with trout rising to insects. Riffle corners might be the most productive, readable, and dependable water types on most big rivers. If you're fishing with guides, many times they like to take their clients out to a corner and fish it for half an hour to an hour before jumping into the boat to float down to the next corner. If you focus on riffle corners when you're not locked onto a pod of rising trout, you'll greatly increase the productivity of your days spent on trout rivers.

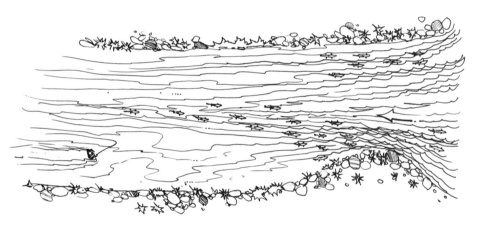

**Contents of boat bag.** Extra fly boxes for big rubber-legged nymphs and streamers; special boxes for specific hatches (one for the various stages of the blue-winged olives, the sulfurs, the spotted sedges, golden stones, salmonflies, and perhaps midges); fingerless wool gloves; rain gear; spare spools for sinking lines; water bottle; thermos of coffee; and minor luxuries of your own choosing, such as camera, binoculars, and lunch.

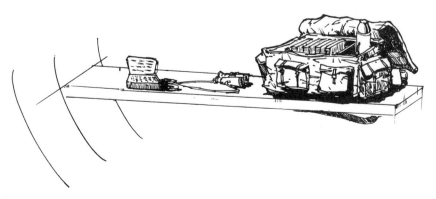

## GEAR:      FREESTONE CREEKS, STREAMS, AND RIVERS

**Shape of the water.** Freestone, a vaguely defined fly-fishing term, has come to signify waters originating from falling rain and melting snow as opposed to water released from dams or rising from springs. Most freestone streams have spring-heads submerged along their courses, and many have dams that insert tailwater stretches into otherwise freestone systems. The term defines a typical structure of repeated riffles, runs, and pools flowing over gravel, rock, and boulder beds, as opposed to slow, meandering flows over marl or silty bottoms.

Freestone streams come in the widest variety of water sizes—our arbitrary creeks, streams, and rivers—and offer the most varied water types, including the primary riffles, runs, pools, and flats, plus all the peripheral boulder, bank, pocket, ledge, trench, and other types of lies. Trout might be found almost anywhere, so be prepared to apply any rig and method to pry them out.

**Nature of the challenge.** If you fish the wide variety of freestone streams, you'll find use for the entire range of rigs and methods described in this book. As you move from one water type to another you must be prepared, both mentally and in terms of your equipment, for any kind of change. You might fish a searching dry fly upstream through a shallow riffle with scattered holding lies that you're unable to see. Then you might get to the head of the riffle and find a long run of deeper water flowing over a bouldered bottom, so you'll want to rerig with indicator and shot and tumble a nymph or two down there.

Above the run, at a bend pool that pushes deep water against its outside edge, you might want to try a streamer swung deep along the bank or a dry and dropper rig fished tight to the bank. Around the bend, you might encounter a long flat with a hatch happening, and you'll find trout rising to sip size 20 blue-winged olive mayfly duns. In this case, you'll need to add 3 feet of 6X tippet to the end of your leader, select your most imitative Blue-Winged Olive pattern, and position yourself off to the side of the rising trout for a reach cast presentation, or perhaps move upstream from the hatch, and fish with a downstream wiggle cast.

Rather than dictating prescriptions, I am suggesting that you make constant observations when you fish freestone waters and be prepared to make fairly frequent changes based on what you observe.

**Basic outfit.** Fishing the wide variety of freestone streams brings one of fly fishing's greatest joys—exploration—which is often best done with a compromise outfit, well-suited to the widest range of rigs and methods. A perfect exploring rod would be $8^1/2$ to 9 feet long, with a moderately fast action—not stiff and never weepy—balanced to a 5- or 6-weight floating line in weight-forward taper. Carry a spare spool with a sinking tip line; you'll use the floater 90 to 95 percent of the time. If you already own a 9-foot rod balanced to a 4- or 5-weight for use on streams and rivers of all types, you'll find that this is pretty close to perfect when it comes time for exploring.

**Freestone stituation.** With their wide variety of water types and broad range of fishing conditions, freestones do not create average situations. Instead, your ability to read water and fish where trout are likely to lie will help you avoid wasting time fishing in spots where trout are unlikely to be and instead might increase your catch two- or even three-fold. At the very least, bounding along a beautiful freestone creek, stream, or river armed with the right gear for exploring will bring you lots of pleasure.

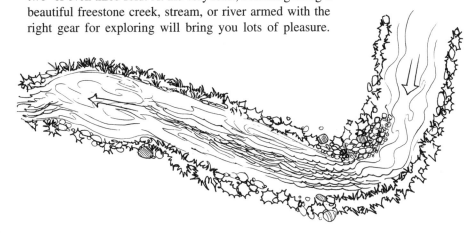

**Packing for exploring.** Keep your fishing gear packed and ready to grab and go. The boat bag that I described for fishing big rivers will come in handy on stillwaters. I also recommend a daypack to hold all the items, including a water filter bottle, miniature binoculars, camera, raingear, hat, fingerless gloves, belt bag, chest pack, or vest, that you might want to carry with you for a day astream. In time you'll want a wader bag for wet waders and brogues, warm socks and fleece pants and jacket, an overburdened vest, and a landing

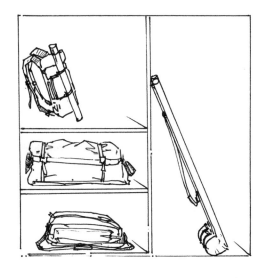

net. Take what you need from the bag, and leave the rest behind in your rig. A two-rod travel tube will protect your rods when the reels are on.

Repack your gear at the end of each fishing trip so that it's ready for the next trip. Such a system will keep you from forgetting things.

**Shape of the water.** Spring creeks of all sizes have constant flows from steady sources and do not suffer the scouring spates that wallop freestone streams when winter rain or spring snowmelt occurs. They have clear water, stable banks with few gravel bars, more grassy undercut edges, and bottoms of finer material than freestone streams. Without scour, vegetation can take root, and fallen blowdowns will not wash away.

Constant flows and aquatic plant growth create a myriad of *microniches,* or spaces where great numbers of aquatic insects and small crustaceans can live. The result is a restricted array of species, with each species having a concentrated population. Since trout in a spring creek often feed on a specific insect or other food form, they will accept only flies that look and act very much like it.

**Nature of the challenges.** Even when no hatch is happening, trout can be selective, feeding on small submerged insects riding the currents down to doom. You might not need to imitate a specific species, but you should fish a very small nymph, or pair of them, drifting as freely as the naturals might. Spring creek trout rarely move far out of their feeding lanes to chase food, so the challenge for a fisherman is to present small nymphs delicately, at the right depth, and within a few inches to either side of a feeding trout.

When a hatch happens, observe which stage of an insect the trout are taking. Capture an insect and note its size, form, and color, and then select an imitation based on those aspects of the insect. If trout are feeding on emergers in the surface film, you don't want to mistake their prey for adults and fish a high-floating dry fly.

Another challenge during a hatch is to take up a casting position that allows you to present your chosen fly to the rising trout without frightening them or warning them that your fly is not the real thing. Many fishermen mistakenly fish from downstream, casting upstream so the line, leader, and fly all pass over the trout's head, land on the water, and drift back down to it. By the time the fly arrives, the trout knows something is not right. When fishing spring creeks, try to attain proficiency with the cross-stream reach cast and downstream wiggle cast.

**Basic outfit.** The presentation outfit is central to fishing hatches, no matter where you find them. This outfit consists of a delicate $8^1/2$- to 9-foot rod balanced to cast a 3- or 4-weight floating line, either double-taper or weight-forward. The rod should load easily and cast gracefully with 20 to 40 feet of line out. Almost all manufacturers rate their rods for a line that most experienced casters consider one line weight too light. When you buy a rod, ask to cast it with the line for which it is rated, and then try casting with lighter and heavier line weights to find the best balance for you.

Buy 10- to 12-foot knotless base leaders in 4X. If the situation calls for small flies, add 3 feet of 5X; for smaller flies, add 1 foot of 5X and 3 feet of 6X, and for the smallest flies, add 1 foot of 5X and 6X, then 3 feet of 7X. When you go smaller and finer at the same time, as long as you keep the leader in balance, your fly will roll out nicely.

**Spring creek situations.** You'll most likely encounter two types of fishing problems on spring creeks: nymphing during nonhatch periods and matching hatches when trout are rising. When nymphing, position yourself downstream and off to one side of the trout or their suspected lies so that your back- and forecasts can be made away from the trout, and your presentation does not plop the line, leader, indicator, and nymphs right onto their heads.

During a hatch, take up a position at a more acute angle off to the side of the rising trout, or even upstream from them, so that your fly arrives first, ahead of the warning line and leader.

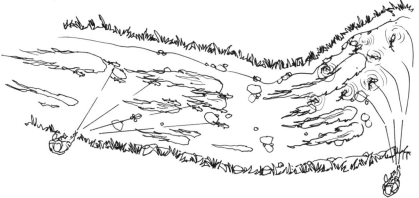

**Observation and imitation.** To spot trout, you'll need polarized sunglasses. Watch the water awhile; then cup your hands around your eyes to block out stray light. Look for parts of trout: tails, shadows, the white of an open mouth, or the flash of a turning flank.

Use your binoculars to watch floating insects; if they disappear in swirls, that's what you want to match. If they don't disappear, try emergers or nymphs. Capture specimens in an aquarium net, and examine them under a 4 or 5X hand glass.

Carry tweezers and a pickle jar lid that is white inside. To get a close look at what the trout might be eating, turn over sticks and stones, or draw up a fistful of vegetation, and use the tweezers to gather the insects and crustaceans you find. Place them in the lid, which you filled with water.

**Shape of the water.** Tailwaters vary depending on the size of the creek, stream, or river on which a dam is built, the type of geography into which it's inserted, and whether its purpose is largely water storage, irrigation, or generation of electricity. At many tailwaters formed by dams on warm-water rivers, cold water released from the impoundment provides the right temperature for trout and their food to live. Fishing on such tailwaters is usually good for 10 to 20 miles downstream from the dam or until the water once again warms beyond trout standards.

Water storage reservoirs help to improve fishing by smoothing out widely fluctuating natural flows. Irrigation impoundments typically release water during the crop season, which causes a reversal of normal flows: When water is held back in winter, the tailwater is low, clear, and fishable; when water is released in summer, the tailwater is high, often cloudy, and in many cases less fishable. Power dams frequently have wide daily fluctuations in flows, depending on the demand for power. Sometimes these changes are abrupt and can be dangerous to the wading angler.

**Nature of the challenges.** First, discern what kind of tailwater you're on: then fish accordingly. Some tailwaters are best bombed with big streamers on heavy sinking lines. Others are suitable to drifting in a boat and dangling a nymph or two beneath a strike indicator as you move along. Those with steady releases of cold flows have conditions similar to spring creeks, so be prepared to fish small nymphs deep during nonhatch periods and small emergers or dry flies when trout are up top feeding selectively.

Most famous tailwaters appear in fishing guide books, have been featured in magazine articles, or even have books written about them. When fishing these waters, do your research, and call ahead to fly shops and guide services to determine current conditions before your trip.

**Basic outfit.** A special outfit is not necessary to fish tailwaters. You can use what you already have for other types of water. A compromise setup—an $8^{1}/_{2}$- to 9-foot rod with 5- to 6-weight—will serve you well on most tailwaters. On tailwaters with heavy hatches of tiny insects, use the same $8^{1}/_{2}$- to 9-foot, 3- to 4-weight outfit prescribed for spring creeks. If you want to fish big streamers, then the rod designated for banging banks of big rivers will work: a 9-foot, 6- to 8-weight.

Don't go out and buy a tailwater outfit, or any other kind of outfit for that matter, unless your fishing experience indicates that you lack it and would benefit from it. By waiting until you have a specific need, you'll know the shape of the outfit that will fill it.

**Tailwater situations.** A tailwater with stable flows resembles either a freestone stream or a spring creek, depending on the nature of the tailwater. Your research should tell you in advance what conditions to expect when you arrive. Arm yourself accordingly with the proper outfit and set of fly boxes.

If the tailwater is subject to daily fluctuations, know the nature of possible changes in advance. Upon arrival at the water's edge, observe current conditions carefully, and fish in the way that the shape of the water demands. Be watchful while you fish, because any change in water level could endanger you.

**Cautions on tailwaters.** All waters emerging from dams are somewhat enriched—stillwaters grow plankton, moving waters do not—and most tailwater bottoms tend to be slippery. Carry a stout wading staff, and wear studded felt-soled wading brogues.

Educate yourself about releases, and know the warnings, whether loud whistles or horn blasts, that announce them. On some rivers, water surges are not announced. Don't be so intent on your fishing that you fail to notice more strength in the current around your legs or water that was once knee deep is now thigh deep. If ever in doubt, get out of the water at once.

## GEAR:      LAKES

**Shape of the water.** In moving water, trout take stations, called lies, and their food is delivered on the current. Lakes, on the other hand, are still. Trout living in lakes have lots of food, but it's not delivered. Instead, they go find it: They cruise and travel in pods. Trout in stillwaters respond to annual cycles of the seasons. They also move in response to daily cycles of food migrations and hatches.

Stillwaters have areas, not always evident, where trout are most likely to be found: inlets, outlets, over drop-offs, weedbeds, shoal areas, and bouldered points. They like coves in spring and deep water in the heat of summer. They return to the shallows in fall and are down in the depths again in winter. Their food—aquatic insects and crustaceans—is always found near the vegetation on which it lives, and trout are almost always found near the aquatic insects and crustaceans on which they in turn live. Keep in mind that if you've found one trout in a lake, you've likely found a pod.

**Nature of the challenges.** The first challenge is to find the trout. Sometimes you'll be able to see them cruising, even rising. If you own a depth finder and a boat, cruise around until you find the location of trout on the screen and then anchor and fish for them. Most often, you'll have to look for the features that attract them—the coves, drop-offs, weedbeds, and other locations that hold their prey—and fish each in its turn until you start catching trout.

The second challenge is to get your fly or flies down to the correct depth. Trout in lakes tend to cruise and feed at a specific level in the water column: in the shallows, near the bottom, over the top of a weedbed, at the upper or lower edges of a drop-off, or at the surface if hatching or migrating insects attract them upward.

Your final challenge is to entice trout to take your fly. More than just selecting the right pattern, you must also retrieve it in the manner that natural food forms might move. A suspended midge pupa moves differently than a prowling leech; a damselfly nymph stalking prey is almost motionless, while one migrating toward shore for emergence is in as much of a hurry as its feeble swimming ability allows. How many trout you catch can be linked to how you retrieve your fly or simply let it sit.

**Basic outfit.** The best tackle for lakes is different than that used for streams. The more water you can cover, the more trout you can catch, so those stiff casting tools designed for distance casting have finally found their place in trout fishing. A 9- to $9^1/_2$-foot rod balanced to a 6- to 7-weight line is ideal, though you'll often use your lighter presentation or exploring outfits for feeding fish. You need some sort of line system that allows you to fish all the levels of a lake, from the surface to the minor shallows down into the dark depths. Start with a weight-forward floater, then extend to a clear intermediate slow-sinking line, and move on to a sinking tip and fast-sinking and extra fast-sinking shooting heads. Finally, your lake fishing will be vastly more productive if you have some sort of transportation to move you around on the water: a float tube, pontoon craft, or boat.

**Lake situations.** Lake situations can be divided neatly into two categories: the times you're nosing around trying to find the fish, and the times you're trying to catch the fish you've found. Often exploring with your fly pattern, either by casting or trolling, will determine at least one way to catch fish. But sometimes you'll have to go through that patient routine of determining what the trout are eating, selecting a fly to match it, and then choosing a line that gets the fly to the right depth. After that, it's just a matter of retrieving the fly the way the trout want it, and you've got them cornered.

**Special items of equipment.** If you already own a boat bag, you'll be able to use it on lakes. If you don't, and you intend to fish lakes out of some sort of watercraft, then get a bag, even if it's just a cast-off gym bag. The bag will hold your line system and any extra reel spools. If you're afloat, it's a good idea to carry two rods rigged. The first, strung with a floating line, lets you respond at once to spotted rises with either a dry fly, nymph, wet fly, or streamer fished shallow. The other, rigged with a sinking line, allows you to change the lines according to the depth you want to fish.

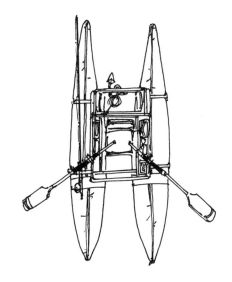

Much of the equipment you already own for fishing creeks, streams, and rivers—vest, waders, rain gear, and landing net, to name a few—will be as useful on lakes as on moving waters.

**Shape of the water.** Ponds are miniature lakes, ranging from half an acre to seven acres in size, but they're far easier to read than larger stillwaters. Fishing ponds is often best in spring, when the water first warms up and both insects and trout become active. Many freestone streams are blown out by runoff at this time, so think about ponds when your favorite moving waters are out.

Ponds can be classified into two types. The first is a natural body of water, caused by water filling depressed ground forms. These are usually shallow all around, unless backed up against a steep hill or cliff, and the deepest water is somewhere near the center. The shape of the surrounding topography—ridges descending to points, lowlands forming broad, flat banks—will tell you almost precisely where the shallow and deep water is located and where you're most likely to find trout. The second type of pond is man-made and usually is created by bulldozing an earthen dam across the slight valley of a headwater rivulet or seep. These are shaped consistently from shallow at the upper end to deepest near the dike, usually with a deep channel following the submerged watercourse.

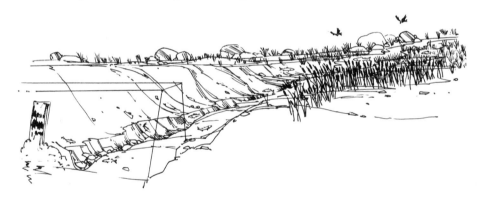

**Nature of the challenges.** Some ponds have stable banks that are clear of obstructions around which you can walk and cast from shore. More frequently ponds have reed-lined edges and mucky bottoms, which are difficult and sometimes dangerous to wade. Most ponds in forested areas are so hemmed in by trees and brush that you can't stand on shore, or wade the edges, and make an uncontested backcast. So the first challenge when fishing ponds is finding a way to get your fly onto productive water. If you can't walk, wade, or hop logs, you will need transportation. Float tubes find their happiest home on ponds.

Your second challenge is finding the fish. If they're not up and feeding visibly, then they're almost always near the bottom, and you will have to look for them either on the bottom of the shallows or on the bottom in whatever deep water the pond might have. To figure out the depth in either of these areas, clamp your everpresent hemostat to the end of your leader and drop it over the side of your tube.

Then choose a rig and method that gets your fly or flies to that depth, and you'll likely have found the trout.

Your third challenge is getting the fish to strike. Remember that a majority of bottom-dwelling trout foods in ponds are small, move slowly, and are the color of the bottom vegetation. You can almost always catch some fish by choosing an olive to brownish-olive size 12 to 16 nymph, counting it down to the right depth, and bringing it back with a handtwist retrieve.

**Basic outfit.** Once again, what you carry for lakes, rivers, or streams will work fine on ponds. In fact, when people ask me at seminars what rod I recommend they buy for pond fishing, I always reply, "Buy a float tube." If you own a long rod, you should use it, and if you own a sinking line system, you should use the rod for which it is balanced. If you don't own an intermediate or sinking-tip line, then buy one. You can do almost all pond fishing with a floating line for the surface and shallows and a sinking-tip line for the minor depths that occur on most ponds. A clear intermediate is great for trolling.

If your pond approaches the size of a small lake and has the same sort of depths, then use the lake outfit prescribed in that section.

**Pond situations.** The two situations that are common on lakes also occur on ponds: Trout are either up and feeding where you can see them, or they seem to be absent and the pond appears to be lifeless. You know by now that you can solve the first situation by discovering what the trout are taking, matching it as closely as you can, and casting the fly to rises and either letting it sit if it's a dry or retrieving it to make it move naturally if it's a wet fly, nymph, or streamer. In the second situation, select a rig that will put a nymph or streamer, or more likely a combination of a small nymph trailing a modest to large streamer, close to the bottom, and use a retrieve that keeps them there, moving slowly, as long as possible.

**Outfitting a float tube.** When fishing ponds, I use a U-tube for easy entry and exit. It's lightweight and can be inflated by lung power, if necessary, though a foot pump firms it up better. Because ponds often require a hike, a backpack tube is ideal. Wear chest-high waders, use tubing fins, and tie a landing net to the side. Keep in mind that landing a big trout from a tube can cause the line to tangle with your fins and force you ashore. Wear your vest, strap your boat bag to the tube on the side opposite your casting arm, and you're outfitted.

## KNOTS

When fly fishing for trout, you will need to know just a few knots. You use the *arbor knot* to attach backing line to the reel. The *nail knot* attaches the backing to your fly line and the other end of the line to a 1-foot leader butt. The *blood knot* attaches your base leader to the leader butt and can also be used to connect rebuilding leader sections and tippets to your base leader. The *surgeon's knot* is quick and strong and used most often to connect fine tapering and tippet sections to the base leader. The *improved clinch knot* is used to connect dry flies and wet flies to the tippet, and the *Duncan loop knot* is used to give nymphs and streamers free movement in their drifts and retrieves. The *surgeon's loop knot,* which can be quickly tied, is used most often with small flies of all kinds.

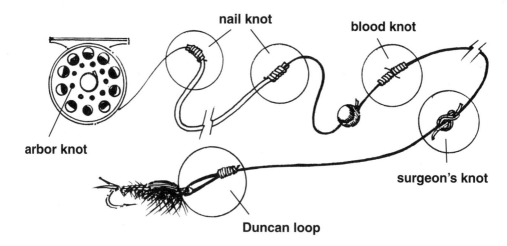

Except for the simple arbor knot and more difficult nail knot, these knots will be used repeatedly throughout your fishing day. Practice them until you can tie them quickly. Moistening monofilament knots by touching them with the tip of your tongue before slowly drawing them tight will help seat them correctly and make them much stronger. For a smooth transfer of casting energy, the leader butt should be 25- to 35-pound test monofilament, the approximate stiffness of the end of the fly line you'll tie it to. To predetermine the correct amount of backing to fill your reel spool, wind the fly line on first, and add enough backing to fill the spool to within about $3/16$ inch of the rim. Then take the backing and fly line off, reverse them, and tie your knots as you respool them.

## Backing to Reel: Arbor Knot

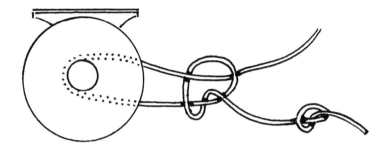

1) Run the tip of your backing around the arbor of your reel spool, tie an overhand knot in the tag end, and draw it tight. Clip the tag.
2) Tie a slip knot around the standing line, draw it tight against the overhand knot, and pull the standing line to snug the slip knot tight to the reel spool.

## Backing to Fly Line and Fly Line to Leader Butt: Nail Knot

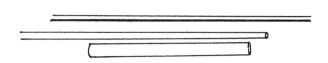

1) Overlap backing or leader butt and fly line several inches. Place the end of a 2-inch section of hollow tube from an ink pen, a drinking or stirring straw, or a WD-40 can nozzle even with the fly line tip.

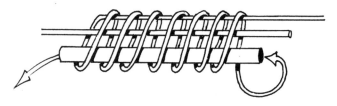

2) Take about five turns of backing or leader butt around the fly line, backing line, and hollow tube together, pinching the turns with your thumb and forefinger as you go.

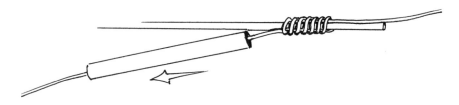

3) Run the tag end of the backing or leader butt through the tube. Draw the tag end out of the tube and pull it snug. Then draw the standing backing or leader butt end snug, taking as much slack out of the turns as possible before you remove the tube.

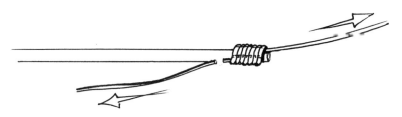

4) Slide the hollow tube carefully out of the knot. Hold the tag end of the backing or leader butt together with the fly line in one hand and the standing backing or leader butt in the other hand. Draw them in opposite directions, seating the knot tightly and neatly. Trim the tag ends.

## Leader Butt to Base Leader: Blood Knot

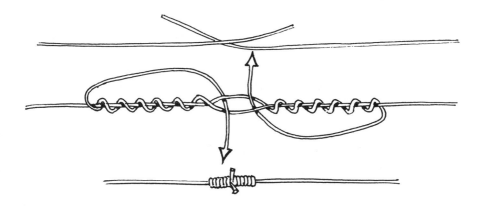

**Note:** This knot can also be used for tying leader sections to each other.

1) Overlap several inches of the leader butt with the heavy end of the base leader.
2) Wrap five turns of base leader around the standing leader butt. Poke the tag end between the base and butt strands.
3) Stabilize the knot junction between the thumb and forefinger of one hand, and take five wraps of the leader butt around the standing part of the base leader. Poke the tag end through the center hole in the opposite direction.
4) Moisten the wraps and slowly draw the knot tight. Trim the tag ends. If the leader butt is much longer than 1 foot, clip it to about that length.

## Tapering Sections and Tippet to the Base Leader: Surgeon's Knot

**Note:** Use the surgeon's knot, never the blood knot, if the two sections of monofilament you're tying together are more than a single X (.001-inch) different in diameter.

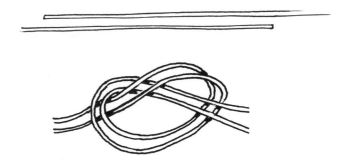

1) Overlap several inches of the two leader sections to be tied together. Take a single overhand knot.

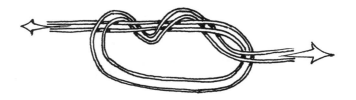

2) Take a second overhand knot.

3) Moisten the knot and draw it tight. Trim the tag ends.

## Tippet to Dry Fly or Wet Fly: Improved Clinch Knot

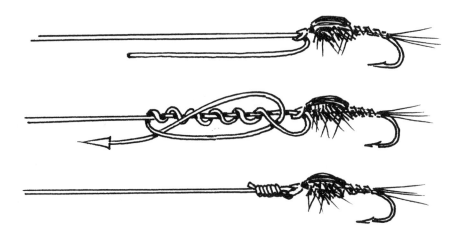

1) Run 2 to 3 inches of tippet through the hook eye.
2) Take five turns of the tag end around the standing tippet.
3) Run the tag end through the gap next to the hook eye, then back through the loop formed by doing that.
4) Moisten the knot and draw it tight. Trim the tag end.

## Tippet to Nymph or Streamer: Duncan Loop

**Note:** You can adjust the size of the loop by moving the knot with your fingers. If the loop collapses against the hook after you play a large trout, you can pinch it between your thumbnail and fingernail and open it again.

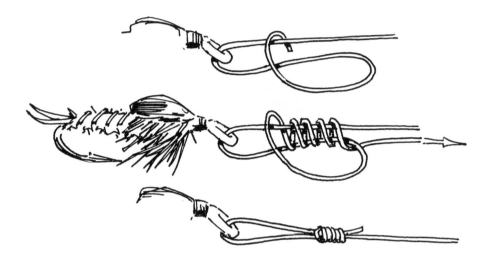

1) Run 3 to 4 inches of tippet through the hook eye. Reverse the tag to make a loop alongside the standing tippet.
2) Take five turns of the tag end through the loop and around the standing tippet.
3) Moisten the knot and draw it tight in a short loop in front of the fly. Trim the tag end.

## Tippet to Small Flies: Surgeon's Loop

1) Run 2 to 4 inches of tippet through the hook eye and double it upon the standing end.

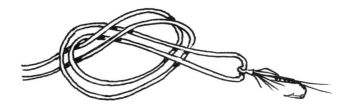

2) Form a loop of the doubled tag end and standing tippet.

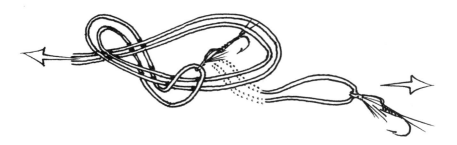

3) Pass the fly through the loop (a second pass through will form a double surgeon's loop, more secure but usually unnecessary).

4) Moisten the knot and slowly draw it tight. You can adjust the size of the loop by pushing the loop closer or farther from the hook eye as you tighten it. Clip the tag.

# CHAPTER 2

# Casting and Control

## BASIC FLY CAST

All fly casting is built around the simple basic fly cast, which consists of a backcast and a forecast. Each back- and forecast is built of three repeated parts: the loading movement, the power stroke, and the stop. The load straightens the fly line in the air and sets its weight directly against the rod tip. The power stroke provides the line speed that makes the cast work. The stop forms the loop of line traveling through the air and keeps the line and fly from driving toward either what is behind you on the backcast or the water between you and where you'd like your fly to land on the forecast. No part of the cast is more or less important than any other. Because the stop is most often overlooked, beginning fly casters often have problems with the line striking the ground behind them or the water in front of them.

During a cast, the rod should move through an arc of no more than 90 degrees straight above your casting shoulder—45 degrees to the front and 45 degrees to the back. Exceeding these limits will result in driving your line into the ground if you're practicing and onto the water's surface if you're fishing.

You can practice the load, power, and stop motions with the butt section of a rod, or even without one, while you sit at your desk, watch TV, attend meetings, or sit at a red light. Simply move your arm slowly back in the load, then snap it forward for speed and power, and stop it abruptly. Repeat—load slowly, power snap, and abrupt stop—until it's ingrained in your muscle memory.

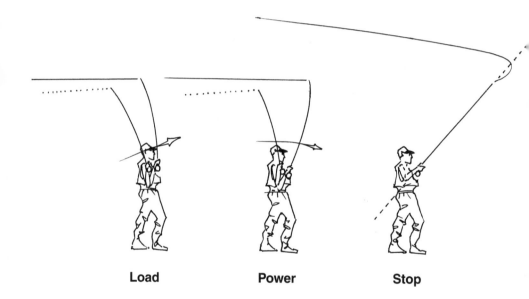

**Load**               **Power**               **Stop**

**The backcast.** To make a proper backcast, you must load, power, and stop the rod with the line in front of you. Start with it on water or grass, but don't power the backcast toward the ground. If your backcast drops toward the ground, you've powered the rod too far past 45 degrees, forgotten the stop, or have waited for gravity to take over before beginning the forecast. Turn your head to watch the backcast unfold and see if it's happening right.

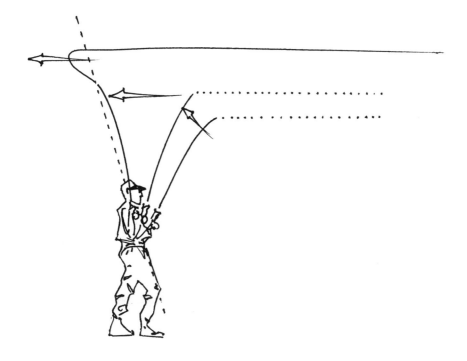

**The forecast.** To make the proper forecast, wait until the line is almost straight in the air on the backcast; then bring the rod forward to load the line against it. Use the strength of your forearm to bring it forward abruptly in the power stroke, and then stop it. Again, if the line drives toward the ground, you've either powered the rod too far or forgotten to stop it.

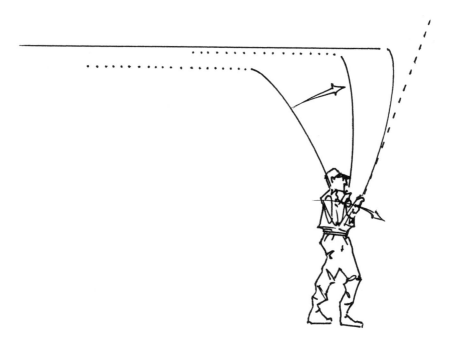

**The delivery stroke.** When you're wading in water and casting flies over trout, aim your final delivery stroke 2 to 3 feet above the water, not right at the point where you want your fly to land. The line and then the leader should turn over and straighten in the air about waist high. Line, leader, and fly should all float softly down to the surface at about the same speed. If you direct your delivery stroke right where you want the fly to land, the line and leader will crash in the water and frighten the trout you're trying to catch.

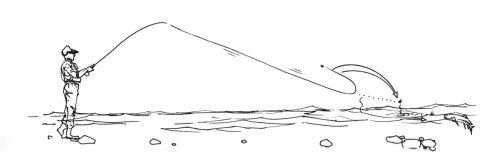

**Loop control.** The more open your casting loop, the more air your line will have to cut through, and the less distance you'll be able to get in your cast. A tighter loop will give you a bit more accuracy, which is important when you're fishing dry flies. When you cast a nymph rig with an indicator, split shot, and two flies on the leader, you'll have to open the loop or you'll get tangles.

To control the width of your casting loop, shorten or lengthen your power stroke, decreasing or increasing the distance the rod tip travels in the air above your shoulder. With a short, fast stroke, you get a narrow, tight loop. With a long, slow stroke, you get a wide, open loop. The point is to strive for control over the width of your loop, so that you can open and close it to suit the demands of the situation in which you're fishing.

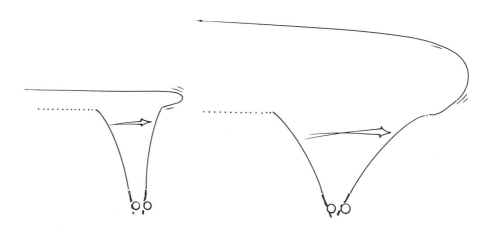

**Tilting the casting plane.** When you're on water with somewhat open banks—an eastern spring creek, a midwestern pastoral, or a western desert stream—the obstacles to your casting will be shrubs, tall grasses, sagebrush, or anything else that grows from head height to rod-tip height behind you. On forested waters, you'll often be able to examine a crowded backcast area and note gaps in limbs and trees that let you loft a backcast in a precise area, as long as you aim it carefully. In all these scenarios, which are common in about a quarter to a third of all trout-fishing situations, you'll be able to fish the water if you're able to loft your backcast above the obstructions. To do that, merely tilt the casting plane of the basic fly cast.

Normal fore- and backcasts move through the air in an even plane, at the height of the rod tip, parallel to the water in which you wade, to the earth on which you stand, or to the eaves of your house if you're practicing on your lawn. If you aim your forecast lower toward the water in front of you and use the normal short load, power, and stop movements, you will keep the backcast in the same plane as the forecast, but tip it up high into the air behind you to clear tall grasses and low shrubs. You also can lift it over trees that are higher than the rod tip. If you turn and observe the unfurling loop of the backcast, you can aim it at holes in a thicket of branches.

There is a limit to how high you can lift the backcast without breaking the level plane of the cast. You cannot extend the forecast until it crashes into the water. If you're standing or kneeling on a high bank, you'll be able to tilt your cast quite high and deliver a normal forecast. If you're wading waist deep, with the bank crowding tight behind you, you'll be limited to a short cast, perhaps to 20 to 25 feet, which is still plenty of length to catch a trout that you normally wouldn't be able to show the fly to, without tilting the casting plane.

## ROLL CAST

The roll cast, a variation of the basic cast, uses the water in front of you to load the forecast, so that you do not need a backcast behind you at all. It is useful in areas where brush prevents a backcast, even with a tilted casting plane. The roll cast is most useful on small and brushy waters. If you're fishing a typical pond or lake with brushy edges and you have no boat or other way to get out onto the water, the roll cast will let you fish where otherwise you might not.

The roll cast works best with long rods of medium to medium-fast action. A stiff rod won't load for the cast, and a weepy one won't travel in a short enough power stroke to form a hoop in the line. But whatever rod you're carrying when you get into a situation that calls for a roll cast will work. Even a short rod will always make long enough roll casts on small waters.

A floating line works best for roll casting. Although a double-taper is preferred for long roll casts, a weight-forward will work fine if the casts you want to make don't exceed the length of the heavy forward section of the line. You can roll cast with a sinking-tip line, though not as far or as gracefully as you can with a floater. You can coax a short roll cast out of a full-sinking line, but only with a certain amount of thrashing to bring the line to the surface. You'll have little luck trying to roll cast with a shooting head line.

It's far easier to roll cast a dry fly than a sunk fly, simply because the fly is afloat and easy to roll off the water. But you can make an adequate roll cast with a sunk fly as long as you draw it close to the surface before trying to roll it into the air.

**Parts of the roll cast.** To make a roll cast, you need the line to be on water. Grass won't work, so you can't practice the roll cast on the lawn like you can with the basic cast. Most instructions for the roll cast start with the line laid out 30 to 40 feet in front of you, but the purpose of the cast is to get the fly out there in the first place. Rarely will you encounter a situation in which you have brush crowded up behind you, a nice pool in front of you, and your line magically already laid out there, straight and ready to be rolled.

**The initial position.** Begin by removing your fly from the keeper on the rod and holding it by the hook bend between the thumb and forefinger of your line hand. With the same hand, strip out the amount of line you'll need to reach the lie to which you're casting. Continue to hold the fly, and wobble the rod tip crisply back and forth to coax line out through the guides. Let this line pile up loosely under the rod on the water in front of your feet. Don't exceed your casting limits; begin with 15 to 20 feet of line plus the leader. Only attempt this on quiet water; if you're knee deep in a rushing riffle, the current will sweep your line downstream and destroy your cast. The roll cast works best on small waters, where you can usually position yourself at the still edge of a pool, with the holding water a short cast away.

**The loading movement.** Draw the rod slowly back in the same arc you would use in a basic backcast power stroke, but without the power. Stop at about a 45-degree angle behind your shoulder, and hold the rod. You are now in the same position from which you would begin a normal forecast, except the line is still on the water and not in the air. The line will be drawn toward the rod tip, sliding across the surface. When the line hangs down from the rod tip in a curve behind you rather than in front of you, you're ready to execute the power stroke. Watch the point where the line contacts the water, and don't let it slide behind you so that the curve collapses and the line hangs straight off the rod tip. Initiate the power stroke when the maximum curve has formed in the line.

**The power stroke and stop.** Drive the rod forward with a brisk, strong movement, using the same motion as the power stroke in the basic forecast. At the end of
the power stroke, when the rod is approximately 45 degrees in front of you, stop the
rod just as in the basic cast. At the same time, let go of the fly still held in your line
hand. The short power stroke and crisp stop are just as important in the roll cast as
they are in the basic cast. If you do not stop the rod and instead drive it toward the
water, your line will lob out in an oversized loop rather than a roll, and the cast will
collapse short.

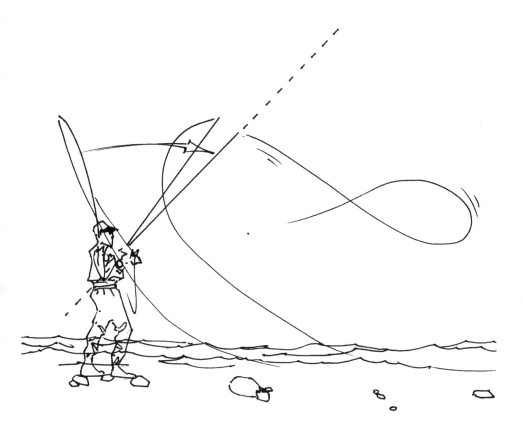

**The shape of the hoop.** If you've executed the parts of the cast correctly, the line should roll out in the air, just above the water, in a fairly small elliptical hoop. If you've driven the rod too far, you'll get a round hoop, or one that is not even closed, and the line will probably travel a short distance on the water rather than a longer distance in the air.

In almost all roll-casting situations, this initial cast, starting with the fly in your hand and the line at your feet, serves to extend the line toward its target. Usually a second roll cast, made on the heels of the first, will put the fly on target. Strip more line off the reel, if needed, and shake it onto the water under the rod tip. Then draw the rod behind your shoulder, let the line slide toward it on the water, and power the rod forward to a stop when the curve of line between the rod tip and the water has sagged behind you.

## SIDEARM CAST

Often when fishing upstream, you'll move along the edges, where overhanging tree limbs might restrict your rod and line from traveling their normal arcs over your head. This problem arises most often on creeks, frequently on forested streams, and more often than you might think when you prowl the banks of big rivers. Your ability to lay the cast over on its side will help when movement of a normal overhead basic cast is restricted.

The sidearm cast is also useful when you're casting to rising trout from a position that is close to them, even when you're wading out in open water. Crouching down to stay out of their sight accomplishes nothing if you begin waving your rod around and throwing the line back and forth over their heads. The sidearm cast lets you tip your forecasts and backcasts off to the side, low to the water, and out of the sight of trout that are intent on feeding.

**Parts of the sidearm cast.** If you have already mastered the basic cast, you will have no trouble with the sidearm cast. You merely tip your casting forearm from a vertical position to one that is horizontal or anywhere in between. Not every cast must be tipped over entirely. Often just dropping the rod tip a few degrees will lower the line's travel out of the way of an obstruction. Very often, dropping the casting forearm halfway to horizontal will clear overhanging tree limbs. But when you're in an area where brush droops low over a lie, especially on a creek or small stream, your ability to lay your rod over until it is parallel to the water will enable you to send a tight loop unfurling far back beneath the salmonberry or huckleberry bushes and cedar or sycamore branches that sweep within 2 to 3 feet of protected lies.

Practice on the lawn until you can almost scorch the earth without catching the grass. Then when you get out on the water, you'll be able to probe places that nobody else is able to touch. Because those lies rarely get pestered, you can imagine the size trout that probably lurk there.

## OFF-SHOULDER CAST

Sometimes when fishing, you'll find that a basic cast off the normal casting shoulder—the right shoulder for righties, the left shoulder for lefties—simply will not work because the trees or brush or whatever blocks you is on the wrong side to make a sidearm cast. It can happen on small streams, where brush encroaches from the casting side, or when you fish upstream along the banks of trout streams and rivers of any size. When brush and trees crowd in on your casting side so that you're not able to execute the rod movements of normal fore- and backcasts, the off-shoulder cast is the answer.

Sometimes a strong on-shoulder wind will menace you with your own fly or drive the line into you, but if you cross the casting arm in front of your body and make your cast from the off-shoulder, the wind will blow the line and fly away from you.

To make the off-shoulder cast, start with your casting forearm in front of your chest and the reel close to your off-side ear. You'll use the load/power/stop sequence

of the basic casting stroke, but your range of motion will be abbreviated. You'll be able to make an almost normal forecast, but only a short backcast, and the power you can apply in both directions will be reduced. Instead of going for distance, use the cast at short to normal trout-fishing ranges, 25 to 45 or at most 50 feet. Once you master it, the off-shoulder cast will serve you well, allowing you to catch many trout that otherwise might have been difficult and letting you continue fishing on windy days.

**The backcast as forecast.** On some large and windswept rivers where open gravel bars are in the backcast area, you can defeat the wind by simply reversing your fore- and backcasts. Face the bank, with the wind on your off-shoulder blowing the line and dangerous fly away from you. Work your line out with normal fore- and backcasts, only with the forecast away from the water you want to fish and the backcast in the direction of the water where you want the fly to land. On the final stroke, after your last "backcast" over the shore, turn to the water and convert this "backcast" into your delivery stroke, placing the fly where you want it.

## OFF-HANDED CAST

Learning to cast left-handed if you're naturally right-handed, or right-handed if you're left-handed, is surprisingly easy and can have some remarkable benefits. I've known very experienced anglers put out of fishing for a year or more by shoulder injuries or tennis elbow. Even without injuries, the off-shoulder cast is not one you'd want to use for more than a few presentations. If you begin giving your off-hand casting arm a bit of responsibility from time to time, before long you will be able to naturally switch back and forth to take advantage of the best positions for casting angles on creeks, streams, and rivers. Believe me, after shoulder surgery, I was glad to be fishing left-handed while my right arm was still in a sling.

**Learning the off-hand cast.** One way to learn to cast off-handed is to follow the same process you used to learn with your dominant hand: Practice the three parts of the proper basic stroke—load, power, and stop—with your forearm alone or with the butt of a rod at home or the office. Then begin casting short on a lawn or over water. Finally, when you get into a fishing situation that is almost impossible to solve with your dominant hand, switch the rod to your off-hand and give it a chance. Begin with short casts. I learned to cast left-handed working up the right bank of Oregon's brutal Deschutes River, taking fat 15- to 20-inch redside rainbow trout on 15- to 20-foot casts.

Another, perhaps easier, way to begin casting off-handed is to pick up a second rod in your off-hand during a practice session and begin casting two rods at the same time. Again, use a short line. You'll be pleasantly surprised how quickly your off-hand learns to follow precisely the movements of your dominant hand. After a few practice sessions, your off-hand will be able to handle the rod without the leadership of the other hand, and you'll be able to switch-hit whenever you want to.

A minor warning here: Distance casting with the off-hand is both beyond my capabilities and my ability to instruct you. Even after about twenty years of being able to switch hands at will, I'm more graceful casting at short distances with my left hand but cannot coax more than about 60 feet of line into the air without risking some confusion that usually leads to a collapse of the cast. Of course, I don't often cast long in my own fishing, and I don't practice for distance. Perhaps my left hand has the ability to cast for distance, and I just don't know it.

   **Control of the line and playing fish.** It took me little more than a season of switching back and forth between hands before I could cast adequately with my left hand, but it took the better part of five seasons fishing that way before I was able to train my dominant right hand to take up its duties as the line hand, stripping in line to take up slack as a dry fly drifted down current toward me, and controlling the line when a trout was on. Learn to fish out casts and drifts with the rod in your off-hand, but when you hook a fish, don't feel bad about switching hands and reverting to your old way of playing and landing it.

## RIGHT AND LEFT CURVE CASTS

When you're presenting a dry fly upstream to a rising trout on water that is at least somewhat smooth, the fly should be shown to the fish ahead of the line and leader. A curve cast can make that happen. If your position is downstream from a boulder lie and you'd like to present a dry to that likeliest of holding places in the soft spot above the boulder, then a cast with a curve in it will keep the line and leader off the conflicting currents below the boulder and give your fly a free drift. If you're able to throw a curve, you'll be able to present flies into many lies protected by brush dangling too low over the water to tackle with sidearm casts, or you can show flies to trout in lies protected by lodged branches protruding from the water.

**Learning the cast.** A positive curve causes a hook to the left for a right-handed caster, while a negative curve causes a hook to the right for a right-handed caster. The positive curve is executed by tilting the rod over into a position to make a sidearm cast, then making normal fore- and backcasts. Overpower the delivery stroke so that the loop, unfolding parallel to the water, flips around rather than straightening out. The fly, leader, and end of the line will settle to the water in a hook to the left if you're right-handed, to the right if you're left-handed. It's easy to master this cast if you keep it short.

Executing the negative curve requires less theory and more practice. The theory is that you tilt your rod over into the sidearm position, work out standard fore- and backcasts, and then deliver the fly with an underpowered final stroke. Because the loop fails to unfurl completely, the fly, leader, and line tip will settle to the water in a curve to the right if you're right-handed, to the left if you're left-handed. Even in the best of hands, the formation and placement of this underpowered negative curve is less than precise.

Because the positive curve cast is not as accurate as a basic cast, it's a good idea to consider improving your position and using a more dependable presentation. Restrict the negative curve cast to situations in which no improvement in your position is possible and no other cast would give you a chance to get a fly over the trout.

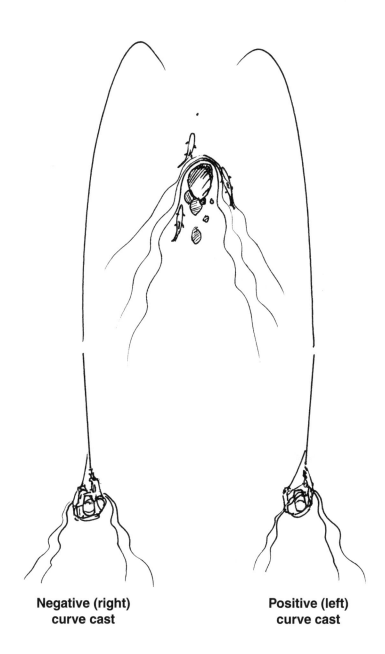

**Negative (right)
curve cast**

**Positive (left)
curve cast**

## OVAL OR BELGIAN CAST

The line loops formed by the basic backcast and forecast unfold directly over the rod tip, with the top and the bottom of the loop in the same vertical plane. On windy days, or when you have any minor casting problems or are just experiencing a bad or unlucky day, the top of the loop can collapse onto the bottom and form what is called a *tailing loop*. The resulting tangle kills your cast and forces you to stop and untangle it. If you're fishing a single dry fly, untangling the line might take just a moment. But if you're fishing a nymph rig with an indicator, split shot or putty weight, and two or three flies on the leader, not only are you more likely to get tangled when all that weight causes the loop to collapse, but you're going to spend a lot longer getting untangled. In the normal course of casting, the basic cast executed with a properly formed and, in the case of a complicated rig, patient casting stroke and open loop will work fine.

The oval cast, also called the Belgian cast, causes the top of the loop and the bottom of the loop to travel on different planes, thus greatly reducing the chance that they will tangle. Many expert fly fishers frequently use the oval cast when fishing, most of the time subconsciously when they're not even aware that they're doing it. Because the oval cast keeps the rod tip in constant touch with the line—the tip is, essentially, always under at least a slight load—the cast provides a better feel for what the line is doing in the air and therefore offers the fly fisher more control over the line throughout all of its travel.

**Learning the cast.** The oval or Belgian cast requires the same load, power, and stop movements as the basic cast, but the movements blend into each other so that the rod moves in a tipped plane on the backcast and comes around into a straight plane on the forecast, and the line responds to the rod tip by following in a much larger oval.

wind direction

The backcast is made with the rod in the same position as for a partial sidearm cast, tipped out just a few degrees to 45 degrees from vertical. After the load, power, and stop movements, the rod drifts back with the unfurling backcast, keeping in constant touch with the line, and at the same time is lifted into the vertical plane for the forecast, or even tipped slightly off to the other side. The line tip and leader will follow the direction of the rod tip and will straighten without tangling. Because the plane is tilted, if weight on the leader causes it to sag, the top of the loop will be to the outside of the bottom and will not collide with it.

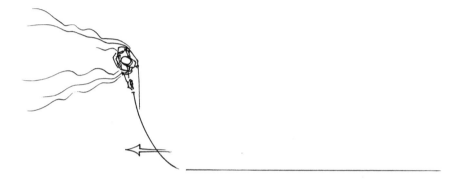

The forecast is made with the normal load, power, and stop movements, but in a longer and more fluid stroke that keeps touch with the line and throws an open loop. If you want, you can tilt the rod over slightly in the opposite direction from a sidearm cast, causing the forecast loop to unfurl with the top of the loop a bit outside of the bottom. Again, if weight on the leader causes the top to sag, it will not collapse onto the bottom.

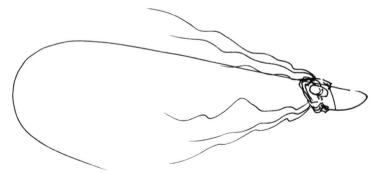

If you're fishing a dry fly, you can use a constant oval to hold the line in the air while you wait for a trout to rise. You can also use a small, fast oval to dry your fly quickly between presentations and get it back onto the water quickly in what some guides call *speed casting*. This lets you make presentation after presentation to the same rising trout, in hopes that one of the casts will put the fly in the right place just when the trout is ready to rise again.

## LINE CONTROL ON THE WATER

The most critical part of any cast is what you do before you make it. First, assess the situation to decide what rig and method you're going to use. Then stalk or wade into the best position before you cast. The closer you can get to trout, or the suspected lies of trout, without alerting them that you're there, the easier it will be to present your fly to them and coax them into taking it.

Once you've made your cast, you must control your line on the water. This consists primarily of three things: gathering slack to remain in position to set the hook, feeding slack to extend the length of a drift, and mending line to eliminate drag.

**Gathering slack.** Whenever you're fishing upstream, whether with dry flies or nymphs, the line, leader, and fly will begin drifting toward you as soon as they land on the water. Slack occurs in the line between the fly and the rod tip, and if you let this slack accumulate on the water, you'll have to remove it after a fish takes the fly and before you can move the hook to set it. To prevent this, always gather slack as soon as it forms, simply by drawing it in through the guides. You can lift your rod to take out some slack, but don't lift it too high so that you have no room left to lift it to set the hook if a trout hits.

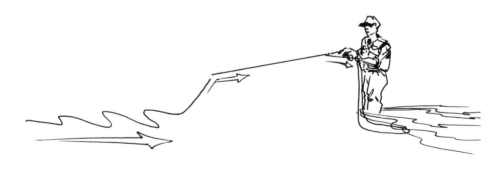

**Feeding slack.** When fishing downstream, you'll find many times when you want to feed slack into the drift in order to extend it. If you are casting dry flies over rising trout, feeding slack can be critical for reaching fish sipping just where your fly might start to drag. When you are shot-and-indicator nymphing, the fly might reach strike zone depth, down near the bottom, as it drifts back even with you. By feeding slack to extend the drift downstream, you keep the fly in that zone a lot longer.

You can feed slack by letting it slip out through the rod guides, although the resulting tension might hinder a drift, even of an indicator rig. Instead, you might want to wiggle your rod tip back and forth to draw slack out through the guides and lay it in S curves on the water in front of you. Then as it feeds out, it will not cause drag.

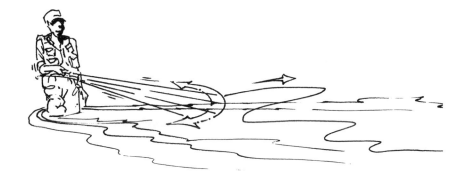

**Mending line.** When you cast across currents, the moving water typically produces more leverage against the thicker, heavier running part of the fly line than it does against the lighter, thinner front taper and leader. This causes the back of the line to move faster downstream, forming what is termed a ***downstream belly*** in the line. Your dry flies will begin to drag, and if you're fishing a nymph rig, the belly will speed the drift of your indicator and lift your fly away from the bottom.

To counteract this type of drag, use an ***upstream mend*** to lift the belly off the water and flip it over into an upstream curve. The dry fly or strike indicator will then

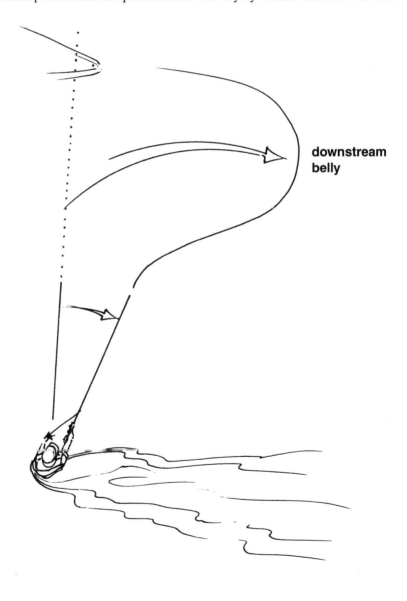

downstream
belly

float without drag until the slack is pushed back out of the line into another down-stream belly, at which time you must mend again. You can use the same mend to slow the swing of a wet fly or streamer. On slow water, you can use a ***downstream mend*** to catch the current and speed the swing of a wet fly or streamer. Most of the time you'll make small to big upstream mends to slow the drift or swing of all types of flies.

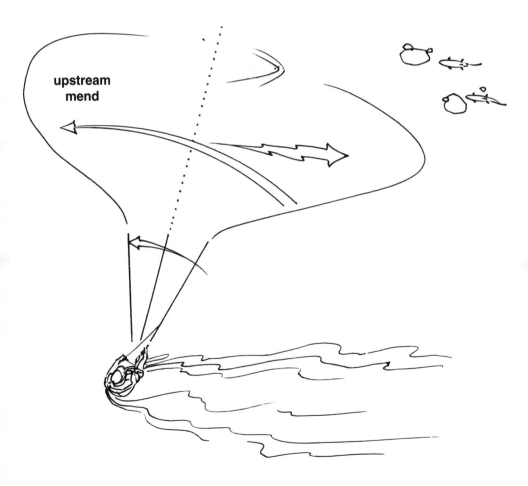

upstream
mend

## SETTING THE HOOK

Setting the hook involves seating the hook in the trout's jaw without breaking it off. I dislike stiff rods for all but distance casting situations, which are rare when trout fishing on moving water. Stiff rods also smash tippets on the hook set. The finer the tippets you fish, the softer the tip of the rod you need to protect them.

Different types of flies send different messages that tell you when it's time to set the hook, and request that you set it in different ways. The most common scenarios follow.

**Large dry flies (size 8 to 12).** Large dry flies are typically fished during non-hatch situations, often on riffled water or in creeks and small streams. Trout take them with speed and assurance. Most often you'll see the fly disappear in a slight splash or a bold boil. Set the hook the moment you notice the take. Lift the rod quickly, though not with enough strength to break off. Upon turning down with the fly, the trout will quickly ascertain that the fly is feathers and fluff, not food, and will eject it soon. Large dry flies fished on fast water require the quickest hook sets.

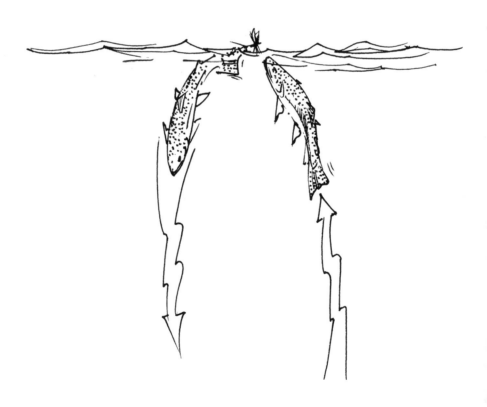

**Small dry flies (size 14 to 22).** Small flies are often fished over trout feeding on small insects, usually on smooth water. Trout take such flies with slow and deliberate sips, and a quick hook set will often pull the hook away before the trout has closed its mouth on the fly. Discipline yourself to wait a beat or two, until you are sure the trout has turned down with the fly, then lift the rod gently. It doesn't take much force to pull such a small hook home. If you miss the strike, a harsh hook set will rip the fly out of the fish's mouth and put the fish down. If you don't miss, a hook set with too much vigor will break you off.

The largest trout take with the slowest rises, perhaps because it takes them longer to close their large mouths on the smaller flies. Whatever the reason, a quick hook set with small flies will almost always succeed with the little fish and fail with the big ones. Be patient, and take your cue from fly fishers in New Zealand, where almost all the trout are big ones. Before setting the hook, they mumble, "God save the Queen."

**Nymphs with indicators.** Noticing takes to nymphs fished with strike indicators takes practice. Takes that cause the indicator to dip are obvious, but some cause little more than a twitch or slight tug in a direction away from the current. Get into the habit of setting the hook any time your indicator acts contrary to the current. By the time the indicator moves, the trout has already mouthed the nymph and will quickly realize that it's not real. You should react instantly, but not violently.

The strike must take the slack out of the line and leader and then move the indicator and any weight on the leader before it moves the nymph. A short movement of the rod will not do it. You have to lift quickly and steadily in a long arc. When nymph fishing, it's very important to remain in constant position to set the hook throughout every drift.

**Wet flies and streamers.** The most common way to fish wets and streamers is on the swing, downstream and across the current, on a tight line. The take usually feels like a sharp rap or sullen tug, and such takes set all but dull hooks. Merely raise the rod to engage the fish and begin playing it. If your hook is large and your leader stout, give another rap if you desire, but don't break off a big fish. If a trout takes a swinging fly going straight away from you, a jerk on your end will instantly cause a snap at the other.

With wet flies, especially soft-hackles, takes are often tiny taps or no more than a slow and steadily increasing pressure against the line. In either case, wait until you feel weight on the line before lifting the rod to begin playing the fish. If you set the hook sooner, you'll almost always pull the fly away from the fish.

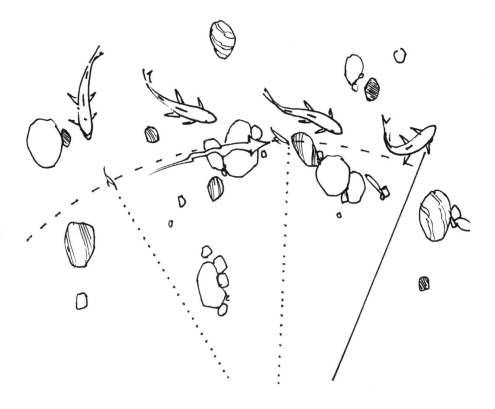

# CHAPTER 3

# Fly Selection

Your flies, like your tackle, should enable you to fish the full range of trout rigs and methods. When trout hold and feed along the bottom, which they do more than half the time, you need nymphs. When they chase baitfish, you need streamers. When they feed on aquatic insects passing through the mid-depths on their way to the surface, you need wet flies and soft-hackles. When they feed on emergers or adults on the surface, you need the right types of flies to entice them to the top.

**Two types of feeding.** When trout see a wide variety of natural insects and crustaceans delivered by the current, they feed opportunistically. Usually they'll hold along the bottom, where they accept whatever drifts to them as long as it looks alive. If the water is fairly shallow, say less than 5 feet or so, they'll also dash up to take insects that float over their heads on the surface. When trout feed opportunistically, you can almost always catch them with searching flies.

Trout feed selectively when a hatch of insects, fall of terrestrials, drift of crustaceans, or any other activity makes a species of food form abundant and available. They focus on one species, or one stage of a species, refusing any fly that does not resemble what they're eating. To catch trout when they're feeding selectively, you must present imitative flies.

**An array of fly boxes.** I suggest that you consider acquiring fly boxes in a logical order, or that you take time to create some order for those that you might already own. First, have a basic *box of searching flies* that includes a short list of the most effective drys, nymphs, wets, and streamers. With this box, you can fish creeks and small streams and also succeed on most other waters when you want to travel light. A box of searching flies is a great place to start. Give it a permanent seat in your belt bag or chest pack, as recommended for creek fishing in chapter 1.

**Opportunistic feeding**

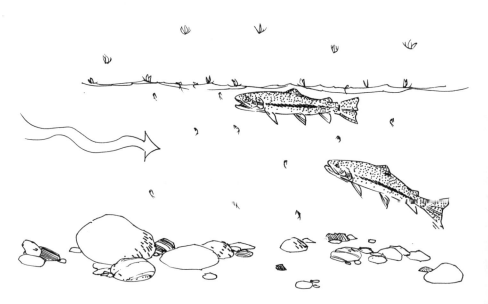

**Selective feeding**

Second, build a ***dry-fly box*** in which you place a narrow selection of both searching and imitative flies at first. Expand this selection over time to cover the full range of surface situations that you encounter. If you often fish hatches of small insects, add an ***emerger box,*** though you could also simply add a few emerger patterns to your dry fly box.

Third, a ***nymph box*** should be filled with those flies you will use when trout are feeding on the bottom. I recommend a big box for nymphs; your flies will surely expand to fill it. Fourth, a ***wet-fly and streamer box*** will cover those times when trout are feeding in the middle depths or chasing in the shallows. Finally, I suggest a separate ***stillwater fly box*** if you fish a lot of lakes and ponds; this box will be covered in chapter 10.

If you find that your trout fishing begins to direct itself to specific hatches, then buy a small box for each important insect that you encounter often—blue-wing olives, sulfurs, midges—and carry that box whenever a hatch is expected.

## SEARCHING-FLY BOX

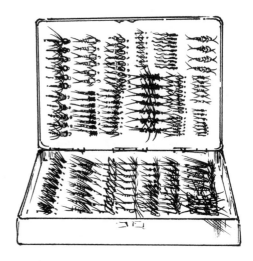

The best searching flies of all kinds—drys, nymphs, wets, and streamers—are almost always based on natural food forms. Two of the best are the Elk Hair Caddis, an adult caddisfly imitation, and the Parachute Adams, originally a mayfly dun imitation. But there are exceptions. The Royal Wulff, with its striped green and red body and white wings, seems to resemble nothing in nature, but get the body wet and it is suddenly segmented dark green and reddish-brown, very natural colors, and its wings help you follow its float on the water. This fly works because it looks like a lot of things in nature, though it doesn't look exactly like any one of them. It fools a great number of trout.

The selection of flies in your searching box should be carefully chosen to cover the broadest range of trout foods. Each fly should be a proven pattern. A suggested list follows, but your own box should contain any favorite flies that have worked for you over the years.

### SEARCHING-FLY SHORT LIST

| | |
|---|---|
| Elk Hair Caddis, size 12 to 16 | A. P. Black, size 10 to 16 |
| Royal Wulff, size 12 to 16 | Beadhead Prince, size 12 to 16 |
| Stimulator, size 6 to 12 | Brassie, size 16 to 20 |
| Chernobyl Ant, size 6 to 12 | Muddler Minnow, size 6 to 12 |
| Parachute Adams, size 14 to 20 | Olive Wolly Bugger, size 6 to 12 |
| Beadhead Hare's Ear, size 12 to 16 | March Brown Spider, size 12 to 16 |
| Whitlock Fox Squirrel, size 14 to 18 | Leadwing Coachman, size 12 to 16 |

## DRY-FLY BOX

Your dry-fly box, which over time might become two or three or even more dry-fly boxes, should contain both searching dry flies for opportunistic feeding periods and imitative flies for times when trout feed selectively. A few patterns will overlap between your searching fly box and dry-fly box and other specific boxes as well.

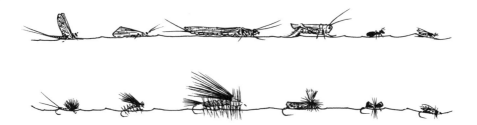

The flies with which you begin to build this dry-fly box should reflect the wide range of floating food types upon which trout feed most often: mayfly duns and spinners, caddis and stonefly adults, grasshoppers, ants and beetles, and midges. It should also reflect the knowledge that mayflies, caddis, stoneflies, and midges—the most abundant aquatic insects—come in a set of repeated color themes. Many pattern styles, such as the Compara-dun for mayflies and Elk Hair Caddis for caddisflies, should be tied in more than one color so that you can fish important hatches.

### DRY-FLY SHORT LIST

| | |
|---|---|
| Adams, size 12 to 16 | Deer Hair Caddis, size 12 to 16 |
| Light Cahill, size 12 to 16 | King's River Caddis, size 12 to 18 |
| Olive Compara-dun, size 14 to 20 | Stimulator, size 6 to 12 |
| Sulfur Compara-dun, size 14 to 18 | Improved Sofa Pillow, size 6 to 10 |
| Parachute Adams, size 16 to 20 | Adams Midge, size 16 to 22 |
| Olive Parachute, size 14 to 20 | Parachute Hopper, size 8 to 12 |
| Sulfur Parachute, size 14 to 18 | Foam Ant, size 16 to 20 |
| Tan Elk Hair Caddis, size 12 to 16 | Foam Beetle, size 14 to 20 |

## EMERGER BOX

You'll use emergers, sometimes called cripples, only in selective situations. If you don't fish hatches often, you can easily omit this box, and thereby lighten the burden in your bulging vest. If you do fish hatches, you'll find that you turn to emergers during hatches of small insects on smooth water.

When rising up for emergence, aquatic insects larger than about a size 16 have enough mass to break through the surface film without getting stuck. Trout feed on smaller emergers far more often than large ones. Insects emerging in riffles and rough runs are not hindered by surface tension, because it is broken up by the seething water. They might drown before they escape the surface or get taken under by the currents, but they don't get stuck in the surface as emergers.

Most of your emerger fishing will be over size 16 and smaller mayflies, caddisflies, and midges on spring creeks, tailwaters, and the smooth flats of freestone streams. On these kinds of waters, hatches are heaviest and trout become selective most often.

### EMERGER SHORT LIST

| | |
|---|---|
| Olive Polypro Emerger, size 14 to 20 | Quigley Cripple, size 12 to 18 |
| Sulfur Polypro Emerger, size 14 to 18 | Olive X-Caddis, size 14 to 20 |
| Olive Sparkle Dun, size 14 to 20 | Tan X-Caddis, size 14 to 18 |
| Sulfur Sparkle Dun, size 14 to 18 | Klinkhamer Special, size 14 to 20 |
| Palomino, size 16 to 22 | |

## NYMPH BOX

You might as well start out buying a big nymph box; as you experiment with nymphs, your supply is going to outgrow almost anything you can buy to hold them. Make sure, however, that the box can still fit in the largest pocket of your fishing vest.

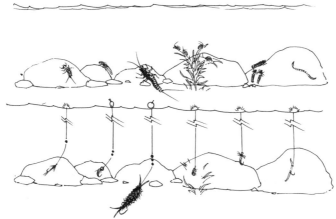

You'll want to fill your box with nymphs that cover all the common food forms: mayfly and stonefly nymphs, caddisfly and midge larvae and pupae, scuds, and even aquatic worms. Some of the most effective searching nymphs, such as the red San Juan Worm, might seem unrealistic, but kick around in stream gravels with a collecting net and you'll realize how abundant aquatic worms can be, and why an imitation for them takes trout in almost all moving waters.

Your nymph box should also contain a variety of searching patterns, such as the Beadhead Hare's Ear and Beadhead Prince. Although they don't imitate any naturals exactly, they look a little like enough of them that trout often mistake them for the real thing.

### NYMPH SHORT LIST

| | |
|---|---|
| Flashback Pheasant Tail, size 14 to 22 | Peeking Caddis, size 10 to 16 |
| Beadhead Hare's Ear, size 12 to 18 | San Juan Worm, size 12 to 16 |
| Whitlock Fox Squirrel, size 12 to 16 | Olive Scud, size 12 to 16 |
| Beadhead Green Rock Worm, size 12 to 16 | Kaufmann's Stonefly, size 6 to 10 |
| Olive Serendipity, size 16 to 20 | Brooks Stone, size 8 to 12 |
| Red Serendipity, size 16 to 20 | Girdle Bug, size 6 to 10 |
| TDC, size 14 to 18 | |

## WET-FLY AND STREAMER BOX

Not many folks fish wet flies anymore, but carrying a few, and knowing when to use them, will solve some situations for you. Wet flies work whenever trout feed opportunistically; they also catch trout feeding selectively on caddis pupae rising for emergence, caddis adults diving to lay their eggs on the bottom, and drowned mayfly duns or spinners. Soft-hackled wet flies, tied with little more than thread bodies and a turn of hackle from a grouse, partridge, or similar land bird, can give the impression of many nymphs, pupae, and drowned adult insects that trout eat, and with their kicking little legs, they look very lifelike.

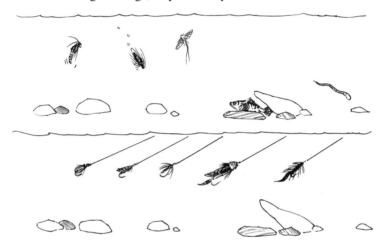

Streamers tend to incite strikes from larger predatory trout. It's a good idea to carry some large ones for big-fish situations, such as on large rivers or smaller waters with deep pockets and undercut banks. But don't neglect smaller streamers, which often induce action when the general run of dry flies, nymphs, and wet flies fail.

---

### WET-FLY AND STREAMER SHORT LIST

| | |
|---|---|
| Hare's Ear Wet, size 12 to 16 | Starling & Herl, size 16 to 18 |
| Leadwing Coachman, size 12 to 16 | Muddler Minnow, size 2 to 12 |
| Olive Sparkle Pupa, size 12 to 16 | Black Marabou Muddler, size 2 to 12 |
| Partridge & Orange, size 10 to 14 | Olive Woolly Bugger, size 4 to 12 |
| Partridge & Yellow, size 10 to 14 | Black Woolly Bugger, size 4 to 12 |
| Partridge & Green, size 10 to 14 | Zonker, size 2 to 8 |
| March Brown Spider, size 12 to 16 | |

# PART 2

# Moving Water

# CHAPTER 4

# Reading Water, Finding Trout

Y ou'll find yourself fly fishing for trout in two basic ways. The first is to
*visible fish*, and the second is to *likely lies*. If you spot trout, you're more
likely to catch them because you'll know precisely where to cast. You'll
also know you're not fishing that bane of beginners—empty water. Since you'll
probably spot the trout when they're actively feeding, they are more prone to accept
the right fly if it's fished in the right way.

Feeding trout, however, are more likely to be somewhat selective, so you must
determine what they're taking. Select a fly to match the natural food form at least
reasonably. Then correctly rig the fly and select the proper method to present it so
that the trout see it the same way as the naturals on which they're feeding. If you
fish the wrong fly right, you'll have a good chance of fooling some fish, but if you
fish the right fly wrong, you're more likely to frighten them.

Spotting trout requires a great degree of patience. I recommend that you don't
begin rigging up until you've stepped to the waterside and taken some time to look
over the creek, stream, or river you're about to fish. After observing the winds and
weathers and the height and color of the water, search for visible trout. Look for
rises in all sorts of water: rough and smooth, in pockets, hidden along the banks,
tucked into eddies. Some rises will be obvious, but many sipping rises will catch
your eye only as something oddly out of place.

To spot trout beneath the surface, you must wear polarized sunglasses. A pair
with amber tint are better than darker gray because they eliminate surface glare
without reducing the amount of light illuminating the trout you want to see. A
billed hat also helps, and you can try cupping your hands around your eyes to block
out extraneous light rays.

When fishing likely lies, as opposed to spotting fish, you must rely on your
ability to read water and assess where trout are most likely to hold in it. To a great
extent, experience helps: The more you fish, the more trout you'll catch, and the

**71**

more your subconcious will build an image of the types of water your flies were in when they were attacked by trout. The next time you see some water shaped that same way, you will know to cast to it, and when your fly gets whacked again, this reinforces that image. Fishing is the best way to learn to read water. You can also read books on the subject, but they won't help as much as going fishing.

A bit of knowledge about the needs of trout, and how moving water meets those needs, will increase your ability to read and find trout. Trout need cool water and oxygen, so you won't find them in stagnant water. In creeks, streams, and rivers, they need current to deliver food, but because they are unable to swim against a strong current for very long, they also need shelter from the same current that feeds them. They require some minor depth of water, or broken water over their heads, to protect them from predators such as kingfishers, ospreys, and you and me.

To summarize, trout need cool and well-oxygenated water with a current to it, some boulders or other obstructions to break that current, and a bit of depth or broken water. That's about it. If you search out water that provides those simple needs, you'll find trout.

Even after you've rigged and begun fishing likely lies, keep a sharp eye out for rises and other visible trout. If you spot them, it will suddenly change the game.

## SPOTTING FISH

You'll spot trout most often by their rises, so you should develop a keen eye to see them. But you'll also add an increment of success to your fishing if you improve your ability to spot trout beneath the surface.

**Trout rising in rhythm.** Most often during a hatch of aquatic insects or fall of terrestrials, trout hold high in the water and set up on stations, waiting for the current to deliver bites downstream to them. When food arrives, they tip up to take it. If nature offers abundance, they often tip up in a rhythm, taking one insect, skipping one or two to a bunch, then tipping up again when ready.

**Trout cruising and rising.** When insects are scattered over a fairly flat surface, trout often move around, watching for them, rather than holding in a single station and waiting for them. When an insect is spotted, the trout moves to take it, anywhere from 1 foot to 3 or 4 feet or more, depending on the size of the insect and the inclinations of the trout.

**Trout cruising and hunting.** Trout out hunting big bites such as sculpins and baitfish, usually at morning and evening, are most often big. Look for them on shallow gravel bars and uplifting tailouts of pools, or down in the more obscure depths of runs.

**Trout holding in lies along the bottom.** The bottom is the most common place to find fish that are not feeding on a hatch. Trout tuck in behind a boulder, into a trench, or along a ledge that breaks the current, waiting to accept what the current delivers to them, including your dead-drifted nymph.

**Winking along the bottom or in the middepths.** When trout feed on fair numbers of insects in the drift along the bottom, or less often when they suspend in the middepths and nip at insects passing through on their way toward the top or bottom, you can spot them by the winks their sides make as they turn to take prey.

**Spooked trout.** If you approach the tailout of a pool, especially on a creek or small stream, and see one to several V wakes arrowing briskly away from you toward the darkest cover or the deepest depths, you just scared some trout that were holding on the shallows. The spooked trout are your sign to forget that pool, but a reminder to slow down and watch the water carefully on your approach to the next one.

## READING LIKELY LIES

When you can't spot trout, either feeding or holding, you'll have to read the water for the most likely lies. These lies will reveal themselves by the way the water gathers and delivers food to the fish, shelters them from the currents that bring the food, and protects them from overhead predation.

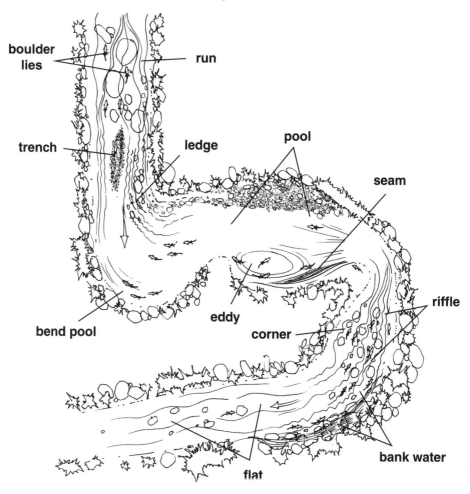

**Riffles.** These fast stretches are richest in aquatic insects and often hold trout where boulders or other obstructions break the current. Trout will be on constant lookout for a wide variety of nymphs, larvae, pupae, and adults drifting or floating by. You'll find trout sprinkled in riffles wherever they can get out of the constant current.

**Runs.** Runs are typically deeper than riffles and have less brisk currents. Trout hold along the bottom of runs wherever any structure gives them shelter. In a shallow run, 3 to 5 feet deep, trout will dash to the top to take floating insects and dry flies. In deeper runs, 6 to 10 or more feet, it will take a hatch to get them to move to the top.

**Flats.** Gentler currents, and sometimes heavy hatches make flats the perfect water to read by waiting for a hatch to draw trout to the top. In nonhatch periods, fish will hold near the bottom, often rooting in vegetation for insects and crustaceans or waiting to accept drifting nymphs, either naturals or yours.

**Pools.** The word *pool* is often used to define any water that holds trout. I use it here to describe water that enters from a riffle or run, carves out depths, and ends in a tailout where the water lifts into faster water downstream. Each pool has a head, depths, and tailout. Trout are usually found in the depths except when food offered at the head or tailout encourages them to move upstream or downstream to take advantage of it.

**Banks.** Three things define good bank water: current to deliver food, shelter from that current, and depth for protection from predators. Though short stretches of good bank water can be found on almost any moving water, the best bank water is usually found on streams stabilized by spring creek or tailwater origins.

**Eddies.** Wherever the bank deflects a current outward, the water will reverse itself and move back upstream along the bank to fill the vacuum, forming an eddy. Eddies have slow currents and gather drifting and floating food. Trout, often large ones, laze around in eddies and feed on whatever the rotating currents deliver.

**Boulder lies.** Wherever a boulder along the bottom breaks the current, whether in a riffle, run, pool, or on a flat, trout will find soft spots just upstream and down from the boulder. Protruding boulders are easy to see. Submerged boulders hold trout just as well, so look for a subtle boil on the surface indicating a boulder below.

**Trenches.** Wherever the bottom drops away into a trench, no matter how slight, trout find relief from the current. Watch for lines of slick water on the surface in riffles and even cascades; these often mark trenches down below and should be fished carefully.

**Ledges.** Ledges that cut across currents break the flow and provide perfect lies just downstream. You'll often find trout lined up at intervals where a ledge breaks a productive riffle, to collect the abundance of food delivered to them there.

**Riffle and pool corners.** When fast water enters a pool, it almost always leaves a slower, shallower wedge of water on the inside edge. Because the corner provides the nearest soft water for trout to hold and dash out to intercept whatever gets delivered from the riffle, these corners are among the most productive water on any creek, stream, or river.

**Current seams.** Wherever two currents of disparate speeds come together, they form a current seam that collects food from both sides and delivers it in a straight line downstream. Trout often line up along a seam to take advantage of this collected drift.

**Pocket water.** Even the most brutal cascades will have spots where the current is broken by boulders, ledges, or trenches. If such soft pockets are big enough for trout to tuck into, to avoid the current and dash out for food swept by, you can be sure that one or two fish will hold in each pocket.

# CHAPTER 5

# Rigs and Methods for
# Dry Flies and Emergers

D rys and emergers are treated together in this chapter because they're fished with the same set of rigs and methods. Dry flies float atop the surface film; emergers are usually fished riding flush in that same film, though some are fished just inches beneath it. To successfully fish either dry flies or emergers, you must solve the same set of problems: choosing whether to use an imitative or searching fly; rigging to present it delicately; keeping the fly afloat; providing visibility to follow its drift; and preventing unnatural and therefore alarming drag once it gets onto water.

**Imitative or searching fly?** If insects are present on the water and trout are rising to take them, then clearly you need to collect what they're eating, examine it, and choose an imitative fly that looks at least a little like it. If no trout are rising, then simply choose a favorite searching fly. If you pick one based on a food form, say an insect that you notice abundant in streamside vegetation or flying in the air but not on the water, then it's more likely to remind the trout of something they've eaten lately.

**Rigging to fish the fly delicately.** Arm yourself with an $8^{1}/_{2}$- to 9-foot presentation rod—except on creeks where the rod should be 7 to 8 feet long—and a 3- to at most 5-weight line balanced to the rod. If the water is small or rough, use a leader about the length of the rod. If the water is smooth, extend the leader out accordingly, to between 11 and 15 feet, with 2 to 4 feet tippet. See the chart on the following page to balance fly size to tippet diameter. The smoother the water, snottier the trout, and smaller the fly, then the longer and finer the tippet you need.

## BALANCING FLY SIZE TO TIPPET DIAMETER

To have your fly turn over in the air properly and land on the water as it should, your leader tippet should be in balance with the size fly you tie to its end.

| Tippet size | Diameter | Fly size |
|:-----------:|:--------:|:--------:|
| 2X | .009" | 6, 8, 10 |
| 3X | .008" | 10, 12, 14 |
| 4X | .007" | 12, 14, 16 |
| 5X | .006" | 14, 16, 18, 20 |
| 6X | .005" | 18, 20, 22, 24 |
| 7X | .004" | 20, 22, 24, 26 |

**Keeping your fly afloat.** Make sure your fly type suits the water type—high floating for rough water, low floating for smooth water. Dress your fly with floatant before casting it to prevent it from soaking up water. Before every presentation, make a couple of brisk backcasts to whip water off the fly. When your fly becomes waterlogged and begins to subside, or any time after you've caught a trout, dry the fly on a handkerchief and reapply floatant. If it's a CDC dry, swish it in water to clean it, shake it in dessicant to dry it, and apply CDC powder to keep it afloat. Never apply paste floatant to CDC flies. When any dry fly or emerger can no longer be refloated, nip it off and tie on another.

**Following the drift.** You want to be able to see your fly on the water to know where it is and whether it's drifting without drag. You also want to notice takes so that you can set the hook. Large searching flies are usually no problem, although using flies with light-colored wings in good light, or dark wings to show against the water in low light, will help. With small dry flies and low-floating emergers, you might have to slip-knot a small yarn indicator 4 to 6 feet up the leader or use a larger, more visible dry fly as an indicator.

**Preventing drag.** Almost all natural insects when afloat on the water surface simply sit and drift without movement. If your dry fly gets tugged around by the tippet, even the most foolish wilderness trout will recognize it as an unnatural movement and refuse the fly. A dry fly allowed to drag rarely catches trout. Therefore, your goal, when fishing dry flies and emergers, is to eliminate drag. The following steps will help.

**Read conflicting currents.** Learn to scan the water where you're about to cast your dry or emerger, and look for currents that go in different directions or flow at different speeds. These conflicting currents will pull in opposite directions, straighten the line and leader, and begin to propel the fly across the surface. Only after you understand what causes drag, and begin to look for it, can you begin to solve it.

**Choose the best casting position.** Once you've studied the currents over which you must cast, you'll be able to determine the best place from which to launch the cast. Get as close as you can without alarming the trout or spooking the lie. You want to place as many conflicting currents as you can behind you, rather than between you and the trout or likely lie. So that you don't alarm the fish or spook the lie, move into position slowly, crouch if necessary, send out no warning wading waves, and do not make sudden broad gestures that attract the eye of the trout.

**Choose the best cast for the position.** Now, choose your method—your cast—to suit the position you've taken. You might, for example, find it necessary to move out of an unsuitable downstream position and into a more suitable cross-stream or even upstream position, to avoid conflicting currents. You would then use a cross-stream reach cast, or downstream wiggle cast, as opposed to the more traditional upstream presentation.

**Control line on the water.** Once you've read the currents, taken the best position, and made the right cast, you can often fish out the cast without any further attention to anything but the trout rising to take your freely drifting fly. Often, however, the line and then the leader will begin to draw taut and cause drag. If necessary, mend to remove a downstream belly, feed line to extend the free drift, and reach with your arm and the rod top to take pressure off the line and leader. Sometimes you'll have to be creative in your cast, and in the mending and tending you do after the cast, to prevent drag.

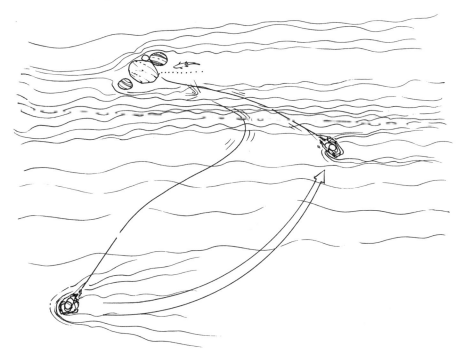

## RIG:          STANDARD DRY FLY

**Purpose.** The standard dry-fly rig consists of a floating line; leader tapered down to a long, fine tippet; and fly tied to the tippet. It is designed to present dry flies on moving water as if they were free from attachment to any sort of restraint. The line can be as light as a 2-weight in windless conditions or as heavy as a 6- or even 7-weight when casting big dry flies over broad, windy riffles. A 3- to 5-weight is best for most dry-fly fishing. The lighter the line, the more delicate the presentation. The leader should be tapered in a way that transfers the energy of the cast from the line through the leader to the fly. It should straighten in the air before falling to the water, but it should not land perfectly straight, or you might get drag. Not only does the long tippet make an invisible connection, but it recoils somewhat after straightening and lands with slack, giving the fly that desired free float.

**History/origins.** The tapered leader originated in horsehairs, which were tied in sections of several hairs together, down through two or three, to a single strand at the point. Later silkworm gut leaders, extruded through holes of ever finer diameter measured in thousandths of an inch, gave us the X system—each descending X being .001 inch finer—and leaders that had to be tied in 20-inch sections, the maximum length of gut strands, and soaked before they could be fished. Modern nylon monofilament is far stronger for a given diameter, is not limited in length, and can be extruded in tapers that eliminate the need for knotted leaders, though many dry-fly fishers still prefer to tie their own leaders.

**Knots and notes.** It's a good idea to nail-knot a permanent 1-foot butt section of heavy leader to your line tip, so you will not have to nip off 2 to 3 inches of fly line every time you change leaders. The base leader should be tied to this butt with a blood knot. If you tie your own leaders, join tapering sections with the blood knot. Tippet sections can be joined with the blood knot or with the faster and slightly stronger surgeon's knot.

Most experienced dry-fly fishers now buy tapered base leaders and add tippet sections with the surgeon's knot to suit the situation. I carry $7^{1}/_{2}$-foot, 3X leaders for creek and small stream fishing and often add 2 feet of 4X, or 1 foot of 4X and 2 feet of 5X, to fish small flies. I carry 9- or 10-foot, 3X base leaders for most stream and river fishing and add a foot of 4X, then 3 feet of 5X, or a foot of 5X and 3 to 4 feet of 6X. It's a very simple system, but it works quite well.

**Adjustments for conditions.** Most necessary adjustments are built into the base-leader-and-tippet system. You can start out fishing large drys, size 6 to 10 or 12, with the short base leader itself. As flies get smaller and trout more selective, lengthen the leader and make it finer at the same time by adding sections of tippet. You can shorten a leader as easily as you can add to it. It's important to keep control of your casts. If your leader is too fine for accurate casts in the conditions you're in, usually a stiff wind, cut it back and retie it with a shorter and perhaps stouter tippet section.

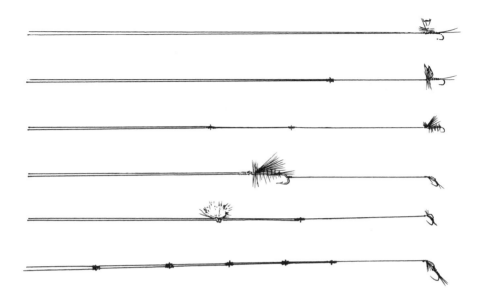

**Rules for the rig.** Always be sure that your leader is helping you, not hindering you, when solving those basic dry-fly problems: presenting the fly delicately and accurately and showing it to the trout on a drag-free drift. If your casts set the fly on the water with a whack, use a longer and finer tippet. If you can't get your fly over a suspected lie or into a trout's feeding lane, cut it back. If your fly drags, add tippet. If your leader does not turn over and lands in a pile, shorten the tippet. You might need to do surgery on the leader, shortening the base tippet before extending it to comply with the size fly.

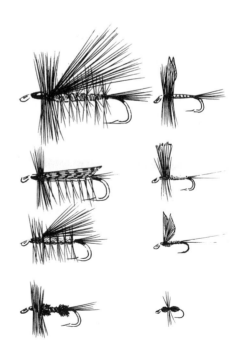

**Appropriate flies.** Given a properly balanced leader, you can fish any searching or imitative dry flies with this basic rig, from size 6 salmon fly imitations to size 24 midge or Trico patterns and any size between.

**RIG:          STANDARD DRY FLY**
**Method:     Standard upstream**

**Situations to solve.** The most common way to travel along a creek, a stream, a small river, and sometimes even a large river is on foot, either wading or hiking the bank, moving upstream, not down. Because trout hold facing into the current, therefore pointing upstream, it's easier to approach them unseen from behind, moving upstream, than it is from the front, moving downstream into their sight. When you come upon visible rising trout, or trout holding in likely lies, from downstream, it's natural to move into position below the trout to keep out of their sight. You'll also find it easier to get a drag-free drift from downstream, since the current pushes the line and leader toward you, introducing slack. The upstream dry fly presents the fewest problems to solve.

**Tuning the rig.** If your rig is already attuned to the size stream you're on and the type of dry fly you're fishing, then you won't have to make any adjustments either for the bit of holding water you'd like to cast to or for rising trout you come upon in your travels. If, however, you've had success working upstream with a searching fly, such as a size 14 Elk Hair Caddis on 4X tippet, and suddenly arrive on a flat where trout are visibly rising to size 18 blue-winged olive mayfly duns, then you need to nip off that Elk Hair Caddis, cut the 4X back a foot, add 3 feet of 5X, and tie on a size 18 BWO imitation.

**Position and presentation.** When approaching a rising trout or a likely lie from downstream, you want to avoid a position directly down current, because that will force you to make your presentation straight over the trout's head. Your line, leader, and fly will all enter into the trout's vision, settle to the water, and then float back down toward it. On very rough water, the arrival of your fly and leader might not alarm the trout. On most water it will.

Take up your position off to one side of the current and your cast will no longer go over the trout or the lie. The fish is not likely to be alarmed by a delicate cast, and the fly will drift toward the trout with the leader off to the side. Any time you find yourself fishing almost straight upstream, even on rough water, move so that you're off to the side of the water you want to fish. Because you now have currents of different speeds between you and the lies you'd like to fish, be sure to work as close as you can to the lies, say 25 to 40 feet. Make your measuring fore- and backcasts off to the side. Only your delivery stroke should be toward the area where the fly will land.

**Control of the drift.** Once your cast is made, begin gathering the slack that the current installs in the line. Don't draw the line tight; just keep enough slack out so that when a trout takes the fly, you'll be able to lift the rod and move the hook to set it. You can lift your rod to take slack out as well, but avoid the most common mistake in dry-fly fishing—letting slack lie on the water and raising the rod so high that when your fly disappears in a splash, you have no room left to maneuver. Setting the hook this way results only in moving slack line, not the fly, and the trout will be gone before you get control.

As you draw in slack, watch your fly carefully. Some dry-fly takes will be violent. Others will be such delicate sips that you'll notice nothing except the absence of your fly. Always set the hook mildly, just in case a trout is out there.

**On the water.** As you move upstream, constantly read the water, watching for likely lies and for rising, cruising, or holding trout. When you spot a trout, or a lie you'd like to fish, determine the best position from which to make your cast, and move into it. Stay out of sight, and don't push any wading waves over the lie or the fish. Keep your line out of sight as you work line out and measure your cast. Present the fly delicately to a point 2 to 4 feet upstream from the trout or suspected lie. Watch the fly carefully in its drift, and be ready to set the hook.

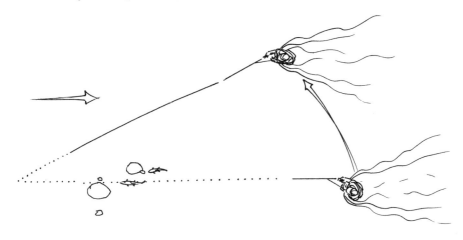

**The trout's point of view.** When you fish an upstream dry fly, the trout will suddenly notice your dry floating on the surface. If the fly looks like something the trout would like to eat, if it's not dragging, and if you have not alarmed the trout with your approach or cast, then the trout is very likely to rise up and either wallop the fly or sip it.

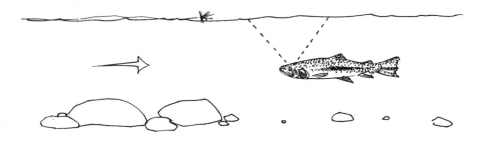

**Situations to solve.** About half the time you spend fishing dry flies on streams of medium size and larger you will be on water types that you know have potential to hold trout. So how do you know precisely where in that water the trout might be located? A broad riffle or run that is 2 to 4 feet deep, the perfect depth to explore with drys, contains rocks, boulders, and small depressions anywhere across the bottom. Trout will be sprinkled in all of these lies, but few of them will send visible indications of their presence up to the surface. That's why you must show your dry fly to any trout that might be holding along the bottom.

**Tuning the rig.** Leader length, tippet diameter, and even fly size will depend on the roughness of the water and the amount of fishing pressure. Adjust your rig to suit the water. If you're on a small mountain stream, a short, stout leader and fairly large dry fly will be most useful. If you're fishing a medium-size foothill stream, you'll cover potential holding water with 9- to 10-foot leaders balanced to a full range of fly sizes. If you're on a big river, fishing riffles with stout leaders and big drys, you'll want to add a 2- to 3-foot finer tippet to balance the smaller flies you'll naturally use when you move to smoother water.

**Position and presentation.** When exploring water to locate trout, move upstream and fish the water as you go. If you want to cover the water well and give yourself the best chance at any scattered trout, try these two techniques. First, take up a position that lets you cast at an angle at least slightly across the current, rather than straight upstream. Second, fish all of the water that you can reach from your initial position with comfortable casts and well-controlled drifts; then move to another position, usually upstream, to cover the next section of water. If you try to cover too much water from one position by extending your casts, you'll soon begin to get drag that you cannot see because your fly is too far away. You also will miss strikes because you either do not notice the striking trout or cannot move enough line to react to them.

From each successive position, make a series of casts and drifts that cause your dry fly to draw parallel lines on the surface 1 to 2 feet apart. Make your first cast close to straight upstream, your first drift nearly under your rod tip. Place the next cast the same distance upstream, just out into the current from the first. Fish the drift down to the same point; then pick up and cast again so that the next drift parallels the previous. Continue until you've covered all of the water or until your casts are stretched to the point where you can no longer control the drift. Then move up to the next position.

**Control of the drift.** At times, if your line crosses conflicting currents, a bit of a mend will contribute to the free drift of your dry. Most of the time when you're covering the water of a riffle or run, in what should be a somewhat disciplined manner, you'll merely have to gather in slack line as the fly floats downstream toward you so that you can react to a strike and set the hook.

**On the water.** Imagine yourself a painter, the water's surface your canvas and the drift of the fly your brushstroke. Cover the nearest drift line with a stroke of the brush—a drift of your dry fly. Continue to cover each succeeding bit of water outward from the first with following brushstrokes. Make sure that every trout holding along the bottom has a chance to see your fly drift almost over its head.

Once you move to position B, stop short of where your fly lit on the water from position A. In this method, your drifts will overlap the coverage from the two positions, and you won't miss any water that might hold trout.

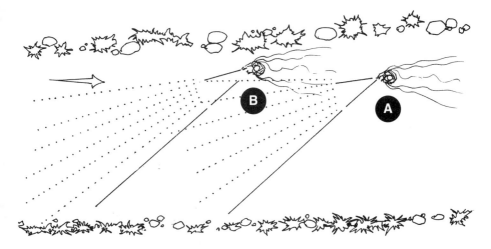

**The trout's point of view.** To trout found down in their sheltered lies along the bottom, the fly should always arrive as a surprise into their sight. They should only see the fly and perhaps the last few inches of the tippet, which, if it's in balance to the size fly you're casting, should allow the fly to float free and naturally.

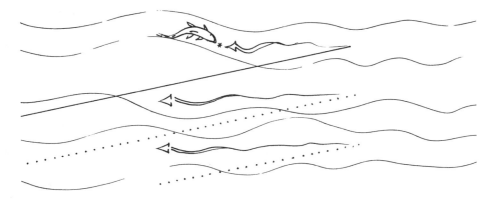

**RIG:         STANDARD DRY FLY**
**Method:      Boulder lies**

**Situations to solve.** A boulder that protrudes from the water forms an obvious lie for trout. Though most folks concentrate their casts in the water directly downstream, the most productive boulder lie is the soft pillow of water directly in front of the boulder. A trout, very often a large one, is likely to hold right near the bottom, at the leading edge of the boulder, feeding on drift or rising to take whatever the current delivers. Other lies are tucked in against each side of a boulder, where the current is deflected out away from it.

The lies directly downstream are usually the most difficult to fish, because the current in the center is running slower than, or even counter to, the currents deflected to both sides. If your cast is more than 25 to 30 feet, then your line will lie across those conflicting currents, and you'll get a very short free drift at best before drag sets in.

**Tuning the rig.** It's not necessary to tune your rig specifically for a boulder encountered in the course of fishing a particular stretch of water. If your leader is the right length for the water you're already fishing, it will almost certainly work for the boulder lie.

**Position and presentation.** Wade into position as close to a boulder as you can get without disturbing any trout that might be lying in the currents broken by it. If the water is fast and choppy, wade to within a rod length or two. If it's smoother, then fish it from farther off, but not much more than three rod lengths. Move in from the side and just downstream from the boulder, rather than directly up the slipstream formed by it.

Make your first presentations to the lie on the near side, placing the fly on the seam where the water deflected around the boulder meets the main current. Your objective is to get a drift down that seam; if you cast too far and cross it, placing your fly on the slow water behind the boulder, you'll get almost instant drag.

Move in closer and place your next presentations on the soft water behind the boulder itself. Your fly will land on slow water, and your leader and line will cross the seam between fast and slow. The instant your fly lands, lift your rod high to keep as much line and leader as you can off the water. If you cannot approach close enough to keep your line off the water, you will not be able to fish the downstream side of a boulder effectively. Let the fly idle in the eddy behind the boulder, and also coax it into free drifts down the center of the soft current for the first few feet below the boulder.

If you can lift most of your leader off the water, then cast to the seam on the far side, and let the fly drift on that interface of fast and slow water as far as it will. The best edge lie on both sides is even with the boulder, not downstream from it.

Make your final set of presentations to that most likely lie just upstream from the boulder. Cast 2 to 4 feet upstream, no more. Lift the line and as much of the leader as possible off the water. Let the fly drift as long as it will, all the way to where the water wells up on the front edge of the boulder. Your strike is most likely to happen just as the fly is about to drag off to one side or the other.

**Control of the drift.** Control the drift of your dry fly in all boulder lies through a combination of short casts and the lofted rod. Gather line in as the fly drifts downstream. An occasional mend, most often flicking just the tip of the line and butt of the leader upstream, will often delay the onset of drag.

**On the water.** Think of trout as being located in four positions relative to the boulder—directly upstream, downstream, and tucked in tight to each side. It's not likely that any boulder will have trout in all of the lies, but you must fish each to figure out which they're using. From position A, fish the near side seam (1), then the downstream eddy (2), followed by the far side seam (3). Move to position B to fish the upstream pillow (4). If the boulder and the currents are shaped right, you can sometimes fish the far seam and the upstream lie by draping the line across the boulder, anchoring it against drag, from position A. But that is not common.

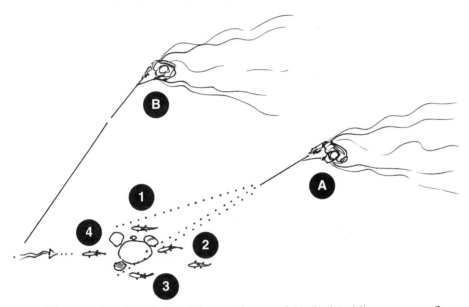

**The trout's point of view.** If a trout in any of the depicted lies sees your fly drag before it sees it drifting freely, then that fish will be alerted to the fraud, and you're not likely to bring it to your fly on any subsequent casts. Calculate each position and cast carefully, and make sure that your first cast to that lie is also your best.

| RIG: | STANDARD DRY FLY |
|---|---|
| Method: | Bank water |

**Situations to solve.** The best bank water is always defined by three things: current to deliver food, depth to provide protection from predators, and boulders on the bottom or indentations in the bank to interrupt the current and give trout places to hold without fighting it. Because of the requirements for current and depth, you'll rarely find places where you can wade out from a good bank and fish back in toward it. Such water does exist, but most good banks must be fished from the bank, not waded.

You must solve three problems when fishing banks: First, navigate through tangles of brush and boulders; second, get your fly onto the water near the edge without catching tall grasses, shrubs, and trees; and third, get a drag-free drift of your fly on currents that are often somewhat seething. Of course, you might find rare banks that are manicured and have even sheets of current flowing along them. If you do, enjoy them. Most folks don't enjoy fishing the average tangled bank, which is why you find so many large trout hanging out in difficult places along them.

**Tuning the rig.** A long rod is a clear advantage along all but creek and small stream banks. The leader should be the length of the rod or a bit longer: 9 to 10 feet. Keep the tippet to a couple of feet and at the heavy end to balance the size fly you're using. Make sure your rig gives you as much casting control as possible; you'll need it in those constrained circumstances. If the currents along the bank you're fishing have lots of conflict, which is common, then dress your leader with line cleaner or fly floatant from the line tip to the tippet knot. It will skate over those currents, rather than getting tugged around by them.

**Position and presentation.** Because you always want to fish into the current, you'll almost always be working your way upstream along a bank, sneaking into a position that gives you the clearest possible cast to the edge water while keeping yourself concealed from the eyes of trout. If the current is reversed in an eddy, then you'll need to position yourself at the upper end of it, face downstream, and fish up current where it sweeps the bank.

Fishing banks does not mean standing on the bank and casting out away from it. Rather, you should creep along and place short casts within a foot or two from the edge itself, rarely more than 3 or 4 feet out. If you can reach a boulder lie just outside the bank, you should fish that as described in the previous section, but without wading unless the water allows it. Your best chance to raise a nice trout will be at the upper edge of the boulder.

Many bank lies allow access only from the upstream side, but often good holding water will be protected by overhanging tree branches. In such a case, you'll need to insert yourself into position to cast downstream to it. Place the fly on the water and instantly begin feeding slack into the drift, letting the fly float freely down into the darkness under those protective branches.

**Control of the drift.** Almost all of your line control on bank water will have to come from the cast. So keep it short and accurate. If you're fishing upstream, gather slack as the fly drifts toward you. If you're fishing downstream, feed slack to give the fly a free drift into guarded lies.

**On the water.** The best bank water is almost always found on creeks, streams, and rivers with stabilized flows. Because erosion is constant at the edges of these waters, the banks are dug deeply rather than sloping off gradually as they do on most freestone streams, scoured by spate. You'll find short to long stretches of bank water on typical streams and rivers, sometimes miles of it on spring creeks and tailwaters.

The sections of grassy undercuts on almost all streams are classic bank water. Be sure that your dry fly floats within inches of the edge; the trout will be tucked back beneath the overhang and might not even notice a fly drifting 2 or 3 feet out. The closer it is, the more eager they'll be to take it. The farther out it is, the more reluctant they'll be to expose themselves to get it.

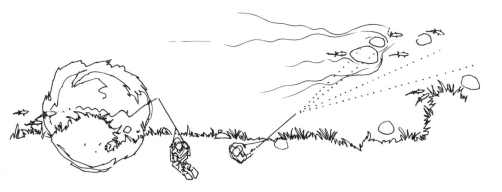

**The trout's point of view.** The bank is the transition line between the aquatic and terrestrial worlds. Food arrives to the trout from both directions. Be watchful for subtle sipping rises at the edge, and be sure to notice any insects in the grasses or shrubs: mayflies, caddisflies, stoneflies, grasshoppers, beetles, or ants. If you see a few, you can bet trout are seeing a lot, and you should be prepared to imitate them.

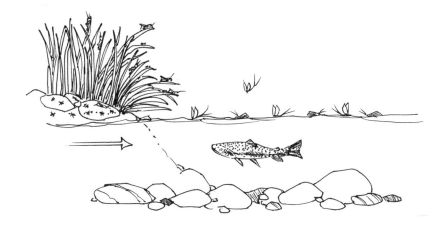

**RIG:       STANDARD DRY FLY**
**Method:    Current seams**

**Situations to solve.** Seams are lines where currents arriving from different directions and at different speeds merge. Seams gather food, both on the surface and in the drift, and deliver it downstream in a condensed stream. Trout move to a seam because bits of food are more than doubled there. They can hold on the soft side, in the slower current, and move in and out of the seam itself or even into the faster current long enough to harvest something on the drift. Trout living in seams are well fed but are able to conserve energy.

When you fish a current seam with a dry fly, your primary challenge is to get a drag-free drift lengthwise down the seam, preferably on the slow side, but sometimes on the fast side as well. You must keep your line and/or leader from crossing the seam, whether from fast to slow or slow to fast. Either way, you'll get drag as soon as the conflicting current speeds have tugged any slack out of your line and leader.

**Tuning the rig.** On any current seam that you're able to fish with casts almost straight upstream, so that the line, leader, and fly all lie in currents of the same speed, you won't have to make any adjustment to the rig you're already using. If the seam must be crossed with your cast, then it's often useful to add 2 or even 3 feet of extra tippet. Cast so the tippet piles up; the current then has extra slack to remove before drag sets in, which translates into extra seconds for the fly to drift freely, enticing trout to take it.

**Position and presentation.** In a seam in which the currents run in the same direction as the flow of the river, with the fast and slow sides at nearly the same speed, you should take your position downstream and make your presentations with standard upstream casts. If you're fishing the slow side, cover it with fairly short 5- to 10-foot drifts, spaced a foot or so apart from side to side, to cover the downstream section of the seam. Then either move upstream a few feet or extend your casts to cover the next 5 to 10 feet of the soft side of the seam the same way. Continue until you've reached the point where the two currents come together and create the seam.

Apply precisely the same sequence on the fast side of the seam. Whether you're covering the fast or slow side, be sure to position yourself so that each cast places the line, leader, and fly in the same set of currents.

If you're covering a seam in which currents of disparate speeds collide from sharply different angles and you have to cast over one to place the fly on the other, then you should take a position as near to the seam as you can get without frightening the fish feeding in it. You'll almost always be fishing from the fast outside current to trout holding and often rising on the slow inside current. Use a pile cast, and underpower your delivery stroke so that the leader piles up rather than straightening out. As soon as the fly hits the water, raise the rod to lift the line and back end of the leader off the water. The more leader tippet you can pile up, and the more line and leader butt you can lift off the water, the longer the fly will sit on that slow current.

**Control of the drift.** If you're fishing upstream along a linear seam, merely gather in slack as it forms. If you're fishing across a conflicting seam, lift the rod, make twitching mends of the line you're holding in the air, feed slack when the current begins to grab the line, and do anything else you can to delay the moment the fly begins to drag.

**On the water.** The most common seams are formed where the current is forced outward from the bank, constricted and slowed at the same time, so that the main current on the outside shoulders up against the slower current on the inside. The easiest and most natural approach to such a seam is from the shallow inside. Avoid casting straight out to such a seam or at a slight angle upstream, since this will lay your line and leader across currents that go from slow at your feet to faster out where the fly lands. Instead, wade out far enough, if possible, to place yourself in position to cast up the length of the seam. This will place your line and leader on currents of at least approximately the same speed and give you a much longer drag-free drift.

**The trout's point of view.** A fly cast across a current seam with a straight line will drag almost immediately, frightening the fish and warning them that the fly is a phony even if it's fished right on subsequent casts. A fly that drifts freely out of a leader piled onto the soft side of the seam has a far better chance to take a trout.

**RIG:        STANDARD DRY FLY**
**Method:    Riffle corners**

**Situations to solve.** When a riffle breaks out of its tipped bed and enters a run or pool downstream, its constricted path leaves corners of soft water at the edges. A riffle is shallow and well oxygenated, and with its myriads of living spaces between stones, is the most productive part of any stream for aquatic insect life. At the downstream end, a riffle corner provides a restful lie, where trout can be at ease but still intercept insects that become dislodged and tumble downstream.

Riffle corners are among the easiest water to read, to approach for casting, and to present dry flies without conflicting currents and consequent drag causing problems.

**Tuning the rig.** If you've been fishing upstream on any size stream, then you'll be rigged about right for any riffle corners that you encounter. Don't change a thing. If you're boating downstream and want to pull in and anchor to fish riffle corners either from the boat or from shore, then you should choose high-floating drys, 10- to 12-foot leaders, and 2- to 3-foot tippets correctly balanced to the size flies you're using.

**Position and presentation.** Riffle corners are always somewhat rough, so they fish best with upstream casts. Take your first position well downstream and inside the water where the depth tapers off too steeply for trout to rise to dry flies, somewhere around 4 to 6 feet. If the water is too deep for you to wade to a reasonable casting position, then it's probably too deep to serve up trout to a dry fly anyway. As a rough rule, begin fishing a river riffle corner about 100 feet below the break, a stream riffle corner 50 feet from the break, and a creek corner from 10 to 20 feet downstream. These numbers should help you avoid the greatest danger of approaching any riffle corner—wading into and through the upper shallows where most of the trout hold.

From your first casting position, begin covering the corner from the inside out. Set your first cast a few feet inside the main current, and then paint parallel drifts out to the current itself. Just as they would along any seam, most trout will hold in the slower inside current, ready to dash out and take whatever drifts by on the faster outside current.

Depending on the size of the riffle corner you're fishing, move upstream and take up subsequent positions, fishing the ever-narrower wedge of water between the shore and the main current and covering all the likely water. Avoid the dead water on the inside, next to shore, unless you see trout rising there. Begin placing your casts where you judge that the water is moving fast enough to deliver food to trout. Then place casts farther out into the current until your last drifts are down the seam and even on the faster side of it.

Do not stop fishing until you have worked casts right up into the very corner of the wedge of slow water, where it might look too shallow and slow for trout to hold. That is often the most productive lie, even on large rivers, and holds the biggest fish.

**Control of the drift.** If you can, wade out far enough so that you can cast nearly straight up into the current coming down from the corner. In this position, all you have to do is gather slack created by the downstream drift of the fly. If your position forces you to cast at a steeper angle out across the currents, then you might need to use upstream mends to keep the fly drifting freely.

**On the water.** Except on creeks and very small streams, rarely will you find it productive to fish the riffle corner on one side from a position on the opposite side. Such a position would require casting across the main current tongue, then lifting all of your line and leader off the faster current. If you can get close enough to accomplish this, it will work well enough, but it is far better to fish up the entire near side first, then move downstream, cross over, and fish the far side from a second set of positions.

Most stream and river riffle corners form good holding water only on one side of the riffle. The other side is either not shaped as a corner at all or comes in with too much swirling turbulence to form lies for trout. Riffle corners are often formed where the stream takes a slight bend so the best corner is on the inside. Only where a riffle enters a run or pool straight will it form fishable corners on both sides.

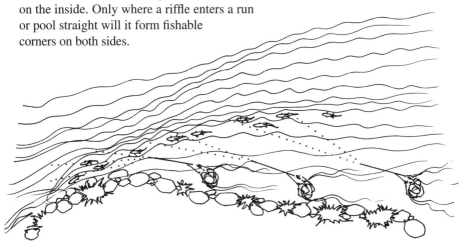

**The trout's point of view.** The trout will almost always be tucked under the rough water formed by the interface of the faster water with the slower water where it bends around the corner. Located on the soft side of the seam, often in water a foot or two deep, they'll be taking mostly submerged nymphs and larvae. However, because their lies are so shallow, they'll be more than willing to dash to the top for a natural, or for your dry fly, afloat up there.

**RIG:          STANDARD DRY FLY**
**Method:      Fishing an eddy**

**Situations to solve.** Eddies are formed where the bank intrudes into the current as a point or peninsula, forcing the flow outward and leaving a vacuum, which is filled by a circular back-current. Currents are always gentle in eddies, and because all sorts of aquatic and terrestrial food forms concentrate there, they are great places for trout to hold and feed. To dry-fly fish in eddies, it's best to look for rising trout, usually in the vortex of the eddy, where their food is twirled slowly around, as on a smorgasbord. However, upwelling and confusing currents make eddies among the most difficult trout waters to solve.

**Tuning the rig.** The most productive way to tune your rig for an eddy is to lighten your tippet as much as possible and lengthen it to at least 3 but preferably 4 feet. A long tippet of 5X or 6X will land with a lot more slack that must be tugged out before the conflicting currents begin to cause drag.

**Position and presentation.** The currents along the bank in an eddy are reversed, so if you judge the bank water to be fishable, then begin from a position at the upstream end of the eddy. The corner where the main river current is shunted to the outside and the eddy current circles up to meet it is a prime lie, so stay back from this location. Your first casts to the eddy should place your dry fly right there. Let it sit, or let the currents slowly escort it around. After you've covered the corner, then cover any likely bank water before turning to the center of the eddy.

Trout that are feeding in eddies are exposed to overhead predators and are therefore wary. Be careful not to loom over them on the bank; don't wave your rod around over their heads, and don't smack your line and leader onto the water on top of them. If the eddy is small, crouch alongside it or take whatever cover you can find. Take your second position near the midpoint of the circular eddy, so that you can cover it all from one place. Watch for rises. When you've pinned a fish, place the fly just a foot or at most 2 feet up current from it. Don't try for long drifts in eddies; the upwelling currents cause drag that is often invisible to you but never to the trout. As soon as your cast lands, loft your rod to lift the line off the near current, giving the fly maximum time to sit without drag.

If the eddy is large, you should fish it from a succession of positions, beginning at the upstream end and covering any rising trout you can from there and then working your way downstream. The position of rising trout in the eddy, and your ability to reach them, will determine the positions you take. Again, once you locate a trout, make your cast tight to it, lifting as much line off the water as you can, and as soon as the slightest drag sets in, lift the fly off the water for the next cast. Avoid letting the trout see your fly dragging. Not only will it ruin your chances on that particular cast, but it will warn trout about that fly on any future casts.

**Control of the drift.** Eddies call on all of your creative abilities to control your line. The current in the vortex of the eddy, where you usually find trout, varies dramatically in speed and even direction from the current at the edge of the eddy, from which you normally need to cast. You will have to employ small flick mends to compensate for the current under the rod, feed slack to extend a drift, and lift your rod to get the line off the water.

**On the water.** Because trout typically feed on a variety of insects caught in eddies, they tend to be picky but not selective. Your dry fly must resemble something they're eating and should be small, delicate, and realistic. Most of all, it must look alive, which means it must float with a perfect drag-free drift.

Trout in an eddy will take as many drowned insects as floating insects. If you've tried the best imitations and presentations you can manage without luck, don't give up. Let your fly soak up water, and then fish it as if it were floating. Don't worry so much about drag now; it can animate your fly in a natural way. Watch for rises where you believe your fly to be. If you see one, set the hook gently. It's likely a trout interviewing your sunk dry fly.

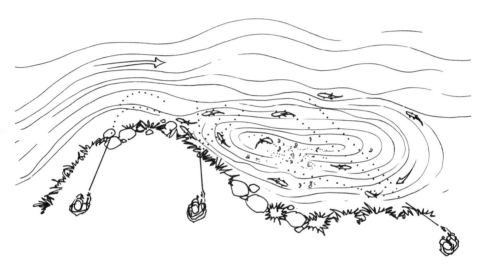

**The trout's point of view.** Trout find eddies places to hang lazily and sip at the small bits of bounty that nature rotates almost endlessly around for them. They usually see and accept more than one type of food, so your fly can fall within a narrow range of mayfly, midge, caddis, and terrestrial types, almost always small. If you're having trouble matching a hatch in an eddy, try a size 18 or 20 Foam Beetle or Foam Ant.

**Situations to solve.** A creek or small stream usually contains trout in its pools. Here, they find satisfaction for all their needs: current to deliver food, shelter from those same currents, and water deep enough for overhead protection. Although trout will also be in riffles and runs, along the banks, and anywhere else that fulfills their needs, most are found in pools.

Most small-stream pools are variations on a basic shape: an entering current tongue, midpool depths, and a tailout where the currents lift up and gather speed for the drop into the next pool. The deepest water in a pool is generally under the main current, whether it's been eroded down the center or pushed to one side. The current also delivers food, so most trout in small pools hold on either side of the main current. Your job is to choose a likely dry fly and give it a drag-free drift over all the water where trout might be lying.

**Tuning the rig.** If you've already tuned your outfit to suit the size stream you're fishing, then you're prepared to fish its pools: a 7- to 8-foot rod, 3-, 4-, or 5-weight line, 8- to 10-foot leader, and 4 or 5X tippet to balance size 10 to 16 dry flies.

**Position and presentation.** You'll be moving upstream and approaching small-stream pools from downstream. When you see or suspect trout on tailouts, fish there first or you'll send them sailing up the pool, frightening other trout. Your first position, therefore, must be downstream from the pool, where you can take advantage of any cover offered. If you're on a tumbling mountain creek, this might be the boulders that form the tailout. Hide behind them and fish over them. If there are none, make your approach crouched or on your hands and knees. Your first short casts to the tailout of a small-stream pool will normally be made from this position.

Because tailout currents get faster as they constrict, an upstream cast will place your fly on currents slower than those on which your line and leader land. Keep your casts short, and lift the line and back end of the leader off the water as soon as the cast lands. Sometimes you can drape the line over a tailout rock, thus anchoring it and preventing drag.

Once you've fished the tailout, the casting gets easier. Take your second position on the corner of the tailout. Remain crouched, and place your casts directly up the current. Cover both sides and the center of the current with several drifts down each line.

Next, move up to a third position that lets you fish the pool corner. Often it's an eddy about the size of your hat, sometimes larger. Set your fly onto it, and let it sit there as long as it will. If the pool has good corners on both sides, you'll want to move up after fishing the one on your side, and cast across the central current to the other corner on the far side. Lift your rod to keep the line and leader off the fast current, and give your dry a chance to rotate around in that corner.

**Control of the drift.** Most line control on small waters will gather slack as the fly floats downstream toward you, so lift your rod to keep the line off the water and avoid drag. Not often will you need to feed slack. Mends can be useful whenever you want to cover slow water on the far side of faster currents.

**On the water.** In spring and early summer, trout are nipping at aquatic insects that are delivered into pools on the entering currents. At that time of year, trout tend to be found in the upper ends of pools, where they can focus on the inflow. In late summer and fall when aquatic hatches tend to trail off and the adults are out laying their eggs, terrestrial insects begin to get onto the water. Most aerial insects land on the water over the broad surface of the pool and are gathered in the currents at the tailout. At that time of year, trout are usually found in the lower ends of pools, where they're focused on those gathering insects.

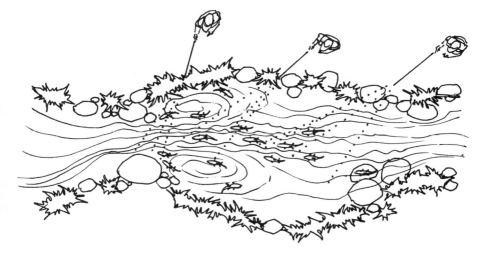

**The trout's point of view.** Trout in small waters are accustomed to seeing a variety of foods, rather than a single species, so they seldom become selective. They do, however, become bashful about size, unless big insects are out, and they can be somewhat selective about color. Always start with a high-floating fly that is easy to see. A useful rule to remember is if trout refuse your first fly, especially with disdainful splashy rises, then go smaller and darker.

**RIG:         STANDARD DRY FLY**
**Method:     Pocket water**

**Situations to solve.** Even in the fastest riffles and cascades, interruptions to the current form small places where trout can hold. Usually these are boulders, which must be approached closely and fished with very short casts. Ledges and trenches show up on the surface as pieces of slick water calmer than the water around it. These slicks—some tiny, some the size of your kitchen table—indicate that the bottom has dropped away below. You can bet that trout will find shelter there.

One of the biggest problems to overcome when fishing pocket water is wading safely into position to fish it. Don't take chances. Wear sturdy felt-soled wading brogues with studs or cleats on water where the boulders are slick, and carry a staff to brace against. While maneuvering in the water, don't scrape your studded brogues on bottom rocks or jab your metal-tipped staff at the bottom. Such noises will scare the trout.

**Tuning the rig.** A long rod will help in pocket water. In such turbulence, trout are not leader shy, so you don't need a leader longer than the rod or a fine tippet. You'll rarely need to imitate any particular insect when fishing pocket water, so choose high-floating drys, usually at least slightly outsized, size 10 to 14.

**Position and presentation.** Approach each pocket from an angle a bit downstream and off to one side. The rougher the water, the closer you'll want to get, and luckily the closer you'll be able to get without alerting the trout. A close position in pocket water is a single rod length away, a distant position two rod lengths. It's not uncommon to catch trout in boisterous water when they come up to take your dry fly right under your rod tip.

Position is about 80 percent of pocket water fishing; casting and control make up the rest. You'll often fish pocket water with your rod in one hand, your staff in the other. Draw out just enough line to make your cast, plus enough to form a loop behind your rod hand forefinger, which should clamp the line against the rod grip. On average, a rod length of leader and another of line beyond the rod tip are about right, though in some pocket water you can control two to three rod lengths of line. When a fish hits, release that loop to get the fish onto the reel.

Make each cast short and precisely to the pocket; then instantly lift the rod as high as you can to get the line and back end of the leader off the water. Coax the fly through a short 3- to 6-foot drift. Don't try for long floats in this kind of water. Pick up and cast again as soon as the fly begins to drag. Cover each line of drift with five to ten quick floats, and keep your parallel drift lines close together, a foot or less. Give trout every chance to ponder your fly. Often they'll hit with a smash, but only after the fly has drifted over their heads several times.

**Control of the drift.** Use small twitch and flick mends to reposition the back end of your fly line between the rod and leader butt and to extend the drift of the dry. You might also try tiny roll casts to reposition the fly into a better drift line. Sometimes you can simply lift the fly off the water and drop it back down exactly where you want it. Luckily, you can get away with a degree of fly movement in pocket water.

**On the water.** Boulders are obvious lies in pocket water, and you want to fish them carefully. Remember that trout tend to lie at one or more of the four poles: downstream, off to each side, and in front, all tucked in tight. The smooth water that tails out from a boulder can hold trout for at least a few feet downstream. Edge up close to it and high-stick your dry fly down that narrow drift line.

Boulders on the bottom of the stream and trenches where the bottom falls away show on the surface only as places where the water is less disturbed than the water around it. Be sure to fish such calms, no matter how small. The size of the slick on the surface is not always indicative of the size trout that will rush up to jump your dry.

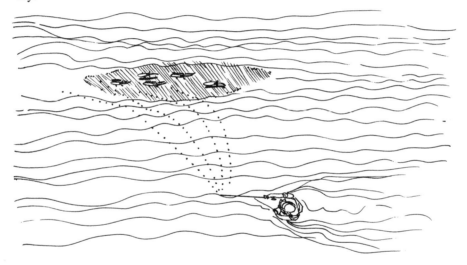

**The trout's point of view.** The current will push the slight calm spot denoting a rock or slight depression downstream from the holding lie itself. Whenever you fish a slight slick in rough water, place your dry at the upstream end of it, and make a few subsequent casts upstream from it, so that the fly floats out of the rough water into the calm. That is the instant a trout is most likely to hit it.

| RIG: | STANDARD DRY FLY |
|---|---|
| Method: | Dapping |

**Situations to solve.** Sometimes you'll find yourself in situations too constricted to allow launching any sort of basic cast or even the roll cast. Brush crowds in behind and limbs sweep low overhead, but the water drives by below the bank on which you perch, and a good lie in such an impossible place can hold a very nice trout.

Such conditions are common on creeks, especially as you move higher into the mountainous headwaters, where annual spates erode channels deeply but do not beat the brush back from the banks. But confined circumstances can occur on forested streams and on rivers everywhere. Surprisingly, brush can be more of a problem on spring creeks and tailwaters than on freestone streams, simply because flows are stabilized, banks are never washed away, and a tangle of vegetation takes root and grows in frequent profusion.

If you can move into position alongside such water, at times you can catch trout, even where you're unable to move your rod in any sort of backcast, forecast, or roll cast.

**Tuning the rig.** Theoretically, dapping is best done with a long rod, which gives you the longest reach, but a long rod is the most difficult to thread through tangles. In truth, when you find the need to dap a fly, you're already going to be fishing a creek, stream, or river and you're not going to gallop back to the car to get the perfect rod for the dap you need to dangle. Simply use what you have in your hand, and keep the leader the length of the rod or a bit shorter rather than longer.

**Position and presentation.** Your position will be dictated by the vegetation around you. Sometimes you'll be standing, other times you'll be crouched or kneeling on the bank, and quite often you'll find yourself snaking into position on your belly. Such positions keep you out of sight of the trout just below you. Just remember that you want to be within a rod's length of the water you want to fish. If you're any farther off, you'll be casting, not dapping.

Poke your rod through the brush and hold it above the water you want to fish. Make every movement very slowly. The primary trout predator in such tight situations is a kingfisher perched on a branch, so any quick movement you make of the rod and line will reveal itself to the trout as just such a threat.

Once the rod is in position, remove the fly from its keeper, and dangle it inches off the water. Trout can see it hovering there and will often slash at it the instant you lower your rod tip enough to set the fly onto the water. If they don't, let the current deliver your fly for a drift of 2 to 4 feet, more if the situation allows it. When you hook a fish, quell your instinct to set the hook hard; you don't want to break your rod tip on the branches above that forced you to dap your fly in the first place.

**Control of the drift.** The only control you have when dapping is vertical: You can lift the fly, reposition it for a second drift, and drop it to the water again. Obviously, your first presentation when dapping is by far the most likely to produce action. Calculate everything out carefully before dropping the fly to the water for the first time.

**On the water.** If you're on small water that holds only small trout, you should be able to lift the thrashing fish out of there, after a brief and exciting dance. If you're on water that has the potential to provide larger trout, then calculate in advance just what you'll do if you hook a fish that is too heavy to hoist. You might be able to step into the water, if it's not too deep to wade, or you might be able to play it out from your original position and then reach down and unhook the fish when it's defeated.

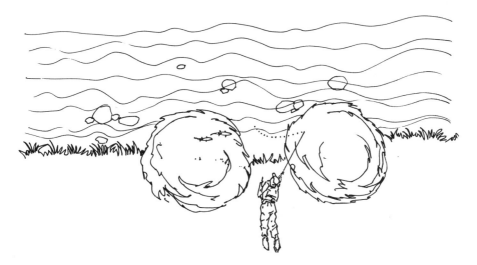

**The trout's point of view.** Trout are accustomed to seeing insects, such as craneflies, stoneflies, and caddisflies, hovering over the water or crawling in the vegetation and dropping to the water. No doubt the trout track them in the air and are prepared to take them instantly once the insects drop down. But trout are not accustomed to seeing anything—the line, the rod, the puppeteer—suspending flies over their heads, so keep your line close to the rod tip, your rod tip close to the bank, and your motions to a minimum.

**RIG:       STANDARD DRY FLY**
**Method:   Cross-stream reach cast**

**Situations to solve.** The cross-stream reach cast is extremely important on smooth currents, when you're casting to trout rising to feed selectively on insect hatches. In such situations, even the best imitation often fails to fool trout if the fly is fished on upstream casts. Trout see the line and leader either in the air or landing on the water and are warned about the fly long before it reaches them.

The reach cast works best when you're fishing to visible, working trout on a fairly broad flat, where the water is not rough and the currents flow in a fairly even sheet without a lot of conflicting speeds between your position and that of the rising trout.

**Tuning the rig.** A long rod, $8\frac{1}{2}$ to 9 feet, will help you get an extended drift with the reach cast. Fortunately, you'll almost always be carrying a long rod for the size waters where the cast becomes important. The leader should be 12 to 15 feet long, with at least 2 feet, and better yet 3 to 4 feet, of fine tippet. The diameter of the tippet should be consistent with the size fly you're casting. Although some large insects provide selective feeding on flat water, for the most part you'll use the reach cast with size 16 down to 22 flies, calling for 5, 6, and sometimes even 7X tippets.

**Position and presentation.** Position yourself either straight off to the side of the rising trout or slightly upstream or down from straight across. If you have a choice, move slightly upstream from the trout instead of down, so that the trout won't glimpse the line and leader in the air or when they land on the water. Move as close as you can, within reason, to the trout: 30 to 40 feet is about right; longer is fine as long as you have no trouble controlling your casts at that range. If you move in closer than 30 feet, keep your profile low by wading or crouching.

When you wade into position for the reach cast, especially if you're at an angle upstream from the fish, it's easy to send wading waves over the trout. When that occurs on lightly fished waters, the trout might fade out of sight and begin rising again after a short time. On heavily fished water, they might keep on feeding but will be on guard against your flies before you make your first cast.

Measure your line for the presentation with fore- and backcasts off to the side of the trout. Carry a few feet of extra line in the air. Make your delivery stroke just as you normally would, aimed 2 to 4 feet upstream from the trout and as close as you can to its feeding lane. As the delivery stroke unfurls in the air, lay your rod over in the upstream direction until it is almost parallel to the surface. At the same time, reach out with your casting arm, and if you want a longer drift, lean your body upstream. The fly will land where you aimed it, but the line will cut across the currents at an angle downstream from the rod tip to the fly. If you were to cast straight across the same set of even currents, you would get a 1- to 2-foot drift, if any at all, before drag sets in.

**Control of the drift.** As soon as the cast lands on the water and the fly begins drifting downstream, follow the drift with the tip of your rod. This will insert slack into the drift and free it up. When the rod, line, leader, and fly are all lined up straight between you and the trout, you can extend the drift farther by reaching with the rod toward the downstream side, eventually extending your arm and even leaning in that direction.

**On the water.** If you're working over trout in a pod, pick out one of them and make your reach cast presentations precisely to it. But don't lift the fly from the water as soon as it has passed the position of that first trout. Often you'll be able to extend the free drift of the fly for as much as 10 to 15 feet, in which case it will have an excellent chance of being accepted by trout lower down in the pod. Also, by letting the fly drift through the pod without lifting it, you lessen the risk of putting the entire pod down when you lift the fly off the water for the next cast. The first cast is always the most important, but you'll often have to make cast after cast to the same fish before everything is aligned right and the trout takes your fly.

**The trout's point of view.** When fishing over selective trout on smooth currents, the reach cast puts you in almost the perfect position to present the fly drifting without any drag and with the line and leader out of the trout's sight. The reach cast is key to your success as you move from fishing the water with searching flies to fishing hatches, a natural progression when fly fishing for trout.

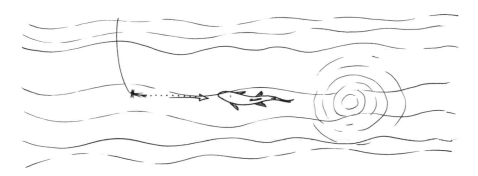

**Situations to solve.** Wiggling the rod tip while the line and leader are still in the air will cause them to land on the water with a series of serpentine curves installed. The current must tug these curves out of the line and leader before drag will set in on the fly. Such slack is critical when you want to fish across two or even more currents that flow either in different directions or at different speeds.

Slack added with the wiggle method is important to the reach cast—you might end up using it more often than not—and helpful with many other types of casts. Even the upstream presentation over fairly rough water—where the currents are seething in different directions—will be more effective with slack added. Most of the time, wiggle is added to cross-stream and downstream presentations, but learning to insert slack by wiggling the tip of your rod in other presentations will allow you to creatively solve situations in which you're forced to combine elements of different methods into one. In this case, it's wiggle added to the reach cast.

**Tuning the rig.** Wiggle can be added into any cast with equipment that is suitable to the size water you're already fishing. You'll find it most useful when you're fishing in fairly smooth water over selective, rising trout. The best rod for wiggling is progressively stiffer from the tip to the butt. It provides the flexibility you need to control the shape of the S curves, from narrow to broad, when they land on the water. Wobble it quickly for a small amount of slack or slowly and more forcefully for broader arcs. A soft rod will wobble its entire length and will not let you put more than two or three large S curves on the water, without any control over them. Likewise, a stiff rod will not bend at the tip and is difficult to control when you're trying to wiggle S curves onto the water.

**Position and presentation.** For the cross-stream wiggle cast, take up the same position you would for the normal cross-stream reach cast—either straight across from the trout, or slightly upstream or down from it. The difference is that your position will not be able to get all the conflicting currents out of the way, and therefore you must lay your cast across them.

The cast is nearly the same as the reach cast: Carry a few extra feet of line in the air, aim at the target point, make the delivery stroke, and lay your rod over as the line and leader unfurl in the air. As they do, wobble the rod tip back and forth briskly. It's as simple as that. The line and leader will land on the water in S curves that vary in size according to how fast and narrow, or slow and broad, an arc you give the rod tip.

**Control of the drift.** If the currents are faster out toward the drift line where the fly will float and slower nearer to you, you can place the S curves in the front end of the line and leader by beginning to wobble the rod as soon as the delivery stroke unfolds. If the currents are faster where you wade and slower out by the trout, you can place more slack closer to the rod by delaying the wobble until the line has almost straightened on the delivery stroke. By learning to control the size of the S-curves and where they're placed on the water, you will be able to solve an increasing number of problems you encounter while trout fishing.

**On the water.** In the standard cross-stream wiggle cast, you'll provide a fairly constant set of curves from the rod tip to the tippet so that the line lands on target with sufficient slack in it. You will have to practice the cast until you master the amount of line to carry, the amount of wiggle to add, and the right time to add it. This skill is best practiced on water over rising trout, so to master it you will have to spend more time on the sorts of waters where trout rise to feed on insects.

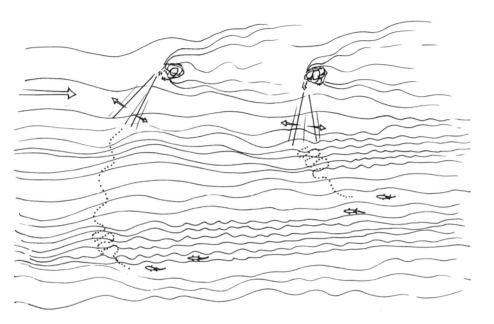

**The trout's point of view.** Make your presentation 1 to 3 feet upstream from the lie of a rising trout, and right into its feeding lane. You'll be surprised how little distance trout are willing to move for flies—or natural insects for that matter—when they're holding a station and rising in rhythm to insects delivered to them on the currents. The slack you've added with the wiggle in your cast will give the fly a free drift so that it arrives in front of the fish without drag.

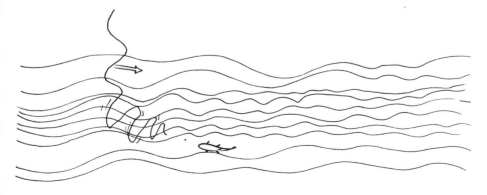

**Situations to solve.** The downstream wiggle cast is reserved for the toughest trout, those feeding selectively on the smoothest and most heavily fished waters. You'll usually use this cast on spring creeks and tailwaters, but freestone streams also have smooth flats, where trout refuse all but the most natural presentations. As the waters you fish become more difficult, you will have to move out of a down-stream position into one off to the side for a reach cast, and if that doesn't work, then into a position upstream, where you can use the downstream wiggle cast. I'm ashamed to admit the number of times I've fished upstream through rising trout and caught nothing, then turned around and fished downstream to the same trout and fooled more than half of them, often on the same flies they'd already refused.

**Tuning the rig.** Make sure your rod is long, neither weepy nor stiff, and that your leader ends in at least a couple of feet of fine tippet, though longer is better. You can execute the downstream wiggle cast with whatever you're using when you want to apply it, most likely on water where you are fishing with light gear.

**Position and presentation.** Once you've pinpointed a trout by its rises, take your position anywhere in an arc upstream from the trout, but never straight upstream. If you make a wiggle cast straight downstream to a trout, you'll only have one good shot at it as the leader and line will follow the fly over the fish. Instead, take a position at least slightly off to one side. Be very careful not to send wading waves over the fish as you move into position. Since you'll be moving right into the trout's angle of vision, stay back 35 to 45 feet, wade deep, or crouch low.

Make your measuring fore- and backcasts well to the side, out of sight of the trout. Work out several feet of extra line in the air, and aim the delivery stroke into the trout's feeding lane, 2 to 5 feet upstream from the trout's lie. As the line lays out, wobble your rod back and forth rather briskly. The line and leader will fall to the water in a sequence of S curves, which will play out and feed slack into the drift of the fly.

You will have to practice this cast to learn to measure the amount of line you need out, the amount of compensation you want to work into the power of your casting stroke for the curves you're casting, and the proper amount of wiggle so the line doesn't land too straight beyond the trout or recoil too far short of the trout. It's better to guess short than long. An experienced fisherman will take one or two mea-suring casts to work the downstream wiggle cast out to the feeding lane of a trout.

**Control of the drift.** Once the fly is on the water, you can extend the drift beyond what the S curves provide by shaking extra slack out of the rod tip and onto the water, but don't wait until drag begins to set in. If the trout refuses, then let the fly drift past it, and tip your rod over in the direction that will pull the line and leader off to your side of the trout. Lift it off the water only after the current has delivered it to where the disturbance of the pickup will not alarm the trout. Repeat until the fly arrives when the trout is ready to feed.

**On the water.** Unlike the reach cast, the downstream wiggle cast is not effective at fishing a dry fly on a long drift through a pod of trout. In the wiggle cast, the line follows in almost the same drift path as the fly, and when you pick up the line for the next cast, it will put at least one of the trout down, alerting the others that something isn't right. Always single out a trout, and work on it. If you're working on a pod with downstream casts, focus on a fish that is on the near side of the pod, or one that is out in front of or behind the others far enough that you can fish for it without alerting the others. Always be aware of the location of all trout in a pod, in relation to your casts, drifts, and pickups.

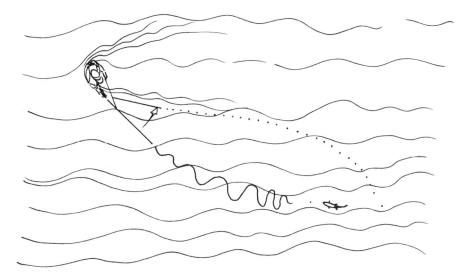

**The trout's point of view.** When you use the downstream wiggle cast, if you see a rise and set the hook very quickly, you'll pull the fly away from the trout. The bigger the trout, the more deliberate its rise, and the slower it closes its mouth whether it's on a natural or your own fly. Learn to wait until the trout has tipped down and then raise your rod gently to set the hook.

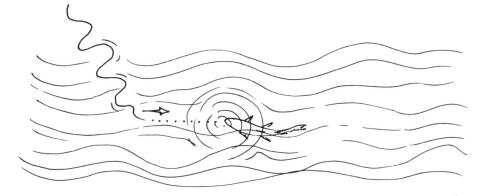

**Situations to solve.** A downstream method older than the wiggle cast, the parachute cast is not as accurate and does not form slack on the water quite as consistently. As a consequence, the parachute is not used as often when casting to specific rising trout. But this cast does allow longer downstream drifts, which are useful when you want to explore for lies and willing trout with downstream casts, or when water conditions prevent you from taking a position downstream.

I find the modified drop and draw more useful than the true parachute cast, so I employ it often. I use it on the riffles and runs of heavily fished streams, where nearly all anglers fish the same water from downstream with upstream casts, thus revealing their line and leader to the trout before showing them the fly. On waters that are not fished heavily, the upstream presentation works well in somewhat rough water, but that is not often true on waters where angling pressure is heavy.

**Tuning the rig.** Simply use whatever dry-fly rig you're already using to fish the water you're on. You'll be rigged right, without the need for adjustments.

**Position and presentation.** The first position is taken at the upper end and to one side of the riffle, run, flat, or pool. If trout are rising, then assume the same position you would for a downstream wiggle cast—upstream and a bit off to the side of the trout.

The cast is measured with quite a few feet of extra line in the air. In the true parachute cast, which you must practice to master, the delivery stroke is made high and long. When the line straightens in the air, the rod is brought back abruptly, just a foot or two at the tip, to bump the line, stop it sharply, and cause it to recoil a few feet. The resulting slack will settle to the water in curves, but the amount of slack and the placement of the curves will not be very predictable. The cast ends with the rod pointed straight up. As the slack feeds out, lower the rod tip and extend your rod arm to follow the drift of the fly, which can be from 10 to even 20 feet. Place the next cast alongside the first, and search a second line of drift for willing trout.

In the drop and draw, overpower the delivery stroke, and release extra line in your line hand as the line in the air unfurls. At the same time, lower the rod parallel to the water and draw it back behind your buttock. The line should flutter to the water with slack, and as this plays out in the drift, move your rod forward to follow it. More slack line can be wobbled from the rod tip and fed into the back of the drift, extending it to the same 10 or 20 feet. Because this method keeps the cast under more control, many experienced fishermen favor it over the better-known parachute cast.

With either of the casts, first fish all the water that can be covered from the first position so that the trout have at least one chance to see the fly. Then move downstream to a new position about 10 feet short of the end of the first series of drifts, and cover the next section of water downstream.

**Control of the drift.** With either the parachute cast or drop and draw, all you have to do is drop the rod, extend your casting arm, and feed slack into the drift.

**On the water.** Cover what water you can with graceful casts from your first position. Then move downstream a few feet rather than trying to extend your casts out of control, and cover the next section of water. Make sure you have at least a few feet of overlap between the water covered from the first and second positions. This downstream approach will give you an advantage over other anglers, who typically would fish the same water with upstream casts, thereby putting their line and leader in the sight of the trout before the fly arrives.

**The trout's point of view.** The fly arriving ahead of the line and leader might be normal and often even necessary on smooth water, but it's something trout don't see very often on relatively rougher water. A trout is far more likely to take a fly that comes dancing into its window of vision on the surface before anything else has warned it. Try the parachute cast or drop and draw on a riffle, or any water you fish often, and see if your take doesn't increase. Just remember to set the hook a beat slower than you would with an upstream presentation.

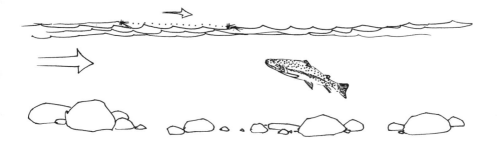

**RIG:        STANDARD DRY FLY**
**Method:    Upstream draw**

**Situations to solve.** Wind makes it almost impossible to drop a dry fly delicately into a trout's feeding lane with a reach cast, a wiggle cast, or any other cast that calls for a soft presentation. When the wind threatens to blow your fly, leader, and line out of there, the upstream draw method allows you to place your fly forcefully on the water just beyond the line where you want it to fish, at the end of a straight line and leader. Then you can skate it back into the right line, before giving it slack for a free downstream float.

The upstream draw method can be effective, both in wind or in calm, for hitting lies on the upstream sides of boulders found in fast or slow water, for fishing slicks on the surface that reflect trenches on the bottom in fast water, and for positioning dry flies in the windows of smooth water that open up and slide down otherwise rough currents. This method is also excellent for placing your fly in the right line to fish down a narrow seam or any other clearly defined drift line. It's most commonly used to align the drift of an imitative dry fly precisely down the narrow feeding lane of a rising trout. I use it extensively when wade or boat fishing big, rough rivers during the giant salmon fly hatch, aligning drifts along brush-shrouded banks and drawing up detonations from large trout.

**Tuning the rig.** If you tune the leader for the type of fishing you're doing, it will work fine for the upstream draw. If it's windy, keep your tippet to no more than 2 or 3 feet.

**Position and presentation.** Your position can be anywhere from almost straight across stream and slightly upstream from the lie or rising trout to almost straight upstream from the lie or trout. Stay away from positioning yourself straight upstream from the line of drift you want to fish. Within this wide upstream arc, choose the position that lets you move in the closest without disturbing the trout and places the most conflicting currents behind you, rather than between you and the lie or visible rising trout.

Measure the fly line carried in the air 2 to 4 feet beyond the drift line you want to fish. Try to place the fly on the water 5 to 10 feet upstream from the lie or feeding trout, and 2 to 4 feet beyond the line of drift. As soon as the fly lands, lift your rod to skate the fly back to where you want its drift to begin. Then lower the rod and shake slack line through the guides and onto the water in front of you. As the slack feeds out, it will give the fly a free drift straight down the line in which you so carefully placed it.

If the currents between you and the line of drift flow in an even sheet, without conflict in direction or speed, you can get a surprisingly long drift, sometimes 10 to as much as 20 feet long, but a shorter 3- to 6-foot drift is more likely. Because the fly floats at the end of a straight tippet, be wary of microdrag, which is often difficult to notice. If you see boils or even rises in which the trout rush the fly but do not take it, then you might want to try a different position or fish with a different method that lets you place the leader on the water with slack.

**Control of the drift.** Although you can't introduce slack into the front end of the line or in the leader itself with this method, constantly feeding slack at the back end of the line, and even mending the line if it begins to form a downstream belly, can extend the free drift of the fly. At some point in the drift, the fly will begin to drag. Never allow this to happen over water you think might hold trout. Lift it at once and cast again.

**On the water.** You can often get 3 to 5 more feet of free drift by combining the upstream draw method with elements of the reach cast. Measure the cast and make your delivery, with your rod arm extended and the rod tipped over at least slightly upstream. If you draw the fly into the drift line while reaching upstream and then toss your slack onto the water, you should have enough slack to play out before drag sets in. Of course, this will depend on having even currents between your position and the drift line. If the water has too much conflict, nothing you do at the back end of the cast will provide extra feet of drift at the front end.

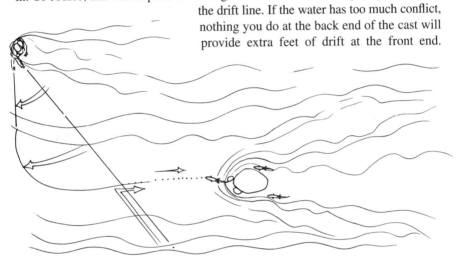

**The trout's point of view.** A lot of commotion occurs when the fly lands on the water and you drag it upstream and across to position it into the drift line you desire. If a trout were to see that, it would probably not take the fly. That's why you want to aim the delivery 5 to 10 feet upstream from the suspected lie or the visible trout. By the time the fly enters the trout's window of vision, it is drifting freely.

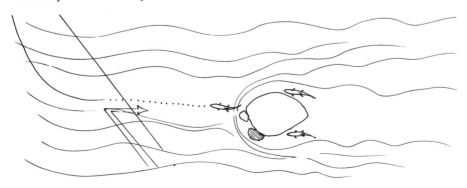

| RIG: | STANDARD DRY FLY |
|---|---|
| Method: | Pile cast |

**Situations to solve.** At times, you'll want a good drift of the dry fly on slow currents, but you first must cast across faster currents to place your fly correctly. This often occurs on a small to medium-size stream, where trout are nosing up in an eddy to the inside of the main, and faster, current. While fishing such a situation is best from a bank on the eddy side, you will not always be able to get there, and sometimes you must wade in from the outside and cast over the fast currents to set your fly on the slow ones. The only way to get a drift with any hope of success is to stack a lot of slack in the front end of the cast, much more than you could with a wiggle cast. The pile cast will usually solve the situation.

Sometimes, the currents near you are much faster than those where the fly will land over a rising trout. You'll often find this when wading a broad but shallow stream or river and casting to rising trout holding near the banks. The water at the edge is slowed by friction with the bank, and the disparity of current speeds makes it difficult to get enough slack with a reach wiggle cast or downstream wiggle cast. In this situation, the pile cast is normally the answer.

A word of caution: If the wind is blowing, the pile cast is never the answer. Forget it.

**Tuning the rig.** The pile cast requires a long leader and long, fine tippet. Usually the situation you're already fishing has the same requirements, but if not, take time to lengthen your leader to at least 12 feet and your tippet to at least 3 feet.

**Position and presentation.** You can take a position downstream, across stream, or even upstream from an eddy lie where a seam separates currents of vastly different speeds. The key here is to be on the fast side with the trout on the slow side. If you're out in open water, casting from fast to slow currents, your position should be at least slightly upstream from the trout, but more often close to straight upstream from it. Keep in mind that when you're straight upstream, you'll get only one shot at the trout. The pile cast is frequently employed in situations where your only hope is a single cast from a position almost directly upstream from a trout rising tight to a bank. In that case, one shot is far better than none.

To make the presentation, measure out a normal forecast, with a few feet of extra line in the air, off to the side of the trout. Aim an underpowered delivery stroke 3 to 5 feet upstream from the trout and high in the air above the water. End the cast by lowering your rod tip almost to the water as the line begins to settle. The end of the line and the leader should tower, then accordion in with the fly sitting in front of a pile of leader.

If the cast has been executed properly, the fly will land in the trout's feeding lane 3 to 5 feet upstream, just ahead of a pile of leader that you normally would not want. In this case, the fly drifts downstream and the tippet and leader uncoil, allowing the fly to drift freely. The pile cast is an extremely effective method, but it does require practice to place the fly accurately with the proper amount of slack backing it up.

**Control of the drift.** After you cast, all you can do is watch the drift unfold and remove all that slack to set the hook slowly if the trout comes up to take the fly.

**On the water.** If your position is directly upstream from the trout, and you get a refusal, the leader and the line will follow the fly over the trout, putting it down. If you are off to the side, however, you can draw your rod over and let the current deliver the back end of the leader and front end of the line downstream from the trout and out of its sight before you lift off for subsequent pile cast presentations.

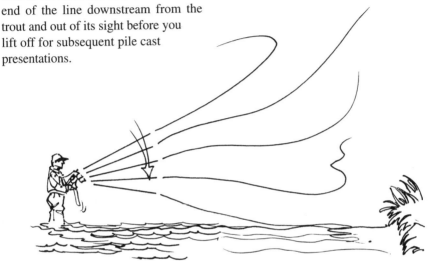

**The trout's point of view.** The trout will see the fly arriving ahead of the line and leader, but unless your presentation happens to be perfect, it could also see a tangle of leader following the fly down. Practice to get the cast down as perfectly as possible. After that, an element of luck will still be involved, depending on how the leader folds up and how the fly lands in relation to it.

| RIG: | STANDARD DRY FLY |
| Method: | The sudden inch |

**Situations to solve.** Leonard M. Wright, Jr., in his book *Fishing the Dry Fly as a Living Insect*, devised the sudden inch to solve the many afternoon and evening situations in which adult caddis either emerge from the water or return to lay their eggs. In my own experience, this happens on more than half of the days of the summer midseason and almost as often in the morning as later in the day. Caddis are skittish; they rest on the water a bit, hop a few inches, take off in short flights, land, and rest again. When they hop or fly, it's always upstream, and when they rest, it's always at a dead drift downstream. When trout feed on such lively insects, they often refuse a dry fly fished with the standard dead drift method, though you should try it first to see if it works.

Recognizing this nervous behavior is important when fishing to trout that rise selectively to winged caddis on smooth flows. If the water is rough, as in a riffle or fast run, the standard upstream dry-fly presentation will usually solve adult caddis situations. Where the water is a flat, smooth run or a slick tailout of a pool, then the lifelike movement imparted to your dry fly by the sudden inch can make the difference between constant refusals and trout dancing on the end of your line.

**Tuning the rig.** If your rod is moderately long, your leader 12 to 14 feet, and your tippet at least 2 to 3 feet of it, you're rigged right for the flat water on which you'll find use for the sudden inch. If not, take time to add a tippet suitable to the size fly you'll use, which should be selected based on the size and color of caddis adults on the water.

The fly itself must be built right to skate, not submerge. Wright tied his Fluttering Caddis on light-wire hooks and made slender bodies, downwings of stiff guard hair fibers, and abundant stiff hackle. If you're unable to get your standard Elk Hair Caddis–style flies to skate, try tying a few size and color variations especially for the method.

**Position and presentation.** The natural caddis will be drifting downstream and hopping or flying upstream on water that is at least slightly flat and demanding, so your best position will be in a narrow arc between 60 and 80 degrees upstream from the rising trout, and within 30 to 50 feet of them, to maintain maximum control of your cast and drift. Measure the cast to place the fly 3 to 5 feet upstream from the trout, but carry several feet of extra line in your line hand.

Deliver the fly gently to the water just upstream from the trout, as close as you can to its feeding lane. As soon as the fly lands, lift the rod tip, draw the line tight, and twitch the fly an inch or so. Immediately drop the rod tip and feed slack into the drift of the fly. If you're working a pod, let the fly drift drag-free as far as it will. If you're working a single trout, after the fly has passed it, lay your rod over to the side, allow the current to deliver the line tip, leader, and fly well out of the trout's angle of vision, and then lift off and make another presentation, again inserting that sudden inch as soon as the fly lands.

**Control of the drift.** Obviously you'll be fishing out the drift of the fly with a straight leader and line tip once you've imparted the sudden inch. Your task from that moment on is to give the drift the most slack you can. Most of the time you can accomplish this by feeding line through the guides and shaking it onto the water beyond the rod tip. You might need to send a soft roll cast down the line to place the slack closer to the fly, but you must do this without moving the fly or causing it to drag.

**On the water.** If your casting position is too far off to the side of the trout, you'll cause the fly to skitter across the current when you give it the sudden inch. You'll also pull it slightly out of the feeding lane of the trout. Although this motion violates the upstream principle of the method, in all likelihood trout will not notice as long as you skitter the fly no more than a short distance and end with it floating down the feeding lane.

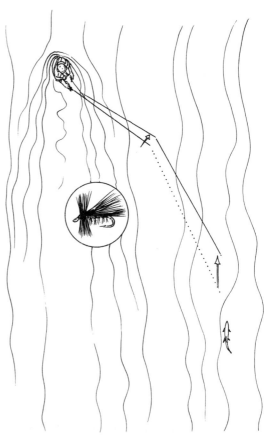

In my own fishing, I always try to catch the trout with a caddis imitation fished dead drift, no action imparted, before trying the sudden inch. I also let the fly float a foot or two before inserting the sudden inch into the middle of the drift. This gives trout that have been eyeing my fly the idea that it's alive.

**The trout's point of view.** The trout might see the slight disturbance of the fly landing just upstream from it, or see it drifting into its window of vision, before the fly makes that sudden upstream skate and comes to rest once more, drifting freely over it. If you can negate any influence of the leader and line after the sudden inch, the trout is very likely to take your fly for the real thing.

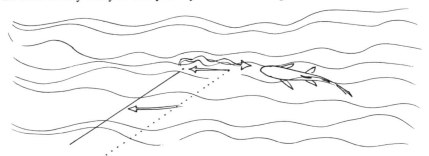

| RIG: | STANDARD DRY FLY |
|---|---|
| Method: | Pop on nose or sound cast |

**Situations to solve.** Sometimes a trout, very often a large one, will hold in a lie that is so tight you cannot find a position that allows you to get a drag-free drift of a dry fly over it. Usually the lie will be close behind an obstruction to the flow, such as a boulder, downed tree, protruding limb, or a ledge with little room upstream to present the fly on an extended dead drift. Often such lies, whether protected by obstructions or conflicting currents, are close to the bank, in an indentation along the bank, or even tucked up beneath an undercut bank. To execute an occasional trout in such a protected lie, either place your dry fly just in front of its nose or set it just downstream with a bit of a smack to attract the trout's attention.

This method also works well against trout rising greedily during a heavy hatch of insects. Popping one on the nose at just the right moment might be the only way to get it to notice your fly among the seeming millions of naturals on the water.

**Tuning the rig.** Tune your leader to hit a target about the size of your hat. It should not be too long, especially if there's more than a breath of wind blowing. The tippet should be 2 feet long and somewhat stout for brushy lies, 3 or 4 feet long and fine if you're casting to greedy trout during a hatch.

**Position and presentation.** You will have to place the dry fly within a foot or two of the trout. Position yourself downstream from the fish at a distance that lets you attain that sort of accuracy. For some folks, this is 50 or 60 feet, but for most of us it's more like 25 to no more than 40 feet from the trout. Your angle to the trout can be anywhere from directly downstream to almost 45 degrees out to the side. The most common position for this method during a hatch is bent over about 20 feet directly downstream from a distracted fish. Put the fly a foot or so in front of the trout, with just that much leader going over its head.

To pop the trout on the nose, measure your cast just a foot or slightly more in front of the trout. If it is rising regularly, try to present the fly just when the trout seems ready to rise again. Quite often the trout, surprised by the fly's sudden arrival, will take the fly without hesitation. The idea behind this cast is to give the fish no time to think things over.

The sound cast, which serves the same purpose and is made from the same downstream position, is used far more often to draw trout out of tight lies. Place the fly about a foot behind the trout and a foot to the side, perhaps 2 feet in both directions if the fly is large. Set the fly down a bit hard so that it catches the attention of the trout, which swings around and engulfs whatever has lit on the water behind it.

**Control of the drift.** Once the cast is made, you will have no control over the drift. The trout will either suddenly take the fly or it won't. If the fish has not noticed the fly, then repeat the cast until you've attracted its attention, or put it down.

**On the water.** This method will not be used often unless you're an observant angler or you fish rivers with very heavy hatches. Trout tuck themselves into bullet-proof lies and grow large there for a reason: Not many folks ever notice them. Look for trout, or the subtle signs of their rises, tight to the banks, up under brush and bunchgrass clumps, or in boulder gardens where the trout can remain out of sight but have sight lines out to anything that lands on their small bit of water. These trout are careful to choose water that is very productive, which keeps them well fed, without the need to go prowling around where it's dangerous.

**The trout's point of view.** Whether you pop a fly on a trout's nose by setting it gently on the surface just a foot or so upstream or bump it on the behind by smacking the fly forcefully onto the water 1 to 2 feet downstream and out to the side to catch its attention, the trout will be taken by surprise. In most cases, you'll get one good shot at a fish, and your chances will diminish on each succeeding cast.

**Situations to solve.** If you're fishing a dry fly or emerger that is difficult, if not impossible, to see at casting range on the water, then you'll also have trouble following its drift. When that occurs, two problems arise: You won't be able to tell if the fly drifts without drag, and you won't know when a trout takes it. This situation can occur if your dry fly is small and drab, if you fish a mayfly emerger or spinner dressing that floats so flush in the surface film you cannot see it, or if the light is low, such as at dawn and dusk, when low-floating spinner patterns are usually most effective.

To solve the problem, try fishing the small or low-floating fly behind a larger and more visible dry fly or adding a strike indicator to the leader. The indicator method is normally reserved for nymphing, but it can work for dry-fly fishing as well. You'll find it solves situations in which you otherwise might harvest nothing but frustration.

**Tuning the rig.** If you're fishing a visible dry fly for a mayfly dun or caddis adult without any luck and want to try an emerger that might be difficult for you to see, then trail the emerger behind the fly you're already fishing and offer the trout a choice between the adult and emerger. If you're fishing a searching fly such as a Royal Wulff or Elk Hair Caddis and want to go to a smaller fly that you might not be able to see on the water, add the smaller fly as a trailer. Use the improved clinch knot to tie a 2- to 3-foot tippet directly to the hook bend of the larger fly, then tie the smaller fly to the tippet. Always use tippet at least one size finer than what you're using with the larger fly; then if you break off the point fly, you won't lose your whole rig.

If trout are willing to accept the fly you're already using but it's difficult to see, slip-knot a $1/2$-inch to 1-inch section of bright indicator yarn into the leader, dress it with fly floatant, and tease it into a fan. Make it as small as possible, and place it 4 to 6 feet from the fly. When tying the slip knot, be sure to form it so that you draw tight the leg leading toward the rod rather than the fly.

**Position and presentation.** You'll almost always use an indicator with a small dry fly or emerger when trout are rising during a hatch of insects or fall of tiny terrestrials. You'll want to apply an appropriate method to solve the situation, and one of the methods designed to cover trout feeding on at least fairly smooth water will almost always work. Depending on the shape of the currents, use an upstream presentation, a cross-stream cast, or a downstream presentation.

**Control of the drift.** Control the drift exactly as you would with a single dry fly, but focus on the larger fly or the visible strike indicator, mending and tending line to give it a free drift. If you see a rise anywhere near the fly, assume a trout has taken the smaller dry fly or emerger, and raise your rod gently to set the hook.

**On the water.** Envision the rising trout at the center of a circle. Take an appropriate position in the 360 degree arc around it, depending on the shape of the currents. If you must cast from directly downstream (A), then pop the trout on the nose. If your position is in the downstream portion of the arc (B), then use the upstream dry-fly method. If the best position is off to the side (C), then try the cross-stream reach cast or cross-stream wiggle cast. If your position is upstream from the trout (D), then use the downstream wiggle cast or parachute or drop and draw.

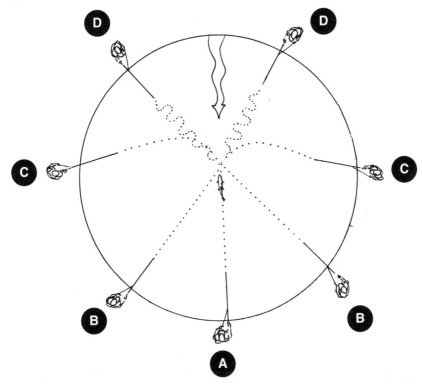

**The trout's point of view.** Unless you've chosen a dry fly or yarn indicator that is large and intrusive, trout will ignore it. They'll rise and sip the smaller fly, and you'll observe either the rise or the sudden movement of your indicator. If your indicator goes under, set the hook at once. If you suddenly can no longer find your indicator, set the hook, but gently.

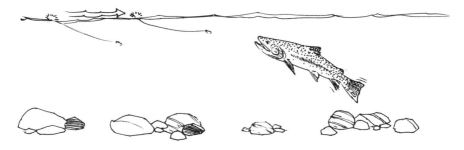

**Situations to solve.** Fishing a dry fly from a moving boat can create quite the dilemma. First, you must constantly watch the water ahead for the most likely holding water, then deliver your dry quickly to that water, in position for the best drift. Then, you must watch your fly for strikes while keeping an eye out for the next bit of great water. You have to watch your fly so you don't miss takes and at the same time watch the water ahead so you don't miss the most likely lies. Meanwhile, your companion at the oars, or worse your guide, will scold you either for missing fish or for failing to hit the most promising water.

Most boat fishing is done to the banks, which helps to reduce the problem by providing a narrower sight plane. You can either keep your eye on your fly while you scan the water ahead out of the corner of your eye, or keep your eye on the water ahead and follow the drift of the fly out of the corner of your eye. Since takes are often detonations, watching for the best water might be the better choice, until you miss a take or two, and your guide tells you how large those trout were that got away.

In time, you will learn to divide your attention among the tasks and even, with more time, to relax while doing it.

**Tuning the rig.** Your rod should be long so you can loft backcasts high above the boat and keep flies out of necks and ears. The leader should be a bit longer than the rod, but not more than a couple of feet longer. The tippet should be 2 feet long and stout so that it balances with the size of the fly. Since you'll usually be probing bank water with large salmon fly, caddis, or grasshopper imitations, a 5- or 6-weight line and leader tapered to 3 or 4X will give you more control than a 3- or 4-weight line and fine leader.

**Position and presentation.** Your position, controlled by whoever is at the oars, should be an easy cast from the bank, say 35 to 50 feet, depending on your comfort range. You should be standing in the stanchions, if there are any, or sitting in the chair, if there are not, facing the direction you want to fish. Keep your focus ahead of the boat and always place your dry fly downstream at an angle ahead of the boat. The current along the bank, where the trout hold, is slowed by friction, whereas the current where the boat floats is a bit faster. When you cast ahead, the boat will slowly gain ground on the fly, enough to introduce slack and give the fly a free drift. If you cast at an angle behind the boat, the boat will draw slowly ahead of the fly, causing drag.

When drifting a fast river, you might find yourself dropping your casts farther and farther back to hit all potential lies, until the fly lands behind the boat. It's better to high-grade the lies, fish the best drift lines ahead of the boat, and let some of the others go. If you find yourself casting at an angle behind the boat, sacrifice some bank, even if it's good, and reposition yourself to cast ahead of the boat. If another angler is in the stern, he will appreciate that.

**Control of the drift.** You might find that your dry is drifting in a good line, about to arrive where you think a trout will whack it, when it begins to drag because of conflicting currents. If you're standing and are high above the water, you can toss mends and even small roll casts at the fly, introducing slack into the line to get a few feet of extra drift. If you can't mend or tend the fly, then get it off the water and cast again to reposition it.

**On the water.** If another angler is in the stern, and you continually drop your casts at an angle behind the boat, you will cut off his chances and force him to fish behind the boat as well. To avoid this, two anglers should work their way along a bank making fore- and backcasts that are close to parallel in the air and aimed at an equal angle ahead of the boat. Not only will this show both of your flies to all the best water, but it will keep you from tangling lines. Tangles cause you to miss a lot of water, and they turn guides to grumps.

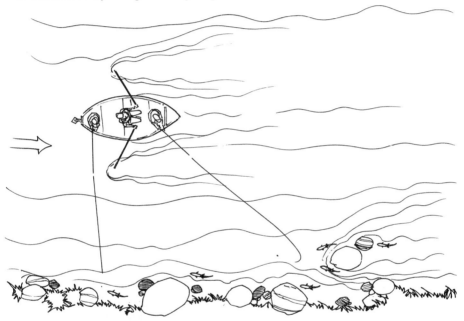

**The trout's point of view.** Your best chances to land a fish is when the dry fly enters into the trout's window of vision on the surface ahead of the line and leader, without drag and without smacking onto the water where the trout can see what happened. When you fish from a boat, try to obtain drag-free drifts of at least 5 and more often 10 to 15 feet to keep from constantly lifting the fly off the water and placing it back down again.

# CHAPTER 6

# Rigs and Methods for Nymphs on Moving Water

You must solve a slightly more complex set of problems when nymphing than when dry-fly fishing. Oversimplified, dry-fly problems are selecting the right fly and defeating drag. Unlike a dry, which sits on the surface where you can see what is happening to it, nymphs, with a few exceptions, probe the invisible depths, so you will need more perception and even some imagination to connect trout to them. Trout make between 80 and 90 percent of their living feeding on subsurface foods, often nonselectively. This means they're easier to fool on the bottom, and once you master nymphing, you're more likely to catch a lot more trout, in a broader set of streamside conditions.

**Determining the right depth.** Most of the time, trout hold on or very near the bottom, where they can take advantage of boulders, depressions, trenches, and other obstructions to the current. They feed on dislodged and drifting aquatic insects, which are also most abundant along the bottom. During a hatch, when aquatic insects rise from the bottom and swim to the surface, trout might suspend and feed on them as they pass through the middepths. Many insects hesitate for some moments just beneath the surface, before penetrating through the surface film and getting on their winged way, and many trout, sometimes including the largest, follow to feed on these subsurface emergers.

If you see clues that trout are holding and feeding in the middepths or just beneath the surface, you should choose a rig and method that will allow you to fish at those depths. In the absence of any clues that trout are feeding on top or in the middepths or subsurface, always assume they're holding and feeding along the bottom.

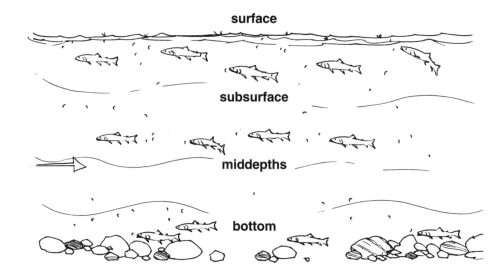

**Choose a rig and method.** Once you've chosen the depth at which you want to fish, choose a rig and method that will show your flies to trout at that depth. If trout are feeding at subsurface, you'll want to rig almost as you would to fish a dry fly, only with a nymph tied to the tippet. If thcy're in the middepths or on the bottom of very shallow water, your rig should be designed to fish nymphs just a foot to 3 feet deep. If the fish and the water are both deeper, choose a rig and method that get your fly or flies on or very near the bottom and allow them to drift along naturally there.

**Controlling line on the water.** Once you're rigged right and have taken up the best position to fish the water you want to cover, make your presentation and then mend the line, feed the line, and high-stick the rod to keep the line off the water. Do whatever it takes to keep your nymph at the proper fishing depth to duplicate the drift of a natural insect. You'll accomplish little even with the right rig if you fail to make it fish in the right way.

**Adjusting for changes in water depth and speed.** As you move along the different water types of a stream, or fish a single but broader water type on a larger river, you'll find that the depth of the water will change as you shift from one casting position to another. Current speed also affects the way you rig to attain a certain depth. It takes more weight to get nymphs down in swift water than it does in placid water. Always be prepared to make changes to your rig if either the depth you're fishing or the speed of the current changes enough to remove your flies from the zone you're trying to achieve, which is usually within 6 inches or so of the bottom.

**Covering the water or high-grading likely lies.** When nymphing, you'll have to decide between covering all of the water or fishing just the most likely lies. If the water is easy to read and you think you can predict where trout might hold, you'll probably want to fish the most likely water. If the surface is more consistent, as on a large flat or in a large riffle, revealing little about where trout might be sprinkled, then you will have to fish it all to find them.

On creeks and small streams where holding lies are usually obvious, you should concentrate on fishing them. On medium-size streams and small rivers where some lies are obvious but many more are not, you should fish most of the water, but give extra casts to the more likely water. On large rivers with a few obvious lies, such as riffle corners and boulders, you'll often have no choice but to cover all of the water.

**Covering visible nymphing fish.** When trout feed visibly, as either subsurface selective feeders or middepth cruisers, or are revealed as flashes and winks as they twist their bodies to take insects drifting along the bottom, your job is to find out what they might be taking, choose a nymph that at least approximates it, then fish it at the depth and in the manner in which trout are seeing the natural insects arrive.

**Detecting takes to nymphs.** Depending on how you're rigged and the method you're using, detecting a take might vary from feeling a thump on a nymph fished on a tight line to noticing the slightest movement of a strike indicator. Next to determining the correct drift at the right depth, detecting takes is the most demanding skill in nymphing. Although explanations and illustrations can help, nothing can substitute for the sixth sense you'll develop only after you've spent enough time nymphing.

**The size of nymphs.** Trout won't pass up giant salmon fly nymphs or big cranefly larvae if they get a chance at them. If large naturals are abundant in the water you're fishing, then fish large nymphs. Most of the time, however, even big trout feeding along the bottom in somewhat turbulent water take insects and crustaceans that average about size 16. You'll do well to fish flies in that same size or smaller. If you fish a two-fly rig, one fly might be large, but make sure the other one is small. You'll enjoy a dramatic upturn in the number of trout you catch if you just drop the average size of the nymphs you fish.

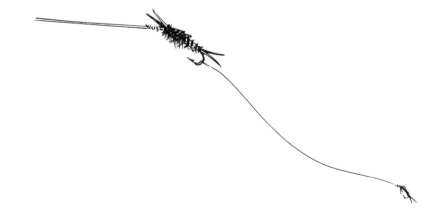

## RIG:        UNENCUMBERED NYMPH

**Purpose.** It might seem surprising that 90 percent or more of the stream nymph fishing you do will be with a floating line. Most of the time, you'll use combinations of weight on the leader to get your flies to depth, strike indicators to warn you of takes, and a floating line to control the drift. However, the unencumbered nymph rig, the simplest floating line rig, is a single nymph tied to the end of the tippet, sometimes with the addition of another nymph trailing the first. This setup is similar to the standard dry-fly rig. If you're fishing dry flies and getting refusals during a hatch, then try nipping off the dry, tying on a nymph to match the immature stage of whatever adult is hatching, and continuing to fish almost exactly as you were.

The purpose of the unencumbered rig is usually to fish nymphs in shallow water from inches to 1 or 2 feet deep. But with methods that use weighted flies, this rig, which is unencumbered by extra weight and indicators on the leader, can be used to get a nymph deep into the water while allowing maximum control over the subsequent swing, drift, or retrieve.

**History/origins.** Nymphs were first fished on silk lines, originally as modifications of wet flies that more closely resembled the immature stages of aquatic insects. The growing popularity and widespread use of nymphs occurred around the same time that coated floating fly lines arrived on the fishing scene. Early nymphs were fished the same way that modern nymphs are now used with the unencumbered nymph rig. Then, when an array of sinking lines became available, these lines were used to move nymphs down farther in deeper water. For a brief time, the advent of sinking-tip, wet-belly, and wet-head lines seemed to provide the solution to fishing nymphs most effectively at any depth, until the arrival of strike indicators and weight on the leader in the 1970s. Once again, almost all nymphing is done with floating lines. The unencumbered nymph rig arises out of the earliest nymph fishing, and it is now used most often to swing a nymph shallow or to nymph a hatch just beneath the surface.

**Knots and notes.** Variations of the unencumbered nymph rig include the base leader, those extended by finer tippets, and two-fly setups that offer trout a choice, often between a large and small nymph. The blood knot or surgeon's knot is used to add tapering sections and tippets to the base leader. The improved clinch knot is often used to attach the fly to the tippet and to fix a dropper tippet directly to the hook bend of the first fly. To duplicate natural nymphs, which move in the currents and look alive, imitations should be tied to the tippet with a Duncan loop on sizes 18 and larger, and a surgeon's loop for smaller nymphs.

**Adjustments for conditions.** Lengthen your leader and fine down the tippet, according to the smoothness of the water and the size flies you're fishing. Start with a $7^1/2$- or 9-foot base leader in 3X, and fish size 6 to 10 nymphs. If you go to size 12 to 14 nymphs, add a couple feet of 4X. If you move down to size 16 or 18, nip the 4X to a foot and add 2 feet of 5X. Anything smaller, nip the 5X to a foot and add a couple feet of 6X. If you add a second fly, use just 12 to 18 inches of tippet one size finer than the tippet to the first fly.

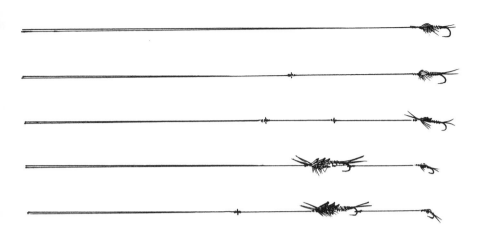

**Rules for the rig.** Be sure that your leader is constructed correctly to let you fish nymphs the way you like. If you're going to fish a small nymph to trout feeding selectively on a smooth flat, use a long, fine leader, just as you would with a dry fly in the same situation. If you're going to fish a moderate-size nymph on the swing in rougher water, then rig with your base leader and a short tippet added. If you're planning to get a large weighted nymph down to the bottom of a deep pool, you might have to lengthen your leader and tippet to give the fly a long enough tether at the end of the floating line.

**Appropriate flies.** Although you can fish the full range of nymphs with the unencumbered nymph rig, size 16 to 20 imitative nymphs work best when fishing selective situations, and size 12 to 16 generic searching nymphs should be used to explore more broken water. Usually when you want to fish larger, heavier flies along the bottom in moving water, other rigs will do it better. But on occasion you'll use large nymphs to probe the depths of slow pools.

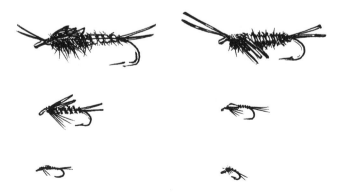

**RIG:       UNENCUMBERED NYMPH**
**Method:    Standard nymph swing**

**Situations to solve.** In our rush to embrace the indicator and shot method, we've nearly forgotten that nymphs were first fished with the old wet-fly swing. This original cast caught a lot of trout, and still does. If you're new to fly fishing, try the standard nymph swing; you're sure to enjoy some success. Let's say you're on a medium to large size stream, or a small to large river, and you want to explore the water to find where the trout are holding. With the standard nymph swing, you can step in at the head of the water you want to cover, usually a riffle or run, slip easily downstream with the current, and make a cast. Fish your fly around on the swing, take a step, make another cast, and show your nymph to any trout that might be out there. Keep in mind that this method is not often effective on creeks and small streams, because they're usually fished upstream and often are too narrow to allow a cross-stream cast and downstream swing.

**Tuning the rig.** Adjust your leader according to the size of your flies and the smoothness of the water. Most of the time on streams, you'll use the standard swing in fairly fast riffles, runs, and current tongues. On big rivers, you'll use it to explore choppy riffles or big runs. Your base leader with a single fly affixed works just fine. Adding a point fly on a short tippet tied to the hook bend of the first fly will increase your chances of taking trout and finding out what sort of fly the trout want.

**Position and presentation.** Never make the mistake of wading right into the most likely lie, the riffle corner. Take your first position 10 to 20 feet upstream from the highest water you want to fish, so that your nymph, on the first series of casts, will swing through fast water with little chance to arrive in the corner with the greatest promise. Make your first cast just 15 to 20 feet, and lengthen each subsequent cast 3 feet or so, until you either are covering streams from side to side or are at the limits of your comfort range on rivers. After getting out the length of line you'd like to cast, begin working downstream by taking a step or two after fishing out each cast.

**Control of the drift.** The nymph must swim at the same range of speed that natural insects do. To accomplish this, you will have to slow down the swing of your nymph. Try casting at an angle farther downstream the faster the current you're fishing. A cast across the current gives the water more bite against the line, and speeds it. A cast closer in, more downstream than out, gives the current less bite and slows the swing. Another way to slow the nymph is with one to several mends during the swing. If you're fishing moderate to fast water, you'll need almost constant mends throughout the swing.

If the water is slow, such as in a creeping but productive pool, then you might have to speed up the swing of the fly to make it look alive. To do this, cast at an angle almost straight across the pool; then toss a downstream mend. If that is not enough, you might want to retrieve the fly, but never do more than inch it along.

**On the water.** When you first get on the water, show the nymph or nymphs to all water that might contain trout. One of the best tools for teaching the art of reading trout water is to cover it with a swinging nymph. Once you do that enough times, you'll soon learn where trout hold and where they do not. As your subconscious begins to sort out what good water looks like, you'll fish it more diligently and your take will begin to creep up.

When fishing a current tongue on any size stream or river, place the nymph in the faster water in the main current, and be sure that it crosses the seam from fast to slow. Trout often hold on the soft side of that seam and feed on things drifting by on the fast side. The most productive moment of any cast occurs when your nymph crosses the seam.

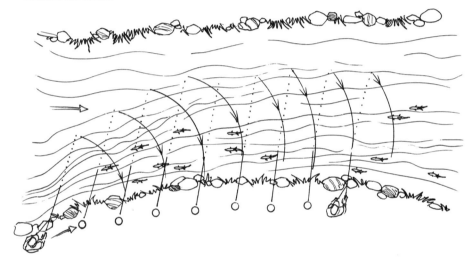

**The trout's point of view.** From its position on the bottom, the trout will see the nymph, or pair of them, swim into view overhead. If the nymph is moving slowly, animated by the current, and looking alive, it will likely be taken. If it's swimming faster than any natural might, or simply hanging as if dead, the trout is unlikely to make any sort of move for it.

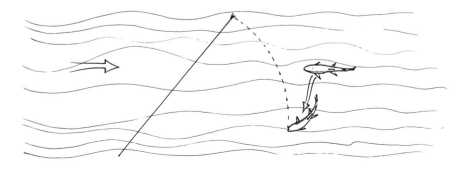

**RIG:        UNENCUMBERED NYMPH**
**Method:     Upstream to feeding fish**

**Situations to solve.** Quite often during a mayfly, caddis, or midge hatch, when it appears that trout are rising to take newly emerged adults off the surface, they are actually concentrating on the nymphs or pupae just beneath the surface. When the take is so near the top that a riseform is sent to the surface, the take appears to be to a floating adult. To see if you're in such a situation, follow closely the drifts of a few adults on the surface. If they run the gauntlet of rising fish and none disappear in swirls, it's likely trout are taking the immatures just inches deep.

To select the correct pattern, you may have to displace the trout by wading out and suspending an aquarium net in the water, then match what the trout are eating, normally with a nymph size 16 or smaller. If you're unable to collect a natural, try a generic nymph the same size as the adults on the surface. Once you've selected a pattern, wade back out and rest the water until the trout return to feeding.

**Tuning the rig.** If you've already been trying to solve the situation with a dry fly or floating emerger, then you're rigged right to fish the nymph. If your leader is not long and fine, add 2 to 3 feet of tippet that is in balance to the size fly, usually 5 or 6X. If the water is smooth, which will often be the case when you use this method, apply dry-fly floatant to the leader from the line tip down to the tippet knot, but be careful not to get any on the tippet or the fly. Watch the point where the leader enters the water. You'll detect takes as either swirls very near it or twitches in the leader tip.

**Position and presentation.** Take up your position much as you would for dry-fly fishing in the same set of conditions—downstream from the trout, but at an angle off to the side. A position directly downstream will give you one shot at the trout, but you will have to pin the nymph almost onto their noses for it to work. Otherwise the line and leader will fly over their heads. The best angle is from 30 to 60 degrees to either side, though on currents that are even sheets between your position and that of the rising trout, you could be directly off to the side and still make the presentation work.

Make the presentation precisely as you would with a dry fly: Pinpoint the position of a trout, and place the fly 2 to 5 feet upstream from it, as close as possible into its feeding lane. If you're fishing over a pod of trout, try to make your presentation to one fish that you've singled out, but if the first trout refuses it, let the fly continue to drift through the pod.

As in dry-fly fishing, you might have to make repeated presentations before everything becomes perfect and the fly arrives in front of a fish at the moment it is ready to feed. Be patient. Avoid putting the trout down, while you make cast after cast. If you've hooked the trout and either put it down or feel it's not interested in the fly you're fishing, then you might want to delve into your fly boxes and try another.

**Control of the drift.** The drift is controlled precisely as it is when making a dry-fly cast upstream to rising trout: Gather slack as it forms, and be prepared to set the hook. Rarely will you feel the take in this type of nymphing, so you must set to any sign that something has happened where your submerged fly drifts.

**On the water.** Trout are spooky when they're holding high in the water column, feeding on insects while exposing themselves to overhead predation. Move into your chosen casting position carefully: Send no wading waves over the feeding fish, and make your measuring fore- and backcasts out of sight of the trout. Don't let the line and leader fly over the trout's head before landing on the water, and cast far enough upstream from the fish so the arrival of the nymph on the water does not alarm it.

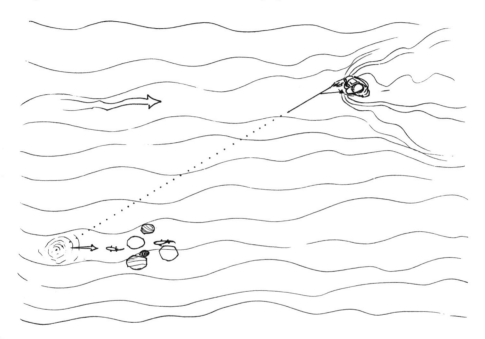

**The trout's point of view.** The trout will be intent on feeding, focused on a narrow drift line, though during some hatches they'll cruise, dashing to take naturals on their way to the top. If trout are on stations, place your nymph gently into their feeding lanes. If they're moving, send the nymph right to a rise the instant you see it.

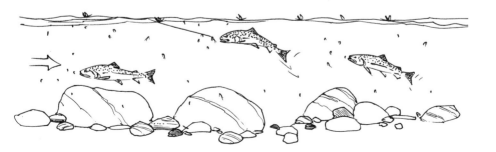

**RIG:        UNENCUMBERED NYMPH**
**Method:    Tuck cast**

**Situations to solve.** This method, originated by the great Pennsylvania angler and teacher George Harvey, is designed to get a weighted nymph to the bottom in brisk water and to fish it tumbling along there with a natural drift, without the addition of split shot or strike indicators on the leader. The tuck cast works well in pocket water 2 to 3 feet deep and for lines of drift a short to medium cast long, say 15 to 45 feet. While perfect for creeks to medium-size streams, it is less effective on larger rivers.

The tuck cast rotates the weighted nymph around at the end of the loop, accelerates the fly, and drives it forcibly into the water. Free of any tension from the line, the nymph sinks quickly and begins almost at once to tumble back toward you. It's a valuable technique to master if you spend time on creeks and streams of average size.

**Tuning the rig.** The leader should be a foot or two longer than the rod, with at least a couple feet of tippet. With an $8^1/2$- to 9-foot rod, the leader will be 10 to 12 feet long, tapered to 3X with large nymphs and 4 or 5X with the more normal range of nymphs. A nymph much smaller than size 14 won't sink quickly. If you want to fish a small nymph with this method, consider adding one as a trailer to a larger nymph that will deliver the smaller one to the bottom.

**Position and presentation.** Take up a position at the lower end of the line of drift you want your nymph to take, either in direct line with the current or off to the side not much more than a rod length or so. Your cast should be straight upstream or nearly so. If possible, position yourself a short cast downstream from the head of the line of drift, so the nymph lands in down-driven current, which along with the force of the tuck, helps escort it quickly to the bottom. This method is especially effective in pocket water, where the current enters in a plunge and drift lines are short.

To make the presentation, align your thumb with the back of the rod grip and your knuckles in a line on the underside. The knuckles should aim at your target, while the thumb drives the rod into a slightly overpowered delivery stroke. Aim this, as the master says, to *shoot to the top of the pool or pocket.* Make your stop with the rod high; you might have to bump the rod back a bit as the short cast unfurls. The rod must be vertical; if it is canted, the resulting tuck will drive the fly sideways rather than straight down.

The abrupt stop and added bump will cause the nymph to arc around while still in the air, and then dive toward the water. The force of the tuck causes the weighted nymph to sink immediately. If the line were laid out straight, rather than tucked, the nymph would either drift high in the water or sink slowly.

**Control of the drift.** As soon as the nymph penetrates to the bottom, begin drawing in slack and lifting the rod to keep slight contact with the nymph and to keep it tumbling toward you. Be careful not to lift the nymph. Avoid taking in line faster than the current causes slack, or you'll lift the nymph and retrieve it downstream. The nymph should drift in the bottom zone, within 6 inches or so of the streambed and at the speed of the current, just as a natural insect, cut adrift in the same water, would move.

**On the water.** Because it is made either straight upstream or at a very narrow angle to one side off the current line to be fished, the tuck cast works well on moderate to fast water where the surface is somewhat rough. On smooth water, the arrival of the line, leader, and fly might alarm the trout. The method is most effective on small to medium-size foothill and mountain streams and least effective on spring creeks, tailwaters, and the larger valley ends of river systems.

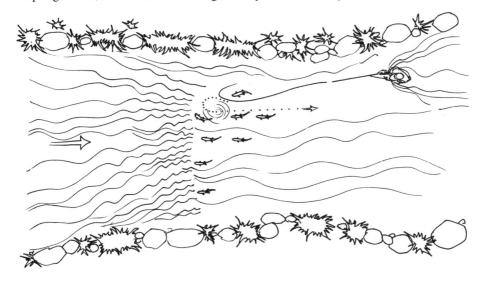

**The trout's point of view.** If the cast and drift are executed correctly, the weighted nymph will arrive to the trout, tumbling along on or very near the bottom at the approximate speed of the current. Takes will at times be felt, but more often will be signaled by a stoppage of the drift, a hesitation in the downstream movement of the line and leader. Set the hook quickly, though not brutally, at any sign of a take.

**RIG:        UNENCUMBERED NYMPH**
**Method:    Lift and drop**

**Situations to solve.** In the half hour to full hour before many hatches, mayfly nymphs and caddisfly pupae get restless. They leave the bottom and swim toward the surface and then change their minds and return to the bottom. When they're finally ready to emerge, they swim all the way to the surface, break through the film, and make the transformation to the adult stage. During prehatch activity, and even during the hatch itself, many trout focus on the rising immature insect, feeding somewhere between the bottom and the top, rather than focusing on the more visible adult floating on top.

You can capitalize on this behavior by rigging with a floating line and weighted nymph, letting the fly sink, and then raising it toward the surface and letting it sink again, repeating the cycle throughout the length of its drift. The rising nymph will look just like those swimming insects. The technique is most useful on modest currents, 3 to 5 feet deep, where fairly even flows lack the turbulence needed to disrupt the rising and falling of the nymph. The limited situations in which you'll find use for this method will be on spring creeks, tailwaters, and broad even sheets of current on freestone streams and rivers.

**Tuning the rig.** You'll need a heavily weighted nymph, based at least roughly on the hatching mayfly nymph or caddisfly pupa, to make this method work. If you have no specific matches, the generic Beadhead Hare's Ear or Beadhead Fox Squirrel comes close enough. A long, fine tippet will allow your weighted nymph to sink the quickest. At least 3 feet, and better 4, of tippet one diameter undersized for the size nymph you're fishing should be about right.

**Position and presentation.** Position yourself at the upper end of the section of water you want to fish, and stay off to the side, close enough to the line of drift that you'll be able to fish it with casts from 20 to 40 feet long, no longer. You want to be close enough that raising the rod results in lifting the nymph. Because you'll cast upstream and across, and fish the length of the drift both upstream and down from where you are, you should be positioned at the side point of an approximately equilateral triangle, make your cast to the upper point, and end the drift at the lower point.

As soon as the cast lands, make an upstream mend or an attenuated roll cast to give the nymph a chance to sink without hindrance from the line. After the nymph sinks 2 to 3 feet, stop the rod and slowly raise it. This will lift the nymph, causing it to swim up toward the surface, much as a natural insect might. When the nymph is near the surface, drop the rod and make another mend or roll. Let the nymph sink, and then stop the rod and raise it again to lift the nymph. Continue to let the nymph sink and lift it again as many times as you can throughout the length of a controlled drift. In many situations, you'll only get two lifts; in some runs, you'll get four or more. After the last lift, take the nymph off the water and make your next cast a foot or two up and out from the first, as you cover the next drift line.

**Control of the drift.** Your ability to make mends and weak roll casts at the nymph will determine how fast it sinks, and therefore how efficiently you'll be able to escort it through its lift-and-drop drift sequences. Drop the rod tip when the nymph is sinking, and raise the rod tip to lift the nymph. As the nymph drifts downstream toward you, take in slack line. After it passes your position, feed line into the drift.

**On the water.** Make your first cast short and upstream, fishing a line of drift not far off the end of the rod tip. Each subsequent cast should be a foot or so out from the one before it, and also a foot or so upstream. In that way, you cover the water in a thorough fashion. Of course, if you see trout working over insects in the middepths or close to the surface, then make your casts and time your lifts specifically to cover those fish. Most of the time, however, you'll apply the lift and drop method blind.

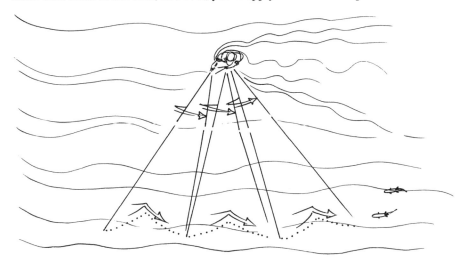

**The trout's point of view.** The most productive part of each drift is when the nymph is animated, lifting from the bottom toward the top. The trout might see the nymph sinking and ignore it but often will turn to take it as soon you draw the line tight and the nymph begins to swim upward, as if alive. As the nymph sinks, however, keep an eye out for any abrupt movement of the line tip that indicates a trout has made a mistake.

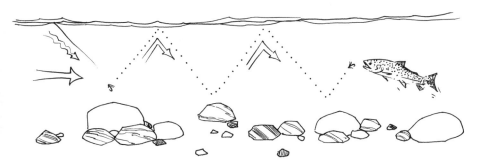

**RIG:        UNENCUMBERED NYMPH**
**Method:    Sawyer induced take**

**Situations to solve.** Frank Sawyer's induced take method will take trout in spring creeks, tailwaters, or any freestone stream with water so clear that you're able to spot fish. Sawyer, a riverkeeper on a chalk stream in England, was the originator of the famous Pheasant Tail Nymph. He tied it with fine copper wire rather than thread to increase its sink rate and make it more applicable to his method, which requires a nymph that will penetrate the surface film upon hitting the water and sink quickly.

The induced take is usually used against trout holding in specific lies, near the bottom but not in deep water, where currents are moderate to slow. In such situations, the current will deliver a constant parade of dead detrital bits, along with the occasional live nymph, past the trout. This method can also be effective with trout holding on the bottom or even in the middepths and feeding on insects rising toward the surface. As long as the fish are not cruising and restless, you can use this method to set up a drift right down their feeding lanes.

The induced take is not effective when you want to search the water or fish in water that is too fast or rough for trout to be spotted.

**Tuning the rig.** The induced take calls for an $8^{1}/_{2}$- to 9-foot rod, a 10- to 14-foot leader, and a 2- to 4-foot tippet of 4 to 6X. At 6X, you may be more likely to hook fish but also to lose them. As Sawyer himself pointed out, the larger the trout, the easier it is to spot, so it's unlikely that you'll use the induced take on tiddlers. To help you notice takes, be sure the tip of your fly line is clean and floating well. Weighted imitations of mayfly nymphs and caddis pupae are always good bets for this method.

**Position and presentation.** Your casting position must be off to the side of the spotted trout and at a sufficient angle upstream so that when you stop your rod, the current will animate your nymph. Get as close to the trout as you can, without alarming it or sending wading waves over it. Usually, this will be between 20 and 40 feet, although Sawyer wrote of using the method out to 60 feet. Just make sure you're able to notice when a trout takes the nymph.

Place the cast far enough upstream from the trout that the entry of the nymph will go unnoticed by the fish and will give the nymph time to sink to the level of the fish. If the nymph is size 16 or smaller and the trout shallow, your cast might be placed just a couple of feet upstream from the trout. In more common situations with size 14 and larger nymphs, the cast will be placed 5 to 10 feet upstream from the trout, which is why the method is most effective where currents are modest and flows fairly even.

Allow the nymph to sink to the level of the trout while you follow the drift with your rod tip. If your cast is placed correctly, the nymph will arrive at the trout's level at the same time it comes within sight of the fish, say a foot or slightly more in front of its nose. When you observe, or more likely calculate, that the nymph has reached that position, stop the rod and lift the tip a foot or two. The dead-drifting nymph will suddenly stop and begin to swim toward the surface within the trout's sight.

**Control of the drift.** You might be able to help the nymph sink and delay its movement by making small upstream mends. The method works best on even flows where line control is not necessary. Just follow the drift with a low rod tip to allow the nymph to sink; then stop the rod and raise it a bit to animate the nymph.

**On the water.** Usually, your nymph will be out of your sight as it drifts and sinks toward the trout. If you're able to see the nymph, then watch it, and be ready to set the hook if the trout takes it. More often, it's best to watch the trout. If the trout makes any unusual movement, or you see the white of its opening and closing jaws around your approaching nymph, raise your rod gently to set the hook. Tiny sideways movements or those flashes of white are the most common signals to set the hook when using this method.

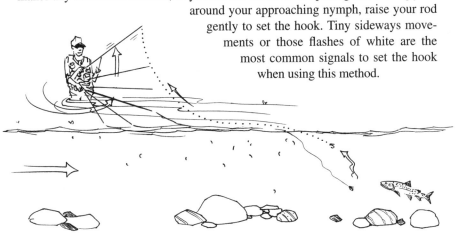

**The trout's point of view.** Trout constantly observe and allow to pass pieces of vegetation, bits of bark, and other dead debris drifting toward them. If you allow your nymph to move through their lines of sight on a dead drift, they're likely to allow the nymph to pass as well. When you use the induced take to animate the nymph close to the trout, the fish will be prompted into an aggressive take.

**RIG:          UNENCUMBERED NYMPH**
**Method:       Plop cast**

**Situations to solve.** When fishing bank water, you'll often come across trout in what seem to be bulletproof lies, areas protected by overhanging limbs, fence-posts, bridge abutments, logs, indentations into undercut banks, and other unlikely items. I once was defeated by a trout rising to sip insects from the shelter of a rusted car body that was installed as riprap to stabilize a river bank. An open door, only half submerged, defended the fish. I failed to catch it.

Sometimes when large insects such as grasshoppers are out, trout can be brought to dry flies popped on their noses or bumped on their behinds. Otherwise, a large dry fly landing nearby is more likely to frighten the trout than to catch it. The plop cast with a nymph operates on the same principle of surprise, but it's easier to draw a trout by sound to a sunk fly than it is to a dry fly.

**Tuning the rig.** Little tuning is needed for this method. The trout's decision to take or not take will be almost instant, and it's not likely to be put off by the diameter of your tippet. Your nymph should be of moderate size, 12 to 16, and slightly, not heavily, weighted. It must penetrate the surface film on impact, but it should not sink out of sight before a trout can turn and take it.

**Position and presentation.** The preferable position for this method is downstream and somewhat off to the side of the located trout. Unfortunately, the nature of such lies makes it almost impossible to get into position to fish them with standard presentations. So try to take the best position the situation allows, and work with it. Get as close to the lie as possible without making the trout aware of your presence as you move into position on it. In rough water, you might have to hit the trout nearly on the head from any direction to get it to notice your nymphs.

The usual presentation places the nymph onto the water with a bit of a plop, near the trout but not on top of it. The fish should hear or more aptly *feel* the nymph's arrival through its lateral line, but it should not see the nymph land. If your position is behind the trout, place the nymph within a foot or two of the fish with the hope that the trout will wheel around and attack. If your position is off to the side, place the nymph 2 to 3 feet away. If your position is upstream, then place the nymph 3 to 4 feet from the trout. All this assumes you are casting over the somewhat smooth water required for this method.

It's a good idea to make a measuring cast 2 or 3 feet away from the point where you think the most effective cast will land. A trout that has not been spooked might be tempted to turn at a longer distance, but don't try to creep casts up to the trout a foot at a time. Land a cast to measure things and give a sensitive trout an opportunity at long range; then fire for effect, close to the trout. The object is to catch the trout by surprise, not warn it.

**Control of the drift.** If you make the plop cast from downstream or off to one side, all you have to do is prepare yourself to set the hook when the trout turns to pounce. If you must take a position upstream and make your cast downstream, you might want to feed a bit of line into the drift, but that's rare. With the plop cast, everything is decided almost at once—fight or flight—and drift is rarely involved.

**On the water.** The most common bulletproof lies are found tight along banks. As you move along the edge, keep your footfalls soft, stay out of sight, and watch the water before you fish it. Sometimes you'll see a dark form materialize into a trout. More often you'll see subtle rise rings emanating out of places you know you can't get flies to. Don't assume that small rises mean small trout. Fish protected by difficult lies tend to remain undisturbed by other anglers and grow large.

**The trout's point of view.** Trout fooled by the plop cast go from totally undisturbed to startled into an attack in an instant. Upon being made aware of the nymph's presence by the slight sound of its arrival, the trout should not have to travel far to investigate whether what has landed should be fled from or eaten.

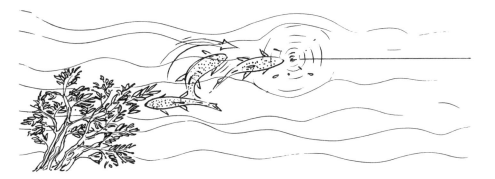

**RIG:        UNENCUMBERED NYMPH**
**Method:     Countdown and slow retrieve**

**Situations to solve.** It's rare to find pools that are ponded almost to stillness, but it does happen, especially late in the season when flows are low on freestone creeks, streams, and rivers. I've also fished tailwaters when the water flow is held back because irrigation or power needs are low. When the current subsides, trout move into pools, where they hold in schools and act as they would in ponds. Except on the largest rivers, most pools are usually 6 to 8 feet deep, ideal for using a weighted nymph rigged with a floating line and long leader.

Trout in such water are rarely selective. Not only do they see a wide array of naturals, but they're hungry enough to take whatever they can get. Use generic nymphs that resemble lots of things, rather than specific imitations. You'll be tempted to choose big flies to go down into the darkness after big trout, but you'll do better with flies size 12 to 14 and even smaller. When in doubt, rig with a medium to large nymph with lots of weight and add a trailing small nymph that is either unweighted or lightly weighted.

**Tuning the rig.** The length of the leader depends on the depth of the pool. If the pool is 3 to 4 feet deep, you can get by with a standard leader 1 or 2 feet longer than your rod. If the pool is 5 or 6 feet deep, you'll have to lengthen the leader 2 to 3 feet. If it is deeper than that, you can probe the depths by adding even more length to the leader, but in truth it might be better to switch to a sinking tip or full-sinking line and apply essentially the same method.

**Position and presentation.** Your primary target will be the deepest parts of the pool, especially the upper end of the deep water, where trout tend to hold to take advantage of what little current enters at the head. So your first position should be at the edge of the pool, close enough to the head that you can place your first casts in the entering current and fish out the casts on the bottom beneath that current. Cover what water you can in a fan from there, and then move to a second position downstream, where your casts should at least slightly overlap those from the first position. The object is to cover all of the water in the pool so that you find the location of that suspected pod of trout. On small pools, you'll fish from just one or two positions. On large pools, you might cover a pool from five or more casting positions down its length.

As soon as each cast lands, flip an upstream mend, assuming there's a mild current, and let the nymph sink. Count it down for two reasons: One, so you'll be able to repeat the fatal cast once you find that pod of trout, and two, to give yourself the patience to let the nymph sink to a sufficient depth. Usually a count between ten and thirty seconds will be all you need, though in rare deep pools you might count up to a minute.

Make your retrieve as slow as you can. Either use a handtwist retrieve, rolling the line hand over and over and gathering in just 3 to 4 inches of line at a time, or use a very slow strip retrieve, drawing the line slowly, with pauses inserted, over the rod hand forefinger that controls it. If you fail to catch a fish or contact the bottom, lengthen your count until you do one or the other.

**Control of the drift.** Beyond occasional mends, focus your line control on the retrieve, which should be designed to creep the nymph, or pair of them, close to the bottom.

**On the water.** Most often, pools that you can fish with the floating line rig and countdown method will be restricted to creeks and small to medium-size streams. On the smallest of them where the holding water is well-defined, you'll be able to cover most of it with a few well-placed casts from one position. If the pool is larger, you'll have to work your way around it. Always be sure to cover any likely lies. If the water is deep along the edges, then place your casts tight against them.

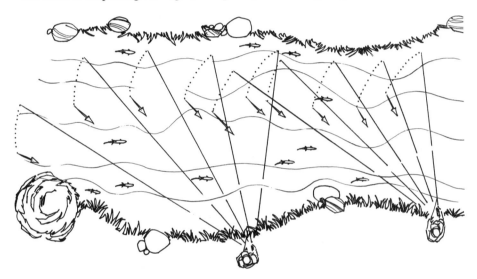

**The trout's point of view.** Trout can be drowsy when holding in still pools, especially in the cold of winter or heat of summer. They're likely to move to nymphs that come close, moving slowly. Fish as close to the bottom as you can, and retrieve as slowly as your patience allows.

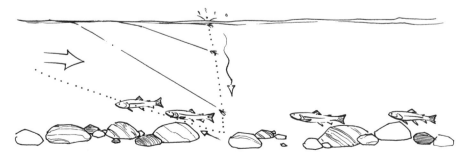

## RIG:           FOTHERGILL OUTRIGGER

**Purpose.** Angler Chuck Fothergill's home waters are rushing Rocky Mountain streams such as the Roaring Fork and Frying Pan in Colorado. His outrigger rig is designed to get a nymph to the bottom quickly in very fast water, keep it there, and tumble it along as a dislodged natural insect might move, while fishing with a floating line that allows him to observe takes. The rig is excellent for pocket water fishing and can be used in riffles and runs wherever the water is fast and the surface broken. It will work in waters of any wadeable depths, from a foot-deep riffle to a 5-foot-deep trench surrounded by shallower but brutally fast water.

**History/origins.** The outrigger rig, developed in the 1960s and '70s, adapted the unencumbered nymph rig for fast water. Fothergill kept the floating line and added weight to the leader. The result predates shot-and-indicator nymphing. In many types of water, especially broad reaches of riffle or run with even depths and current speeds, the more recent shot-and-indicator rig is more effective. But in pocket water situations, the outrigger rig is still very useful, and one you should know about and be able to apply against trout when you want to get nymphs down to them abruptly.

**Knots and notes.** Add tapering and tippet sections to the base leader with either the blood knot or surgeon's knot. The nymph should be tied to the tippet with a Duncan loop knot, which gives it freedom of movement throughout its drift. The tippet in Fothergill's formula should be 18 inches long, and the tippet knot is used to keep the weight from sliding down the leader to the nymph. Fothergill originally used strips of Twist-On weight, which are still effective, although you can substitute the more common split shot. I prefer putty weight molded around the tippet knot, because it catches in crevices along the bottom slightly less often.

Although not part of the original rig, a second nymph can be added as a trailer to the first to give trout a choice about flies. If you do, the first nymph should be moderately to heavily weighted and of medium to large size, and the trailer lightly weighted and two to four sizes smaller. Use an improved clinch knot to fasten a 10- to 12-inch section of tippet, at least one size finer than the tippet to the larger nymph, directly to the hook bend of the first nymph. Then use either a Duncan loop or surgeon's loop to fix the smaller nymph as a trailer.

**Adjustments for conditions.** In a shallow, bouncy riffle, you might get away with a weighted nymph and half a strip of Twist-On weight, a single small split shot, or a pinch of putty weight. As water depth and/or velocity increase, you'll want to add weight, always being sure that at some point in each drift the weight taps bottom. This might mean three full Twist-On strips, heavy split shot, or sections of putty weight to keep the nymph in touch with the bottom in fast water 4 to 5 feet deep.

As the water deepens, you should lengthen the leader to get the nymph down while leaving the leader tip afloat on the surface, where you can still see it. Fothergill's leaders averaged 13 to 15 feet. Because the leader tip is your strike

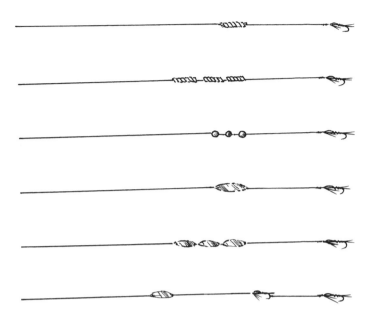

indicator on most casts, it's important that it float. Dress it with floatant or line cleaner, and if it begins to sink, dress it again.

**Rules for the rig.** Use a long rod, $8^1/2$ to $9^1/2$ feet, and floating line with a tip that floats rather than sinks. Because you'll be casting short most of the time and will have a lot of lead to control on the leader, you might find it advantageous to overline your rod one line weight. Always cast with a slow, long stroke that produces a patient, open loop. If you cast with tight loops, you'll deal with constant tangles.

**Appropriate flies.** The best flies for the outrigger rig are generic beadheads or imitations of insects that live in fast water. They should be weighted, though in most cases not heavily. The weight on the leader delivers the nymph to the bottom, where you want it to move naturally. The Brassie was designed specifically for fast Colorado waters where the method originated. Caddis larva and stonefly nymph patterns are also excellent.

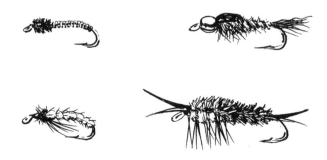

**RIG:        FOTHERGILL OUTRIGGER**
**Method:     High-sticking**

**Situations to solve.** You'll use the Fothergill outrigger rig and high-sticking method almost exclusively in fast water, usually in streams and small rivers that descend swiftly through the lower slopes of the mountains and the upper slopes of the foothills. In such situations, you'll be able to read the water and narrow prospective lies to water slow enough that trout can hold in it. However, you'll still have to prospect the bottom of the tumbled water with your nymph or nymphs, since you'll not be able to tell exactly where trout might be holding.

Fishing with the Fothergill outrigger and high-sticking method becomes a matter of reading fast water for the most likely lies, wading as close as you can to the water you want to fish, and then placing cast after cast to show your flies all along the bottom.

**Tuning the rig.** On creeks and small streams, where most of the holding water will be no more than 2 feet deep, your leader might be 8 to 9 feet long, about the length of the rod. On larger streams and on small or large rivers, the leader will have to be longer, 10 to 14 feet, to give the nymph more scope to sink quickly. The main adjustment you'll make is the amount of weight on the leader. You'll want enough weight to hit bottom at times during the drift. Current speed and water depth combine to determine the amount of weight you need. If the water is fast but shallow, you might need just modest weight. If the water is slow but deep, the same weighting probably will work. As you move to water that is faster, deeper, or both, add weight, and in slower or shallower water, remove weight.

**Position and presentation.** Wade into position at the downstream end of the piece of water you want to fish, and off to the side. In the type of water where this method works best, you'll usually be able to fish with casts of one to at most three rod lengths. Make your initial casts 5 to 10 feet upstream from the water where you believe the trout might lie, giving your nymph plenty of time to reach bottom and begin fishing in the most productive water. If the lie is wide from side to side, fish the nearest side with your initial casts, and work subsequent casts first toward the middle and then to the far side of the holding water. Make at least three or four casts to each prospective line of drift.

If the line of holding water is longer than you can comfortably fish from your first position, then take a second position a rod length or two upstream. Be sure that the water covered from the second position overlaps what you covered from the first.

**Control of the drift.** Line control is the most important part of the method. As soon as your cast has landed, roll a mend upstream to place your line tip in line with or even upstream from the nymph. Then lift the rod as high as you can, and follow the drift of the nymph. The more line you can hold off the water, the better your chance to hook trout. Be careful not to keep the line and leader tight to the nymph, or you will hinder its sinking. As you let the nymph tumble freely, keep the rod tip as near as you can to straight above it, and turn to follow it after it has passed your position. Then drop your rod toward the end of the drift to extend the time the nymph remains in productive water. When it has reached the extent to which you can follow it and still keep it on the bottom, let the current lift it, and then lob it into the next cast either into the same drift line or a foot or so out from the first.

**On the water.** Wading from lie to lie, from current seam to boulder to trench, is the most difficult part of fishing the high-sticking method. If the water is so forceful that you have trouble wading upstream, then let the current ease you downstream through it. Keep in mind that your position should still allow you to turn and make your casts upstream and across the currents. A word of caution: Don't use a metal-tipped wading staff, and don't knock rocks together, or you'll be fishing empty water.

**The trout's point of view.** A trout should see the nymph, or pair of them, either tumbling toward it in the soft water where the current is slowed by friction with bottom rocks, or drifting along just above that soft water, much as a natural cast loose from its moorings might be washed along. The weight should be below the nymph and bump the bottom from time to time, but it should never anchor the nymph in one place.

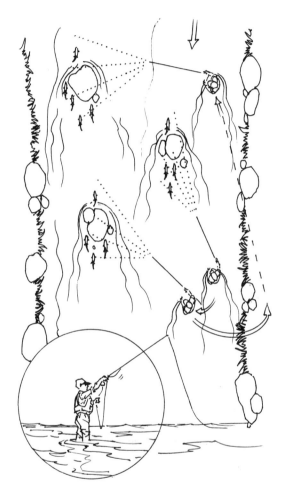

## RIG:          NYMPH AND INDICATOR WITHOUT WEIGHT

**Purpose.** This rig essentially adds an indicator to the unencumbered nymph rig. The indicator, which is usually small—either hard or a bit of bright yarn—can serve several purposes. In cases where you're casting small nymphs to trout rising and feeding during an emergence of insects and the takes are difficult to notice, an indicator can make the difference between total frustration and the satisfaction of fooling very selective trout. The rig is also excellent when you're fishing nymphs upstream in shallow water, whether the trout are lying along banks in somewhat slow water, holding along the bottom in weedy spring creek or tailwater currents, or holding along the bouldered bottom of shallow riffles, runs, and even pools of creeks and small streams.

**History/origins.** The specific origins for this method are sketchy, but it likely cropped up in many different places at the same time, perhaps when somebody having trouble following the progress of a drifting nymph tied a big, bright dry fly into his leader. I began using the method on small streams in the late 1970s, when I was fishing trout that were reluctant to take dry flies but were happy to take nymphs. When nymphs fished with the standard indicator-and-shot method got too deep in such shallow waters, I began rigging with a weighted nymph and small fan of yellow yarn 2 to 4 feet up the leader. It worked wonders, and I still use the same rig on small waters almost every time I fish them.

**Knots and notes.** The leader should be standard for the size water you're on. It will vary from the length of a short rod on a creek to a few feet longer than a long rod on a spring creek flat. Use the blood knot or surgeon's knot for tapering and tippet sections, and tie the fly to the tippet with the Duncan loop or surgeon's loop to ensure freedom of movement in the drift.

After tying on the fly, you can add stick-on foam indicators to the leader. Hard indicators are usually slipped over the leader before you tie on your nymph. My favorite indicator is a quarter- to half-inch length of yarn, folded in half and slip-knotted into the leader an appropriate distance from the fly, depending on the depth I want to fish.

**Adjustments for conditions.** The distance between the nymph and indicator will depend on the depth and speed of the current you're fishing. If you're fishing with a weighted nymph on creeks and small streams a foot or two deep, then the indicator should be no more than 2 or 3 feet from the fly. If you're fishing small flies over feeding trout on smooth water, then the indicator should be 4 to 6 feet from the fly. Unless trout are visible and feeding high in the water column, adjust the indicator to get the nymph as near to the bottom as you can.

**Rules for the rig.** Three rules should be followed. First, the indicator should be high enough up the leader to get the nymph to the proper depth. Second, the indicator should be of sufficient size to float, given the size and weight of the nymph over which it is fished. Third, the indicator should be small, unobtrusive,

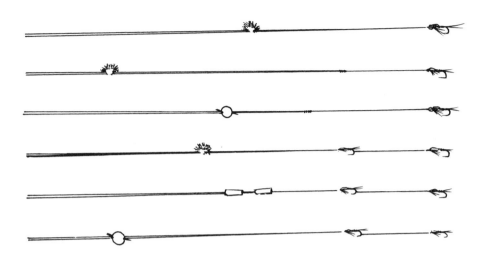

and far enough away from the nymph so as not to spook trout away from the nymph. Surprisingly, you can often place the indicator close to the nymph without bothering trout. When fishing unsophisticated trout on underfished creeks, sometimes just a foot of tippet is enough. Most often, however, the indicator should be at least 2 feet up the leader, and in some situations, usually when fish are feeding selectively, the indicator should be near the line tip.

**Appropriate flies.** Though you can fish large and heavily weighted nymphs beneath either monstrous fans of indicator yarn or hard indicators that are portly and bobberlike, usually you'll use the nymph and indicator rig without weight on the leader to fish flies of moderate to very small size, weighted moderately to lightly. My favorite flies for this rig are almost all standard searching patterns and beadheads, such as the A. P. Black, Beadhead Hare's Ear, Fox Squirrel, and Prince, usually in size 12 to 16.

**Situations to solve.** Whenever trout feed during a hatch, especially on mayflies, midges, or caddis, observe carefully to determine the level at which trout are taking the naturals. Look for the trout's noses breaking the surface film or bubbles left in the rise-rings, indicating surface takes. The absence of such signs means the trout are feeding just below the surface but so close that it looks like a surface rise. When this happens, you can fish dry flies until the trout come home, but you will never catch any. Instead, try fishing an imitation of the emerging stage—a mayfly emerger, midge pupa, or caddis pupa—inches deep. The unencumbered nymph rig will work, but adding a visible strike indicator to the leader will always make it easier to fish and will often increase your take.

**Tuning the rig.** Use the same leader you would to fish a dry fly on the same water. After failing to bring trout to drys, and observing that the fish are actually taking emergers subsurface, you'll want to switch to the nymph and indicator. Just nip off the inappropriate dry fly, tie on the appropriate nymph, slip a small indicator 4 to 6 feet up the leader, and return to fishing. Keep the indicator as small as possible; I like to use a slight fan of yarn rather than a hard indicator. Make sure the nymph has enough weight to penetrate the surface film without sinking deep and tugging the indicator under. A few turns of lead wire wrapped around the hook shank or a beadhead nymph should be sufficient.

**Position and presentation.** When fishing a nymph and indicator to rising trout without weight on the leader, take up the same position and use the same presentation you would when fishing a dry fly or surface film emerger to the same trout on the same water. Most often you'll be on a flat or somewhat smooth run where the best position will normally be either downstream from the trout and slightly off to one side, or across stream from the trout. The best presentation will depend on the position you've taken. If you're downstream, use the standard upstream dry-fly presentation; if across stream, use the reach cast just as you would with a dry fly. At rare times, you'll want to fish a nymph downstream to feeding trout with a wiggle cast.

**Control of the drift.** Fish the indicator like you would a dry fly. You want the nymph to suspend itself just inches below the surface and to trail the indicator into the view of the feeding trout. If you're fishing from downstream, gather slack as the indicator approaches you. Avoid drag, just as you would when fishing a dry fly, though drag with a shallow nymph is not as often fatal as it is with a dry fly. If you're fishing with a reach cast from across stream, then follow the drift of the indicator with the rod tip, again giving it a free drift, without drag, just as you would a dry. Let the line feed out, with a downstream wiggle cast, to show the trout the nymph on a free drift.

**On the water.** The indicator will help you detect takes. If you see it hesitate, move, or dip out of sight, then set the hook. The indicator also marks the location of your invisible nymph. If you see a wink, a rise, or anything that hints to you that a trout has moved near it, lift the rod to gently set the hook. If a trout has taken the fly, you'll bring the hook home. If not, your gentle hook set will not rip the indicator and fly out of there.

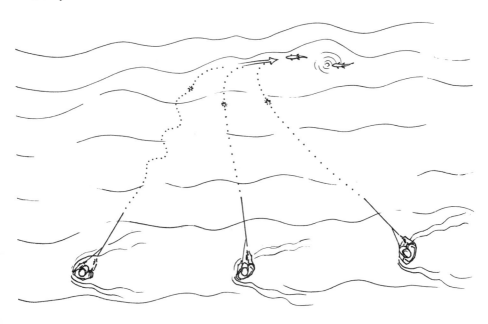

**The trout's point of view.** Like the naturals on which the trout are feeding, the fly arrives just inches deep. If you've done your homework, the fly should be approximately the same size, shape, and color as the natural nymph, emerger, or pupa the trout are taking.

**RIG:          NYMPH AND INDICATOR WITHOUT WEIGHT**
**Method:       Upstream along banks and to current seams**

**Situations to solve.** When trout hold along the banks, they're usually tucked into an indentation or sheltered from the current behind a boulder or in a depression in the bottom. There they can feed on whatever falls into the water from land or is delivered toward shore from the opposite direction. Feeding opportunistically, they almost always are willing to take a generic searching nymph, such as a Beadhead Hare's Ear or Fox Squirrel Nymph, fished just above the bottom.

Trout holding along shallow current seams, those from 1 to 3 feet deep, will again be along the bottom, usually on the soft side of the seam, but will dash into the faster water to accept whatever it delivers. Again, they'll be susceptible to generic nymphs fished 1 or 2 feet deep.

**Tuning the rig.** The leader should be the length of the rod and adjusted to the size water you're on: short on small streams, medium on most streams, and longer on larger trout streams and small rivers. The nymph should be smaller than you think—size 14 to 16—and fairly heavily weighted. Nymphs with tungsten beadheads are excellent for those situations where you want a nymph to sink quickly but not much more than a foot or two. The indicator, whether yarn or hard, must be big enough to float the size nymph you're using. Depending on the depth and speed of the water you're fishing, the indicator should be just 2 to 4 feet up the leader.

**Position and presentation.** When fishing a bank, take a position either on the bank itself or wading just outboard from it. The most effective presentation will be upstream. Cast as tight to the bank as you can: The closer you are to the bank, the easier it is to lay your indicator and nymph in the same line of drift parallel to the bank. If you're wading at a substantial angle out from the bank and the nymph lands close to the bank, the indicator will be farther out and will draw the sinking nymph toward it, away from the water you'd like to fish. Try flicking a quick mend after your cast, to lift the indicator and flip it inches toward the bank in line with the nymph.

When fishing seams, you want your position to be downstream on the soft, or slower, side of the seam. Your cast should lay the line and indicator and nymph all in the same current, rather than crossing the seam. If that's not possible, then you might have to mend downstream if you're crossing from fast to slow, or upstream if crossing from slow to fast. Be sure that your nymph drifts down the slow side, the fast side, and the center of the seam. Your position and presentation should give the nymph time to sink to fishing depth before it reaches the line of drift you want to fish.

**Control of the drift.** With your casts almost always upstream, you will have to do little more than gather slack as the indicator drifts downstream toward you. In rare cases you'll have to mend and tend the drift to place the indicator where you want it. On some casts, you might have to extend the drift downstream from your position. If your nymph is not reaching the depth you'd like despite sufficient spacing between nymph and indicator, a roll mend, made the instant the nymph and indicator touch down, will place the indicator upstream from the nymph and let it sink deeper.

**On the water.** Expect dashing takes along banks and in current seams, and always be prepared to set the hook quickly. If you have slack to gather, the trout likely will be gone before you get control of things. In calculating your position and presentation, be aware of how you'll show the nymph to the fish, either along the bank or down the length of a current seam, and then prepare yourself to hook any trout intrigued by your nymph.

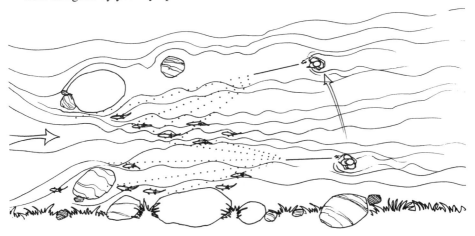

**The trout's point of view.** Whether a trout is holding near a bank or beneath a seam, it will be close to the bottom, shifting its focus from the bottom to the top. If your nymph drifts by almost anywhere in that zone, the trout is likely to respond. But more likely, a trout will take a nymph that comes closest to its depth.

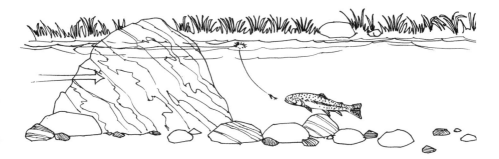

**Situations to solve.** Whenever trout seem immune to dry flies on small waters, I first try removing the dry, replacing it with a medium-size generic nymph, and slip-knotting a small fan of bright yellow yarn just above the tippet knot. After the dry fly, this simple way to show a nymph is my favorite method of fishing for trout on small streams. I use the dry and dropper setup, an extremely effective two-fly combination that is popular with many anglers, only to figure out what type of fly small-stream trout might want. Once I've figured it out, I'll switch to either the dry or the nymph after snipping the other fly out of the equation. I don't want a second hook dangling when I land a trout and release it—that hook becomes a danger both to me and the trout.

**Tuning the rig.** Rarely will you fish a nymph more than a foot or two deep on small water. The leader should be at most a foot or two longer than the length of your rod, the tippet about 2 to 3 feet of that. Tie a size 14 or 16 A. P. Black, Bead-head Hare's Ear, Beadhead Fox Squirrel, or your favorite searching nymph to the tippet, and add a small yarn indicator 2 to 3 feet up the leader. The fly should be modestly weighted, never heavy. Don't let it sink too far. Trout in small streams are accustomed to looking up and rarely will let a nymph drift over their heads without rushing up to inhale it.

**Position and presentation.** Since creeks and small streams are too narrow to cast across and too difficult to fish downstream without frightening the fish, you'll almost always fish them while moving upstream. Take a position downstream from the water you want to fish. If the water is a creek or small-stream pool, approach it cautiously, keeping a low profile and sometimes even making your prayerful initial casts from your knees.

Fish the tailout of the pool or run first, and then work your way up the pool or holding water, drifting your nymph down the center or deepest main current and through any peripheral lies that look deep enough to hold trout. Edge lies, especially those with overhead cover such as drooping branches of brush or trees, hold more trout as the season progresses, especially through summer and into fall, when terrestrial insects drop in from the heights more often than aquatic insects emerge from the depths.

**Control of the drift.** All you have to do with this method is to gather slack and keep yourself in position to deliver a brisk hook set whenever your indicator makes the slightest movement. Often after noticing no more than a slight shift or tilt in the way the floating yarn sits on the water, I will set the hook and discover a nice fish on the end. You have to be intent. With little movement of the indicator, trout will move out of a sheltered lie, flare their gills to ingest a nymph, and turn back, probably in an attempt to dislodge the nymph.

**On the water.** As you work your way up a small stream with the nymph and indicator rig without weight on the leader, be sure to cover all possible holding water. The more heavily a stream is fished, the more attention you should pay to those least likely lies. If you learn to work the pocket water, edge lies, and difficult lies where most folks are reluctant to risk flies, you'll discover where the trout go when they get driven out of their normal lies.

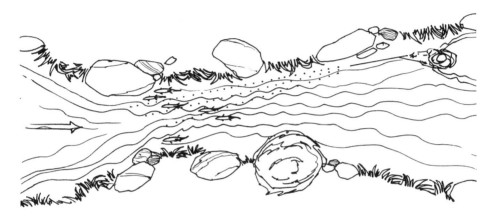

**The trout's point of view.** Small-stream trout will intercept almost any nymph that is not obtrusively large or outlandishly colored and does not arrive with a warning splash. Use small flies in natural drab colors, and rig with a small yarn indicator that lands lightly on the water and suspends the fly 1 or at most 2 feet deep.

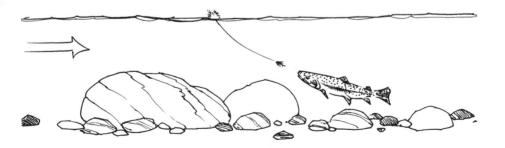

**Situations to solve.** Many mountain and foothill creeks, small streams, and even medium-size trout streams descend through a series of stairstep benches. Within this steep geography, the current plunges over a step of boulders from 6 inches to a foot or two high and then rushes over a 10- to 30-foot bench before reaching the next drop and repeating the process, sometimes for miles. A flat will have from one to five current tongues racing across it, each formed where the current finds a gap to probe through the step.

Depending on the size of the stream, the holding water on these brisk benches will be from 1 to 4 feet deep, rarely more than that. Such water is excellent for fishing with upstream dry flies, if trout accept them, and if the water is not too cold to prevent the trout from coming up for drys. Knowing how to fish stairstepped benches with nymphs can greatly increase your catch.

**Tuning the rig.** Unless overhanging branches will hinder your cast, arm yourself with a long rod, $8^{1}/_{2}$ to 9 feet, to help loft the line off the stairstepped water. The leader should be the length of the rod or a bit longer, and the nymph should be modestly weighted, not so light that it fails to sink quickly, but not so heavy that it plunges to the bottom and gets hung up. The indicator can be yarn or hard, whichever style you prefer, since the water is generally so fast that trout will not notice the arrival of a large indicator. Place the indicator 2 to 5 feet up the leader, depending on the depth and speed of the water, and be prepared to adjust it constantly as you move from step to step.

**Position and presentation.** Since you'll be fishing upstream, take your position downstream. If the stream is average size with the benches 20 to 30 feet long, you'll want to stand on the bench immediately downstream from the one you're about to fish. If the water is tiny and the benches short, you may have to take a position two benches down. If the stream is large, take your initial position one bench down, and fish the lower end of the bench above, but then move up onto the bench itself to fish its upper end.

Fish each current tongue that races across the bench separately. Place your nymph and indicator on one side of the current, then down its center, and finally down the far side. Lay the line, leader, indicator, and fly in the same line of current, if possible, to keep them all moving downstream at the same speed. In very brisk water, make at least two to three casts to each line of drift since trout might not notice the fly on the first cast. If any rocks, boulders, or trenches offer obvious lies, cover them with extra casts.

If you can place your cast right at the head of each current tongue, where the drop plunges over and dives into the bench below, your fly will sink more quickly and be at the depth you want for the entire length of its drift.

**Control of the drift.** Because you'll be on the bench downstream with the current racing over a drop between you and the water you're fishing, keep your rod tip high, and gather slack fast enough to hold your line above that swift drop. If your line catches, it will rush your fly out of the water you want to fish. To eliminate this problem and if the bench is long enough, move up onto it to fish its upper length.

**On the water.** Trout accept and reject flies quickly in fast water. Set the hook the *instant* you see the indicator hesitate, dip under, or shoot to one side. Once you hook a trout, do your best to draw it downstream through a gap in the drop and then play and land it on the bench from which you're fishing. Not only will the trout be easier to handle, but you'll reduce the chance the trout will thrash around and frighten all the other trout on the upper bench before you finish fishing it.

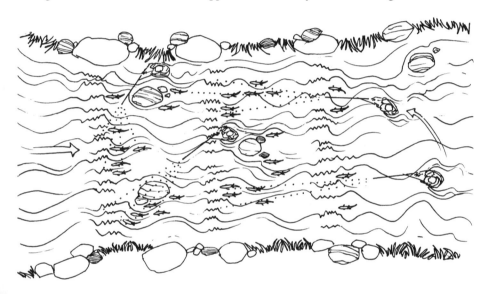

**The trout's point of view.** The turbulence of the water as it dashes down a series of drops and benches may mean the trout will need extra chances at your fly. Focus your fishing on the current lines that form and cross the bench, but make several casts that show the fly down each line of drift before moving on to the next.

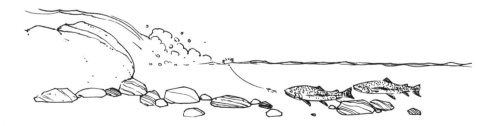

**Situations to solve.** On spring creeks or any other stream or river where the water is clear enough to spot trout, you'll often find them holding along the bottom, almost always in a position where they're able to feed on the drift. At times they'll seem cryptic, not moving, but usually their inactivity will be caused by a lack of opportunity—not much is drifting by. If something arrives, they'll usually accept it, though they might not move far for it. At other times when they're actively feeding, you'll see them shifting from side to side, moving to take something, then returning to their lies. Since they'll move farther to take your nymph, these more active fish will be easier to catch, but you still have to get the nymph down to their level and drifting as freely as a natural might.

**Tuning the rig.** Your rig will vary depending on the clarity of the water, the spookiness of the trout, the depth you need to attain, and the speed of the current. Typically, you'll be working over a wary trout holding on the bottom in 2 to 4 feet of water, usually with rooted vegetation adding to your troubles. In this scenario, your leader must be long, 12 to 15 feet, with 3 to 4 feet of that fine tippet, 4, 5, or even 6X. Your fly should be small, size 16 to 20, and more than modestly weighted. Tungsten beadhead nymphs are excellent for sight fishing because they sink quickly. The indicator should be as small as it takes to suspend the nymph and be made of yarn or putty rather than hard. Place it about 1 foot or at most 2 feet more than the depth of the water above the nymph.

**Position and presentation.** Because the water will be clear and the trout will be wary, you must take a position downstream from the spotted fish, but avoid a position directly downstream where a cast will line the fish and end your chances. Work off to one side, and get as close as you can. Crouch to keep your profile low, and make no fast movements. Never send wading waves over the trout.

Your first cast, although not your only chance at the trout, will be the one with the best chance for success. Before launching the cast, calculate the sink rate of your fly against the depth of the water and the speed of the current, and translate that into an estimate of how far upstream from the trout you must place the cast. Make all fore- and backcasts off to the side, and set your delivery stroke onto the water as delicately as you can. Follow the fly through its drift, if you can see it, and adjust your delivery upstream or down depending on whether the fly drifted too high or too low.

**Control of the drift.** If you're dealing with conflicting currents, you might be forced to make upstream or downstream mends to encourage the free sink of the nymph toward the trout. It's best, however, if your position eliminates this need. As the nymph descends and drifts toward the trout, try to split your attention between the fly and the fish. As they come together, watch for any movement of the trout— a slight move forward or turn to one side, or the white flash of its mouth opening and closing. If you see any hint of a take, lift the rod quickly but gently to draw the hook home. The trout can take the nymph in and spit it out in an instant. If you think that has happened, change flies before casting again. If you cannot see the nymph, use the indicator to mark any takes.

**On the water.** This method depends on your ability to spot trout before they spot you. You might have to shoulder your rod and spend more time looking than fishing. If you ever take a trip to New Zealand, where the water tends to be clear as air and the trout are scattered but lunkers, you'll find out that the guides prefer to spot trout rather than casting blind. You'll employ this method more than any other, but the flies will be large and heavily weighted. Be sure to practice accuracy with a heavy nymph and long, fine leader before rather than during your trip.

**The trout's point of view.** The first cast to a visible fish is always the most likely to hook it. But if your first drift is high in the water column or a bit too far off to one side or the other, or the nymph gets by while the trout is focused the other way on a natural, keep trying. Continue fishing, even changing flies if you want, until you have reason to suspect the trout is not going to respond. Then rest the trout for an hour or so before coming back and trying again.

## RIG:                STANDARD NYMPH, INDICATOR, AND SPLIT SHOT

**Purpose.** Before the indicator and shot rig arrived, the biggest problem with fishing nymphs in moving water was getting the fly to the bottom and then receiving news about takes on the surface. Fishing nymphs on the swing, where takes are felt as raps, is easy and effective. But nymphs on the swing rarely get more than a foot or two deep, so this technique only works on the shallowest bottoms. Though possible, it's not easy to get heavily weighted nymphs at the end of a floating line to the bottom in 3- to 6-foot depths, and it's even more difficult to know when trout take them.

With the advent of the indicator-and-shot rig, it suddenly became easy to get a nymph, or brace of them, to the bottom of a stream, where trout spend most of their time and do most of their feeding. The nymphs could be fished tumbling along freely, just as natural insects might move in the same water, and with some practice, fishermen began to be able to tell when a trout intercepted the nymph in its drift.

**History/origins.** The rig, and a wide variety of methods used to apply it against trout, arose in the late 1960s and early '70s, pioneered by such great anglers as Dave Whitlock and Gary Borger. First codified in Borger's 1979 book *Nymphing* (Stackpole Books), the rig has been expanded upon in many magazine articles and books since then, including my own *Nymph Fishing* (Frank Amato Publications, 1995).

**Knots and notes.** The standard rig starts with a floating line, either weight-forward or double-taper, from 4- to 7-weight. The leader should be 8 to 12 feet long, with a strike indicator toward the butt, split shot or putty weight jammed against the tippet knot, and a nymph on a 10- to 14-inch tippet. The tippet knot, also used to join any leader sections together, can be the blood knot or surgeon's knot. The nymph should be tied to the tippet with a Duncan loop or surgeon's loop to provide freedom in the drift. If you use more than one fly, attach the second tippet directly to the hook bend of the first fly using the improved clinch knot.

I prefer yarn indicators with light rigs and hard indicators with heavier rigs; a yarn indicator big enough to support much weight becomes too much of an air-resistant fan to cast easily. I usually use putty weight, molded around the tippet knot, so that I can vary the amount and to decrease snags—split shot is standard but easily gets hung up in rock crevices. Be prepared by carrying yarn, hard, and putty indicators, a dispenser of removable, nonlead split shot that contains a variety of sizes, and putty weight.

If you're boating, you should keep one rod set up for nymphing and another for dry flies. Make sure the nymphing rod is slower to enable you to cast the open loops that keep indicator, shot, and weighted nymphs separated in the air. If you're having trouble with tangles, try overlining your rod with a line one weight heavier to slow it down.

**Adjustments for conditions.** As you move between water of varying depths and speeds, you will have to adjust the position of your strike indicator and the amount of weight on your leader. As you move from deeper to shallower water or faster to slower currents, either move the indicator closer to the nymph or remove

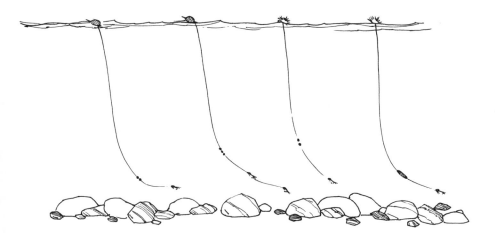

weight from the leader. If you move from shallower to deeper or slower to faster water, either move the indicator farther from the nymph or add weight to the leader. If you don't bump bottom occasionally, you're fishing too high in the water column. You'll be amazed how often adding a single small shot to the weight already on your tippet will turn what appears to be empty water into water full of trout.

**Rules for the rig.** Begin fishing with your strike indicator at twice the depth of the water up the leader from the fly. If the water is slow or shallow, you'll quickly notice that you're not getting a free drift of the fly and therefore need to shorten the distance between indicator and fly. If the water is fast or deep, you'll never bump bottom and consequently will need to adjust the indicator farther from the fly. If you choose to weight with split shot, use a size shot that lets you begin fishing with two or three small shot rather than a single big one. You can add or remove small shot one at a time to quickly adjust to the depth you're fishing.

**Appropriate flies.** There are few restrictions on the types of nymphs you can use with the standard indicator and shot rig. Since you're using weight on the leader to get them to the bottom, avoid heavily weighted nymphs that reduce your ability to adjust for depth and current speed. In big, fast water, however, you might need a heavy nymph and added shot to make contact with the bottom.

**Situations to solve.** In water in which you're uncertain where trout lie, your only option is to show your nymph to all the places where trout might hold. They'll be on the bottom, so you must search it all. Whether you're fishing a broad flat, run, or riffle on a creek, stream, or river, all will hold trout in scattered lies that you cannot read. Rather than holding in pods, the trout will typically be in singles, sprinkled here and there. Gary Borger's shotgun method, detailed in his book *Nymphing,* will help you find them. The key to the method is to imagine a grid, with 1-foot squares, laid over the bottom. Take a series of positions, and from each position make a disciplined set of casts so that your fly drifts through every square foot of that grid.

**Tuning the rig.** The rig must suit the water you're on. If the water is big and boisterous, rig with a large hard indicator, ample weight on the leader, and perhaps a midsize weighted nymph and a smaller beadhead nymph in tandem. If the water is smaller and shallower, rig with a yarn indicator, small split shot or dab of putty weight, and a couple of lightly weighted nymphs. Whenever you use two nymphs, be sure that they offer trout a distinct choice: large and small, drab and bright, beadhead and standard, stonefly and mayfly, scud and midge pupa. If trout consistently take one or the other, nip off the one that is not working to reduce the chance of harming yourself or the trout.

**Position and presentation.** Take up your first position near the lower end of the water you want to cover, and to one side. Imagine a grid over the bottom upstream and just outboard from you. If you can manage a position in the center of the stream, imagine grids to both your right and your left. In either case, cover all of the water you can fish comfortably from the first position before moving upstream or out into the stream into the second position.

Your first cast should be made at a comfortable distance, 25 to 40 feet, and almost straight upstream. Fish out that cast past you to almost the same distance downstream. Then make your next cast a foot outside of the first, and fish a drift that is parallel to the first. Continue laying parallel casts a foot or so apart until you've covered all the water you can reach with comfortable casts from the first position. Make it a rule never to stretch your casts when nymphing with the standard indicator and shot rig, and you'll greatly reduce the number of tangles.

Move into your second position, a cast either upstream or out into the current, and cover the second grid section the same as you did the first. You might have to adjust your indicator and weight if you move out into deeper water.

**Control of the drift.** As the indicator floats toward you, gather in slack and raise your rod, always keeping yourself in position to set the hook if the indicator twitches. Do not pick up the cast when the indicator reaches your position. Instead, let it drift past you, lower your rod, and follow the drift. Then feed the gathered line, letting the indicator float downstream. When it has reached the end of its tether, let the current lift the nymph or nymphs from the bottom, and then let the water load the rod for the next forecast. Often you will be able to place the cast properly for the next drift without any further fore- and backcasts. On casts that are at an angle across the current, you will have to throw one or two upstream mends during the drift to keep the line as straight as possible between the rod tip and indicator.

**On the water.** To make sure you cover all of the bottom, and no trout are missed, your imaginary grids over the bottom should overlap. The lower end of each drift from your second position should cover the upper end of the drift made from the first position. In most trout stream and river situations, you'll have to move your indicator farther up the leader and add a shot or two as you move out from the bank and cover grid lines that are deeper and swifter. If you're fishing your way up a run or riffle from the deep lower end toward the shallower upper end, then do the opposite: Move the indicator down and remove a shot or two.

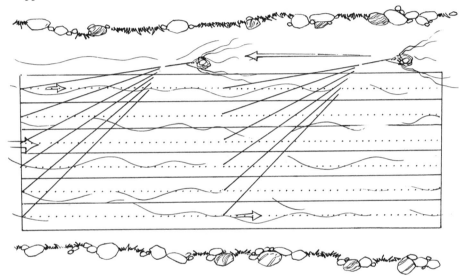

**The trout's point of view.** Bottom-hugging trout might lift up into the current 6 inches to a foot or so to take a fly, but they often are reluctant to move much more than that. If your fly is not ticking bottom now and then—you'll feel hesitations of the indicator to which you should set the hook—then you're fishing too shallow.

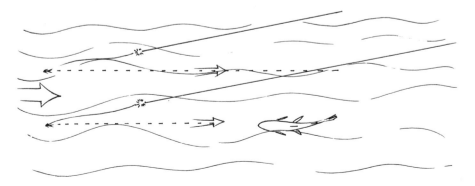

**RIG:          STANDARD NYMPH, INDICATOR, AND SPLIT SHOT**
**Method:      Covering boulder lies**

**Situations to solve.** Boulders form obvious lies for trout in moving water, but knowing where the trout will lie in relation to a particular boulder can be difficult: Are they upstream, tucked under one side or the other, in the slipstream immediately below the boulder, or in the long run of eddied water that trails out behind the boulder and eventually merges into a current seam several feet downstream? To be safe, you must cover all of these prospective lies.

Some boulders will be mavericks, isolated in a bit of surrounding water with little potential to hold trout. You'll want to fish these as if the water around them did not exist. Most times, you'll be fishing with the previous shotgun method, covering all of the water, when you discover a boulder in the water. Continue fishing the water as you were, but be sure to cover all of the potential boulder lies effectively with at least a few extra casts.

**Tuning the rig.** If you're already fishing the water surrounding a boulder, you probably won't have to change your rig. If you're moving into a bit of water specifically to fish a boulder and its lies, then rig according to the shape of the water around the boulder. If the water is deep and fast, go with a hard indicator, lots of weight on the leader, heavily weighted flies, and a distance of two to two-and-a-half times the water depth between the nymph and indicator. If the water is shallower and slower, rig with a smaller indicator, less weight on the leader and flies, and a distance between nymph and indicator of one-and-a-half to two times the water depth.

**Position and presentation.** Begin fishing a boulder lie from a position downstream from the point where the currents moving around the boulder merge to form a seam. Make your first series of casts to cover the outside, then the center, and finally the far side of this seam. If necessary, move to a second position a bit upstream and off to one side. From here, you'll be able to effectively cover the long run of eddied water downstream from the boulder. Continue to fish the outside of the currents that slip around each side of the boulder, but focus on getting good drifts down the softer water below the boulder. Trout like to hold there and dash out into the faster currents to intercept food rushing by.

If you're fishing a big boulder with a long slipstream behind it, try a third position by tucking several casts tight against the downstream side of the boulder and to each side of it. The casts on the downstream side should almost hit the back of the boulder. The casts to the side should be placed far enough upstream so that the nymph, or brace of them, is on the bottom when it reaches the boulder.

Finally, move up and cast a few feet in front of the boulder, so that the nymph reaches bottom right at its leading edge. Trout often tuck in there.

**Control of the drift.** As the indicator drifts toward you, gather slack and lift your rod. To fish the drifts downstream, lower the rod and feed line into the drift. On casts that cross the current seam below the boulder, when you want the indicator to drift down the slower center line, you'll have to almost constantly make upstream mends to keep the line from bellying and dragging the nymphs toward the surface.

**On the water.** If you're on small water, you might be able to cover all of the lies around a boulder from one position, just downstream from it and slightly off to one side. Cover the near and downstream lies first, working them consecutively upstream and out, so that any trout you hook don't spook those you might hook later. If the water is large, then you'll have to fish from more than one position. You'll also want to be sure your nymphs and added weight are adequate to quickly get them down to the desired depth. If they're swept several feet downstream before they reach the depth you'd like them to attain—the bottom—they'll go far over the heads of the trout.

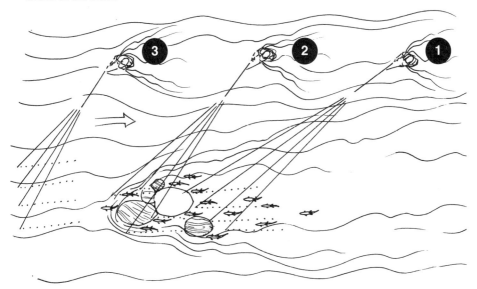

**The trout's point of view.** You know the promising lies—upstream, downstream, and to both sides of the boulder; now be sure your nymph or nymphs probe into those remote places, where trout can see them, and be sure they're deep enough when they do.

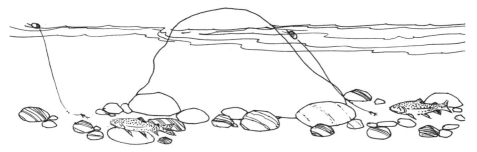

**RIG:**        STANDARD NYMPH, INDICATOR, AND SPLIT SHOT
**Method:**     Covering a ledge or trench

**Situations to solve.** A trench is a long and narrow area of streambed, where the bottom falls off to at least slightly deeper than the streambed around it. A ledge is a line of rock or gravel, a few inches to a few feet higher than the bottom below it, that lies in line with the current or cuts diagonally or at an angle across it. The deeper water of both structures provides trout protection from overhead predation and shelter from the current, which is broken in the bottom of a trench, and on the downstream side of any ledge.

Trout tend to line up, or even stack up, in the bottom of a trench. If you fish a riffle or run and find it barren and then suddenly begin catching trout after trout in one small spot, you've found a trench. Trout generally line up along the length of a ledge. If you're able to read the water right, you can often work your way up a ledge parallel to the current, or across one that lies contrary to the current, and pick off the trout one by one.

**Tuning the rig.** The standard shot-and-indicator rig is designed to fish your fly or flies right on the bottom and therefore is ideal for fishing ledges and trenches. When adjusting your rigging, estimate the depth of the water at the bottom of the ledge or trench, not the shallower water surrounding it. To be effective, your nymph must tumble over the lip and plummet right to the depths, where the trout hold. When encountering either kind of holding lie while in the process of covering a larger bit of water, move your indicator a foot or two up the leader and pinch on another split shot.

**Position and presentation.** Take up your position at the downstream end of the likely lie, and a rod length or so off to one side. Ledges are obvious from the line of break they make across the surface currents, but trenches are often difficult to notice, sometimes forming only a slightly calmer area in an otherwise broken surface. Position yourself according to what the surface reflects about the bottom below it. You must be able to place your cast a few feet upstream from the lip of the ledge or trench and fish the cast through the depths of it.

Make your first cast 2 to 5 feet upstream from the inside, or near edge, of the lip, depending on the depth of the water and speed of the current. In some brisk rivers, you'll have to cast as far as 10 to 15 feet upstream from the lip. The object is to get your fly to the bottom just as it reaches the lip of the ledge or trench. It should be weighted heavily enough, and the indicator should be positioned high enough, so that the nymph, when reaching the lip, tumbles over it and into the deeper water below. The fly should then fish out its drift on the bottom of the trench or in the depths along the length of a ledge. Use subsequent casts to cover all of the bottom of the trench or to work your way out along the length of a ledge cutting laterally across the current.

**Control of the drift.** Control the drift just as you would with any other shot and indicator cast: Watch the progress of the indicator to be sure it is getting a relatively free float. You will have to lift the rod and gather slack as the indicator drifts toward you and lower the rod and feed slack as the indicator passes you and drifts downstream. Toss occasional upstream mends to keep any belly out of the line.

**On the water.** The trick with this method is being able to recognize a ledge or trench amid other water that is a constant depth, and then rigging for the depth of the ledge or trench, not the shallower water surrounding it. This need to constantly adjust the distance between your nymph and indicator, and the amount of weight on the leader, becomes magnified when you fish water prone to ledges and trenches. But if such lies can be found in a riffle, run, or flat, you can bet that trout will be down there.

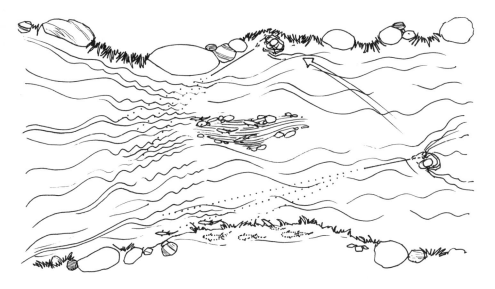

**The trout's point of view.** The fly should drop in on the trout, reaching the bottom at the lip of the ledge or trench, then plunging down to where the trout are sure to hold. If the fly is tethered short, so that it rides high over the drop, few trout will notice it, and even fewer will rise up to take it.

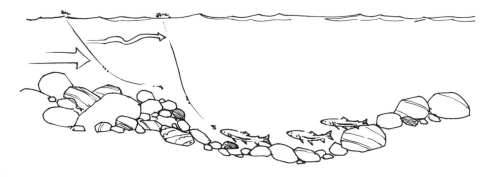

**Situations to solve.** Pocket water, whether in a mountain or foothill creek, stream, or river, is largely a jumble of various water types: boulder lies, ledges, trenches, plunge pools, stairsteps, short runs, or glides of somewhat smooth water. Most often the individual holding lies are separated by boisterous water, the kind where trout don't hang out. Your success fishing pocket water hinges on your ability to recognize places where trout might find some shelter from the current, and food delivered on it, and then having recognized such lies, your willingness to change rigging and tactics to fish each lie accordingly.

**Tuning the rig.** Tune for the depths, not the shallow water around it, and for the fast currents in which pockets of holding water are found. Use hard indicators, perhaps a bit oversized to ensure they float and will be visible in turbulence. A tandem of one large, heavily weighted fly trailed by a smaller and lighter fly will help you get the flies down to where trout can make a choice. The weight on your leader should be substantial and easily increased or decreased. Use putty weight or several small split shot that let you adjust at will. The correct weight will keep the distance between your nymph and indicator no more than one-and-a-half or two times the depth of the water. You need maximum control.

**Position and presentation.** On small to medium-size streams, you'll be able to wade upstream, fishing holding lies as you encounter them. Fish each from an ideal position, in close but slightly downstream and off to the side. Approach to within a rod length or so of most lies so that you won't scare the trout unless you knock rocks together. Make any adjustment necessary for the depth you want to fish; then "shotgun" a small grid of holding water, using several casts to cover it all carefully. The entry of the fly onto the water should be 2 to 6 feet upstream from the piece of bottom you expect to cover. Hold the rod high, and escort the indicator the length of its drift, which will usually be just a rod length or two. Let the current lift the fly, then lob the next cast, and fish it out. Make three or more casts to the same line of drift before moving the next set of casts outboard a foot or so. In rough water, trout don't always notice a fly the first time it rushes through a lie.

If you're on a large stream or river and the current is too pushy to wade upstream against, you might be able to let the current ease you downstream from position to position. Because this can be dangerous, only do it along the edges, where you can always wade out to shore. Don't descend in the center, where you might get stranded in a position in which you won't be able to wade back up the way you came. When working your way downstream through pocket water, move into the same sort of position you would when working upstream—a bit downstream and off to the side from the water you want to fish. Then fish the water as outlined above, covering all of the bottom in a potential lie with several passes of your deep nymph through each drift line.

**Control of the drift.** As always, draw in slack and loft your rod as the indicator floats toward you; then feed slack and lower the rod as it passes you and drifts downstream. With a short cast and high rod, often held almost directly over the indicator, you'll be able to flick slight mends that adjust the indicator into precise lines of drift that look good to you.

**On the water.** When you move into position on each bit of holding water—a boulder lie, ledge, trench, or plunge pool—take a moment to observe it before you fish it. Lean on your staff, assess how the currents shape themselves to shelter and feed trout, and then adjust your rig so it will fish your nymph or nymphs the same way that the current might deliver a tumbling natural. Such a reflective pause not only gives you a rest, which you'll need when fishing pocket water, but it also increases the chance that you'll fish the water right and extract trout from it.

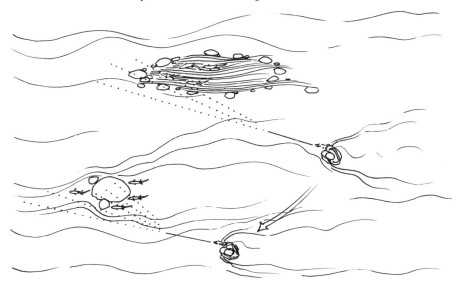

**The trout's point of view.** In pocket water, trout hold in bubbles of calm water amid turbulence and feed on dislodged nymphs rushing by on the current. Such trout make fast decisions, taking naturals or imitations with a swift strike and at once dashing back to their bubble of calm. Sometimes your indicator will suddenly dip under, but at other times it will merely hesitate in the current. Either way, set the hook abruptly; no fine tippets here.

**RIG:         STANDARD NYMPH, INDICATOR, AND SPLIT SHOT**
**Method:    Nymphing trout winking along the bottom**

**Situations to solve.** If you're observant enough, you may notice trout feeding by the winks from their flashing sides as they turn to take natural nymphs, larvae, and pupae adrift on the bottom currents. Usually they'll be winking along the bottom in water that is moving but far less than brutal—a flat or the center slot of a long run. They'll almost always be in a strung-out pod, feeding eagerly and sending almost constant flashes up to the surface, though sometimes you'll find a single fish feeding with the same winks along the bottom. The times you observe such feeding might be merely the tips of icebergs: If you see one trout, there are likely others; if you see them once, most likely they feed in the same place regularly but without the eagerness that causes the tipping and consequent flashing. But what you do know is that when you can see them flashing down there, they are not only present but actively feeding and therefore vulnerable if you can find the right nymph and fish it the right way.

**Tuning the rig.** Rig with a yarn indicator, as small as possible, to allow a delicate entry into the water. Try wading in at the lowest end of the currents, seine what the trout are taking just upstream, and then match it. If you can't collect a specimen, rig with a two-fly setup, one a size 14 or 16 beadhead and the other a tiny standard dressing such as a size 20 Pheasant Tail Flashback. Add just enough weight to the leader to attain the depths at which you see the feeding trout. Fix a small indicator two to two-and-a-half times the depth of the water above the top fly.

**Position and presentation.** Take up your first position at the lower end of the water in which you can see the visible fish. Make your first cast to the inside edge of the holding water, the same 25 to 40 feet upstream you would use with the shotgun method. In essence, you cover the water precisely as you would with that method, making sure your fly covers every square foot of an imaginary grid you place over the water. The difference is that now you know that the water under the grid contains trout.

Once you're fishing the correct depth and getting a good drift through the trout, then the search for a successful pattern begins. If you fish more than fifteen to twenty minutes without any hits, begin working changes, but be aware that the problem will be depth more often than it is fly pattern. Add split shot or putty weight, and extend the distance between your fly and indicator, until you're bouncing on the bottom frequently. Only then should you begin to experiment with different fly patterns.

Once you've figured out what the trout want, work your way up through the pod. Try to play each hooked trout downstream, so you don't frighten the trout above it.

**Control of the drift.** Mend and tend the line just as you would in any other standard nymphing situation. You'll usually be fishing somewhat even, constant, and shallow currents; otherwise you'd not be able to spot the trout. Take in line and raise your rod as the indicator floats toward you. Make mends as required to keep the line as straight between the indicator and rod tip as possible. Lower the rod and feed line into the downstream part of the drift. Takes will generally be subtle so set the hook at the slightest movement or hesitation of the indicator.

**On the water.** If you can see the trout, they can probably see you. Wade into position slowly, keeping a distance of two or three rod lengths from them, and don't send any wading waves over them. Keep your rig as light as you can, and cast with as gentle an entry into the water as your rig allows. Unless the water is smooth, the trout will not be bothered by a delicate cast, but you can bet they'll cease winking if you rig with a big hard indicator, large and heavily weighted nymphs, and lots of splashy shot.

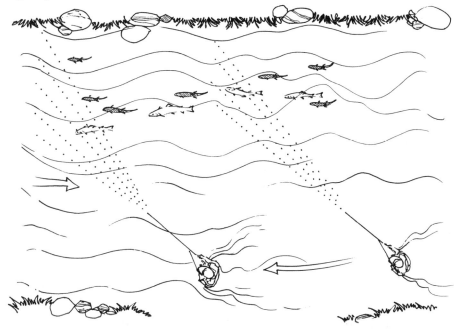

**The trout's point of view.** In almost all cases, the trout will be feeding on natural insects that are small and adrift on the currents rather than swimming. Your nymph or nymphs must arrive to them the same way—tethered to the weight that delivers them to the bottom, but on a fine enough leader that they have some freedom in their drift along the bottom zone.

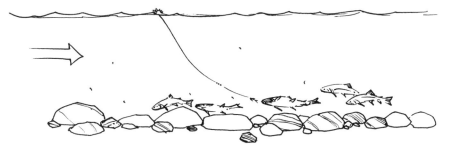

**Situations to solve.** Riffle corners shelter trout from currents, protect them from overhead predation, and feed them well. In fact, riffles are the most productive water for aquatic insects, which get knocked loose and set adrift in those brisk currents. Trout line up to intercept them in the nearest soft water downstream, usually the corner where the riffle breaks over into the run or pool below. Though riffle corners provide excellent fishing with drys, they're even more productive for nymphing. If you're new to nymphing or haven't yet figured out how to read indicator movements and interpret them into trout takes, then reexamine whatever water you're fishing, and focus on its riffle corners.

Trout will be spread out in the fairly shallow water on the inside of the corner, as long as there is at least a foot or more of water to protect them from bird predation and a substantial current to deliver food. Corners are also found on the inside and outside of the seam where the faster entering current meets the slower inside current. Often a few trout, sometimes even the biggest, will be tucked right into the apex of the corner, where they get first shot at the food drifting by.

**Tuning the rig.** Rig first for the depth and speed of the inside water toward the deeper lower end of the holding water. Be sure you have sufficient weight and enough space between nymph and indicator so that your nymph or nymphs reach the bottom: Riffle corners are excellent locations to explore with a two-nymph setup. As you move up toward the head of all but the smallest riffle corners, you'll probably have to shorten the distance between the indicator and nymph and pinch off a small shot or a bit of putty weight.

**Position and presentation.** Take your initial position at the lower end of water you think has potential to hold trout. This will vary from 10 feet downstream from the corner on a small stream to 100 feet down on a big river, but it will be limited by the deepest water you can wade and still cast. Always begin on the shallower inside edge of the riffle corner, and work your way out. Shotgun the water you can reach from your first position, covering the slower and shallower water to the inside of the seam, the seam itself, and a few casts on the outside of the seam.

Move into a second position upstream just far enough that the downstream end of each drift will overlap the same water as the upstream end of your first position's drifts. Again, shotgun the water you can reach, fishing the slow inside of the seam first, the seam next, and the outside of the seam last. Some small riffle corners can be covered from a single position; large corners may require three or four positions. Work your way up until you can cover the apex of the corner, and as you move up, be sure to adjust for the changing water depth.

**Control of the drift.** Use all the standard techniques to control the drift: Gather slack and lift your rod, mend if necessary, lower your rod and feed slack, and let the current lift the nymph. Water-load the rod and place your next cast a foot or so outside the one before it.

**On the water.** When you first approach a riffle corner, stay out of the water, or step in no more than ankle deep, and assess the situation from there before you ever make a cast. Chances are you'll catch most of your fish from the average corner while wading shin to knee deep, though in large corners you might have to work your way out to deeper water to continue catching trout. Anglers unfamiliar with riffle corners often wade in and frighten the trout they'd like to catch.

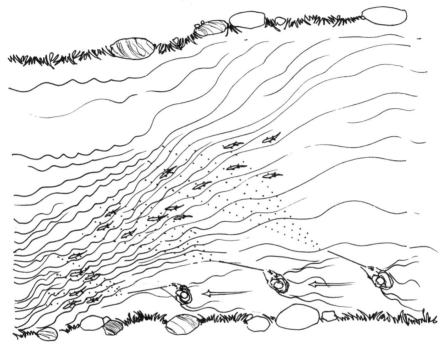

**The trout's point of view.** Trout in riffle corners are accustomed to seeing all sorts of aquatic nymphs and larvae tumbling downstream out of the fast water into the slow water below. They're not often selective. Generic beadheads and standard nymphs are usually all you need, though be sure to use a size 16 nymph as a trailer if it's not your main nymph. Even large trout will take a small nymph in a riffle corner.

## RIG:          HINGED NYMPH AND INDICATOR

**Purpose.** The hinged rig is designed to get a nymph, or pair of them, to the bottom both quickly and with less weight on the nymph and the leader than what is required with the standard indicator-and-shot rig. The thin tippet between the indicator and nymph, which is not tapered, allows the nymph to sink quickly. Once the nymph is on the bottom, it drifts freely and therefore looks alive, more like a natural nymph cast loose from its moorings than a fly anchored by its own weight or tethered to an anchor of split shot. The primary advantage of the hinged leader system is that you can better sense what your nymph is doing throughout its drift. The method works best on waters with constant currents and level depths. It has less success in currents of varying depths and speeds.

**History/origins.** The hinged indicator rig was devised by Dean Hickson and David Schubert of Oakland, California, for fishing Hat Creek and Fall River, two spring creeks with lots of the level flows needed for this rig to work best. It was recorded in detail in John Judy's 1994 book *Slack Line Strategies for Fly Fishing*.

**Knots and notes.** Variations on the hinged rig include one- and two-nymph setups and weight on the nymph alone or with split shot pinched or putty weight molded to the leader. The base leader is just 4 feet long and stout, tapered down to about 2X. Judy recommends cutting a worn-out leader back to that diameter and then cutting off the butt so the leader is left at 4 feet. Fix this to a floating line, preferably a double-taper or long-belly for the mending you must do. Five-, 6-, and even 7-weight lines handle the large fans of yarn better than lighter 3- and 4-weight lines. Tie an outsized fan of yarn to the 2X end with an improved clinch knot— Judy uses polypropylene macrame yarn in yellow for daytime and pink for the low light of evening. The long tippet is usually 4X or 5X, 6 inches to 1 foot longer than the depth of the water. Tie one end of the tippet around the base leader with an improved clinch knot and slide the 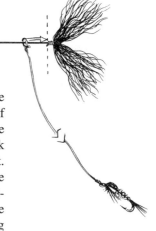 knot against the indicator knot. Tie the nymph to the other end with a Duncan or surgeon's loop knot. If you want a dropper, use an 8- to 10-inch tippet one size finer than the main tippet, and tie it to the hook bend of the first nymph with an improved clinch knot.

**Adjustments for conditions.** Adjustments can be made in the size of the indicator, the length and diameter of the tippet, and the amount of weight on the nymph or on the leader above it. For delicate spring creek and tailwater situations, cut the indicator down to the size of a pea, use fine tippet just a bit longer

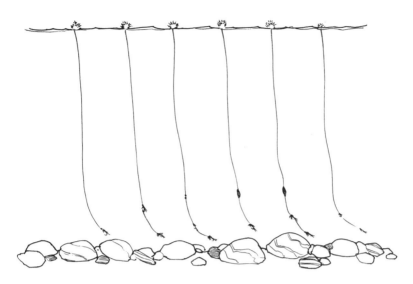

than the depth of the water, and tie on small and lightly weighted flies. For more boisterous waters, use a fan of yarn the size of a quarter or larger and a stouter tippet a foot longer than the water depth. If needed, add small split shot or putty weight to get the flies down.

**Rules for the rig.** The critical rule is to toss a roll mend, to lift the indicator off the water and place it upstream from the nymph, the instant the cast hits the water. If this is not done, the indicator will float ahead of the nymph, keeping it on a short leash and preventing it from sinking. With the mend, the indicator is placed upstream from the nymph, and the nymph plunges quickly to the bottom, only lightly hindered by the thin tippet. The roll mend is made exactly as you would make a roll cast, except that the power is attenuated a bit so the indicator is lifted from the water and flipped upstream, but the nymph is not pulled from the water. It takes practice but is not as difficult as it sounds.

**Appropriate flies.** The most common rig for big freestone rivers is a weighted salmon fly nymph trailed by a smaller mayfly nymph or caddis larva imitation. For smaller spring creek situations, the most useful rig is a single slightly weighted scud dressing, sometimes trailed by a smaller Serendipity or Pheasant Tail Flashback. If any food form is dominant in the water you're fishing, try to match it, or at least approximate it.

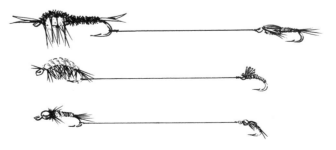

**RIG:        HINGED NYMPH AND INDICATOR**
**Method:    Nymphing the bottom zone**

**Situations to solve.** The hinged indicator nymphing rig is best used on flat water, whether it's smooth or somewhat riffled, with even depths and current speeds and on the inside areas of broad riffle corners, where flat shallows are fairly extensive. In essence, the rig and method work best where you can fish a fairly long reach of water, a cast or more in length, with an even sheet of currents on the surface and an even depth along the bottom. Trout seek out this water for the relatively peaceful holding lies along the bottom. The method is not effective in boisterous riffles, broken runs, or pocket water.

**Tuning the rig.** In calm and shallow water, such as weedy runs often found in spring creeks and tailwaters, use a tiny indicator, one or two lightly weighted flies, and a fine tippet just a bit longer than the water depth. Beadhead dressings and standard nymphs, with just two to six wraps of lead around the hook shank, work well. As the water gets deeper and the current stronger, increase the size of the indicator, add to the length of the tippet, and use heavier flies, or add weight to the tippet 8 to 12 inches above the top nymph. Tungsten beadheads are perfect for the hinged indicator method.

**Position and presentation.** Take your initial position toward the lower end and slightly off to the side of the long and broad sheet of currents you want to fish. Lay an imaginary "shotgunning" grid over the water, and make sure your casts cover each square foot of bottom. Since lies along the bottom of the waters fished with the hinged system are rarely revealed, you will have to cover all of the water to find the fish.

Make your first cast just a few feet outboard from straight upstream. Keep the cast short, 25 to 40 feet, unless you're on smooth water where you can control the drift out to 50 feet, as long as you can throw a roll that far. As soon as the line touches down, make a roll mend, lifting the indicator and flipping it upstream from the nymph. If you don't feel that your indicator is positioned right, make another quick roll mend to put the indicator just upstream from the sinking nymph.

Calculate subsequent casts so that the nymph drifts in a line parallel and about a foot out from the first cast. After you've covered all the water you can reach comfortably from the first position, move upstream into a second position and begin covering a section of bottom that overlaps with the first. In many of the broad sheets of water suited to this method, you can also move out farther into the current and cover a second section of bottom alongside the first.

**Control of the drift.** After the initial roll mend, fish out each cast in the normal sequence for indicator nymphing: Gather slack and lift the rod as the indicator floats toward you, making mends as necessary to keep the line fairly straight; lower the rod and feed slack as the indicator floats downstream past your position; then let the current lift the nymph and water-load the line for the next cast, placed parallel to the first.

**On the water.** After the roll mend, your indicator will often land on the water upside down or sideways. The slight tug that occurs when your nymph first contacts the bottom will pull on the indicator knot and cause the indicator to tilt into proper position with the fan floating up. This initial tilt is your message that the nymph has arrived where it should fish. As it drifts, it should tick the bottom frequently, registered by slight hesitations in the float of the indicator. At first, you'll set the hook to all of these movements, but in time you'll learn which are bottom brushings and which are the slightly more animated movements that indicate a trout has taken the nymph.

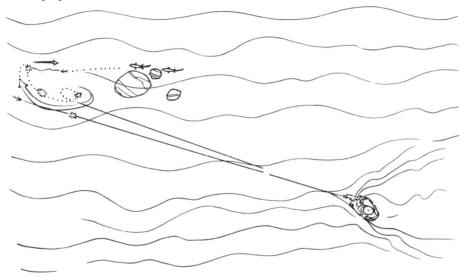

**The trout's point of view.** The nymph, or brace of them, will bump-bump-bump along the bottom, just as a natural nymph or larva when cast adrift makes contact with the rocks, loses its grip, and strives to make contact again. It's a very lifelike way to fish nymphs along the bottom in the right kind of water.

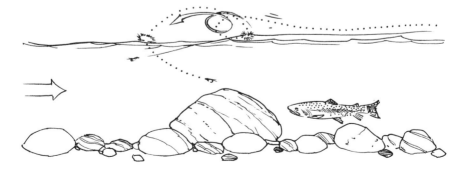

**RIG:        HINGED NYMPH AND INDICATOR**
**Method:    Nymphing suspended trout**

**Situations to solve.** Quite often, in waters with abundant populations of small aquatic insects and crustaceans—midges, mayflies, caddisflies, scuds, and aquatic sowbugs—trout will suspend a foot or two above the bottom and pick off nymphs, larvae, pupae, and anything else that is either drifting at a constant depth or rising toward the surface for emergence. These situations almost always occur on spring creek and tailwater flats with abundant rooted vegetation. Occasionally, you'll find trout suspended and feeding in freestone streams, but not often. Whenever and wherever you find these suspended trout, you'll want to hang a small nymph or two, and fish them as delicately and freely as you can. The hinged nymph and indicator rig offers an excellent way to accomplish that.

**Tuning the rig.** As always, adjust your rig for the situation in which you'll use it. Because you'll usually want to suspend nymphs on weedy flats in gentle currents, where trout are spooky and difficult to approach, rig with a small indicator, 5 or 6X tippet a foot or so shorter than the depth of the water, and size 16 and smaller nymphs, either beadheads or lightly weighted. Tungsten beadheads are excellent for such situations. If the water where trout are suspended is deeper and/or faster, you'll want to use a larger indicator, longer tippet, and heavier flies.

**Position and presentation.** On typical smooth flats, glides, and runs where the suspended nymph method works best, approach your trout or their suspected lies very slowly, from downstream and off to the side, without sending any wading waves over them. Take a position at a more open angle off to the side rather than straight downstream, so that your line and heavy base leader do not fly over the trout's heads on any cast. Typically, you'll fish a suspended rig at an angle that is more across the current rather than up it.

Make your initial cast to the inside edge of the water you want to fish. Place the indicator and nymph onto the water 6 to 10 feet upstream from the point where you'd like the nymph to attain depth and begin fishing. This will give the nymph time to sink and keep the arrival of the terminal end of things out of sight of the trout. As soon as the cast lands, make a roll cast to lift the indicator and place it above the nymph, without lifting the nymph from the water.

Subsequent casts should fish drifts parallel to the first, and subsequent positions should let you fish overlapping sections of stream either upstream from the first or farther out into the current from it.

**Control of the drift.** After that initial roll mend, controlling the drift should be no different than with any other nymphing method, except that your casting angle, which cuts more acutely across the currents, will ask you to make more frequent upstream mends. Gather slack as the indicator drifts downstream, and lift your rod tip, making mends as necessary. Lower your rod and feed slack as the indicator passes your position, then let the current lift the nymph and load the rod, and place a second cast alongside the drift line of the first cast.

**On the water.** Your suspended nymph should never contact the bottom to pull the indicator out of proper attitude. Early in the drift while the nymph is still sinking, you might need to tug on the line to set the indicator at the right angle, fan up, on the water. After that, any movement of the indicator will be caused by trout, so you should quickly but gently set the hook if you see any movement.

**The trout's point of view.** Trout will observe the nymph, or pair of them, arriving adrift on gentle currents, along with the many naturals on which they're feeding. Because spring creeks and tailwaters tend to have a narrow set of food forms in great abundance, the trout likely will be selective. In no other type of nymphing is it more beneficial to collect a specimen and try to match it as closely as you can.

**RIG:          HINGED NYMPH AND INDICATOR**
**Method:     Nymphing from a moving boat**

**Situations to solve.** On many big and rich rivers, mostly tailwaters, guides lead clients to trout by rigging with a hinged indicator system, a couple of nymphs, usually one of modest size and the other tiny, and a bit of weight on a long leader. Clients instruct this rig to be cast overboard and set adrift at the speed of the current. The indicator floats unimpeded, at times for two or three times the distance that you could get out of a cast nymph, at other times for hundreds of feet downstream without another cast. During that time, the nymphs are suspended just above the bottom or dangled down far enough to touch the bottom now and then. If you're ever on a guided trip, you'll likely learn the method from an expert. If you own your own boat, you can put it into play yourself.

**Tuning the rig.** You'll be fishing smooth water, usually 4 to 6 feet deep. Adjust the size of your indicator to the weight of the flies you'd like to suspend; the length and strength of your tippet to the depth of the water and the size trout you expect to catch; and the flies to the natural foods that are most abundant in the water you're going to fish. Aquatic worms and sowbugs are common in the types of rivers where this method works best. A common combination is a San Juan Worm trailed by a tiny sowbug imitation, with a bit of putty weight to deliver them to the bottom or near it.

**Position and presentation.** If you're with a guide, position yourself in the bow or stern stanchions, at his direction. If you're on your own or rowing while friends fish, position your boat in the same set of currents you want the flies to drift down. If you position yourself outside the currents and fish inside them, your indicator will drift at a different speed than the boat, thus shortening your drifts. Fishing across currents will also necessitate a lot of mends, which are not bad on most waters, but on smooth water, and from an elevated position in a boat, they are frightening to trout.

Make the cast to the side of the boat and at an angle slightly downstream, giving the boat some time to slowly catch up with it. If wind or the shape of the currents causes the boat to move slower than the indicator, make your casts to the side and at an angle behind the boat, giving the indicator time to catch up with the boat. The cast need not be long, but the farther you get it from the boat, the more chance your flies will drift through water where trout are not disturbed by the passing of the boat. About two rod lengths are minimum; if the boat looms into a trout's view at the same time your nymphs drift into its sight, the trout is not likely to take them.

You will have no opportunity to make second drifts parallel to the first to cover the water. Often guides set up a daisy chain, in which they drift down through a good stretch of water, hook a trout or two, reach the end of it, get into the slower or eddied water off to the side, row back to the top of it, and then drift back through, thus enabling their clients to fish productive water over and over. You can do the same, but be sure not to disturb wading anglers.

**Control of the drift.** You want to eliminate the need for control once the cast is made. That's why guides love to use this method with inexperienced clients. If your line does belly, however, it's better to mend the belly out to keep your flies fishing at depth a lot longer than to pick up and make another cast.

**On the water.** As with all other hinged indicator methods, nymphing the bottom from a moving boat works best in long stretches of water with even current speeds and constant water depths. It does not work well in rough water and even less well in water that varies in depth as you move from one water type to another. Use it on long and broad flats, down the length of runs, and even on riffles if the water is not too rough, as long as the bottom holds its depth.

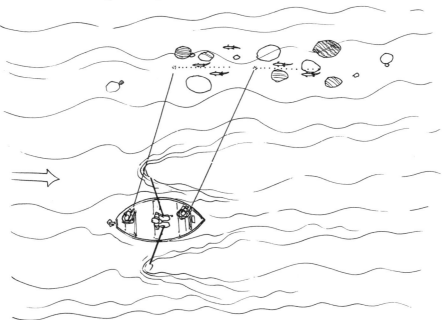

**The trout's point of view.** Most trout taken by this method will be holding on the bottom or suspended in the zone of soft water 6 inches to 1 foot above it. They might pursue your nymph, but the closer you can get your nymph to the bottom, the more trout you'll catch. If your nymph drifts a couple of feet off the bottom, you might think you're fishing empty water, when in truth the water is full of fish holding just a bit deeper.

## RIG:          TWO INDICATORS, PIT RIVER STYLE

**Purpose.** This two-indicator rig was devised to get a nymph, or pair of them, to the bottom almost instantly in short pockets and runs in fast, tumbling water, while also providing news about takes almost the instant a trout intercepts the rushing nymph. The problem with using the standard indicator-and-shot rig in short bits of holding water is the 3 to 5 feet of current it takes for the nymph to get deep enough to be fishing. If the length of holding water is shorter than that, your nymph will be out of the holding water before it reaches bottom.

The two-indicator rig, fished with at least one heavily weighted nymph, two to three split shot or molds of putty weight, and indicators that are small enough to submerge but still be seen, gets down in the holding water almost instantly. It lets you fish short pieces of holding water where you'd otherwise not be able to show a nymph to the trout.

**History/origins.** I was first introduced to the two-indicator rig and the high-sticking method used with it on Northern California's Pit River. Many of the rivers descending the west slopes of the High Sierra are swift and brutal, but because most are dammed, their flow regimens don't encourage the broadening of banks that would make them more typical of freestone streams. Their granite baserock beds are studded with big boulders, and holding water forms as pockets and short runs where the water ricochets and briefly glides between these boulders.

The resulting rig necessary to fish such water evolved into a sort of continuum up the leader from a heavy nymph to some spaced weight to a couple of spread indicators. The nymph, or brace of them, plunges to the bottom almost at once, and the spaced weight allows the quick transfer of any signal about a take. The relative position of the submerged indicators will suddenly change if a trout takes the nymph.

The two-indicator rig and high-sticking method are effective on mountain creeks, streams, and small rivers, wherever the water is swift and the holding lies are short.

**Knots and notes.** The leader should be the length of the rod or at most a little longer. Tie a heavily weighted nymph to a fairly stout tippet with a Duncan loop knot; trout in such waters are not leader shy. If you want to add a point fly, tie a 10- to 14-inch tippet at least one size finer to the hook bend with an improved clinch knot, and then fix the smaller nymph with a Duncan loop or surgeon's loop.

Pinch a small to medium split shot or mold a clump of putty weight to the leader 8 to 10 inches from the first nymph, then another the same distance above the first weight. Sometimes you'll need a third shot or piece of putty weight. Two or three small to medium weights are better than one large one, which would hinder messages about takes. Mold a bit of putty indicator to the leader approximately the depth of the water above the first nymph—you also can use stick-on or small hard indicators—and add another indicator 6 inches to 1 foot above the first, closer in faster, shallower water and farther apart in slower, deeper water.

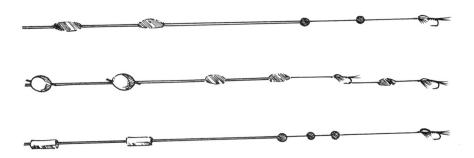

**Adjustments for conditions.** If your nymph is anchoring on the bottom, reduce the weight on the leader. If it is riding too far above the bottom and failing to tap rocks or to get hung up now and then, add weight. If your indicators are riding much more than a foot or two deep, where you're unable to watch them carefully, adjust them higher on the leader. If they're both floating when the nymph is fishing right, then adjust them lower on the leader, closer to the weight and nymph, so at least one is almost always submerged.

**Rules for the rig.** You want enough weight on the nymph and leader to get the nymph down almost instantly. The indicators are not designed to float, but to follow the drift of the nymph. Both can be submerged as long as you can see them and note quickly any change in their relative position. Your casts should be short and made with open loops, almost lobs, at very short range. If you get fancy with the string of nymphs, weights, and indicators strung out on the leader, you're going to get tangles.

Always wade as close to any lie as you can. If you're like me, you'll be leaning on your wading staff with one hand and fishing with the other. Aggressive waders have the advantage in this type of fishing. But don't take chances; the waters where this method works best are almost always leg breakers.

**Appropriate flies.** The most effective nymphs will be rough renditions of the most prevalent natural insects living in the waters you're fishing. Imitations of stonefly nymphs, stout crawler mayfly nymphs, and free-living caddis larvae, size 10 to 14, heavily weighted and often beadheaded, are effective. If you want to use a point fly, it should be smaller and lightly weighted.

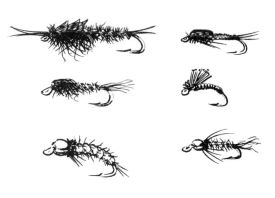

**Situations to solve.** A mountain or steep foothill creek, stream, or small river has sections of water that plunge swiftly through boulder fields, where the current glances and ricochets from boulder to boulder and then forms short glides alongside and between them. Many streams in the High Sierra, Cascades, Rocky Mountains, and Appalachians descend through such reaches. Some have unrelieved miles of such holding water.

The two-indicator rig, which originated on the swift and brutal streams draining the west slopes of the Sierra Mountains, is designed to get a nymph down fast and keep it fishing there. The high-sticking method is useful with many other nymphing rigs, but almost mandatory with a heavily weighted rig in this sort of water.

**Tuning the rig.** The rod should be $8^1/2$ to $9^1/2$ feet long, and the leader should be the length of the rod, no longer. The floating line can be a weight-forward or double-taper. The tippet should be 8 to 12 inches, mostly to give you a tippet knot against which to brace the first split shot or around which to mold putty weight. Use two or three split shot or putty weights spread 8 to 10 inches apart. Mold a putty indicator, big enough to be visible but not large enough to float the rig, at the depth of the water up the leader, and add another the same size 6 inches to 1 foot higher. The nymph, weight, and indicators should be in the front 3 to 4 feet of leader if you're on small water, the front 4 to 6 feet on medium water, and the front 6 to 8 feet on larger water.

**Position and presentation.** Take up your initial position alongside the lowest piece of holding water in the stretch of stream you're wading. Move in as close as you dare, a rod length or at most two from the holding water, and directly off to the side from it. In such rough water, you should be able to nearly loom over the trout without alarming them if you don't bang the bottom and don't make fast movements.

Make your first short cast to the inside edge of the run or glide at the upstream end. Then make an immediate upstream mend, not much more than a twitch, to place the indicators straight above the nymph. Give the rig a moment to sink; then lift the rod to straighten the leader from the indicators through the weight to the nymph. Don't lift the nymph itself, but keep in near contact with it. Follow its drift downstream, lifting the rod as the nymph approaches you and dropping the rod after it passes. Your drift will be short; rarely will you have to gather slack in the upper part of the drift and feed it into the lower part.

When the drift has fished out the length of the holding water, let the current lift the nymph and water-load the line. Then lob the next cast upstream either to the same line of drift or at most a foot out from the first. In this sort of rushing water, cover each line of drift with several casts, and keep your lines of drift very close together, so that the trout have a chance to see the nymph more than once.

**Control of the drift.** Lift and lower the rod through the drift to keep the two indicators in sight, drifting one above the other at the same speed as the current. If necessary, throw small mends to keep the indicators either straight up from the nymph or a little upstream from it. You don't want them leading the nymph through the drift.

**On the water.** The relative positions of the two indicators through the drift will tell you how the nymph is drifting and when you have a hit. If the nymph is anchored to the bottom, the indicators will get tethered. If the nymph never taps bottom, the indicators will not hesitate in their drift. Look for the subtle shift in the relative positions of the indicators to tell you when a fish takes the nymph. Lift the rod quickly to determine whether it's a trout or the bottom. A fish will have the nymph in and out of its mouth in a hurry, so you must react almost instantly.

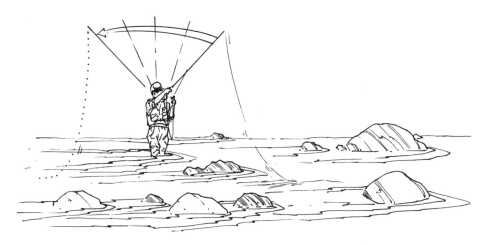

**The trout's point of view.** The trout will always be holding in some soft spot of broken current along the bottom. Your nymph must get down into that same soft water and drift as freely as possible there. If you're not tapping bottom and thus making false hook sets every other cast or so, you won't be catching any trout.

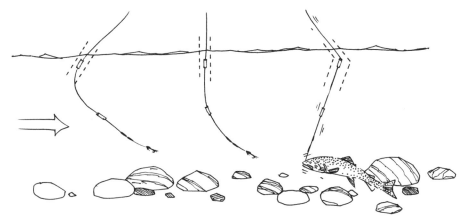

## RIG:       WET-TIP/BELLY/HEAD OR FULL-SINK LINE SYSTEM

**Purpose.** Having a variety of sinking line types is at times advantageous for fishing nymphs at different depths and current speeds. However, in almost all moving water situations, the wider array of lines has been replaced by the single floating line and a set of rigs based on weight and strike indicators on the leader. Most modern employment for sinking lines is found in stillwaters, and treatment here for moving waters will be condensed. More than 90 percent of my own creek, stream, and river fishing is done with floating lines, whereas I use some sort of sinking line for more than half of my stillwater fishing.

The few situations in which you'll use a sinking line in moving water will usually involve the need to get down to substantial depths in runs and pools on medium to big waters, where floating lines and long leaders cannot reach bottom. But you'll also find use for sinking lines in situations where creek, stream, and river pools are ponded almost to stillwaters. For example, in the low water of late summer in all sorts of streams, and in tailwaters where the water flow is nearly shut down either seasonally or daily, your fishing becomes more related to stillwaters than moving waters.

**History/origins.** The revolution in fly-line technology that began in the late 1950s and early 1960s led to sinking lines that in their early days provided the best ways to deliver nymphs to the bottom, even in shallow moving water. Anybody who fished for trout during those early years can recall trying to find methods that would fish nymphs deep and still provide information on when a trout took the nymph. Quite likely, many more strikes went undetected than trout were ever caught. We can also remember the sense of relief that came when the indicator-and-shot method displaced sinking lines for most situations. However, sinking lines are still useful for swinging nymphs deep in runs and for probing the depths of pools with little current.

**Knots and notes.** Sinking lines can be classed in two ways. First is by the length of the sinking forward part of the line: *wet-tip* (10-feet), *wet-belly* (20-feet), and *wet-head* (30-feet), all followed by the normal length of floating fly line, and *full-sink,* with no floating line behind it. The second way to class sinking lines is by sink rate, using such terms as *slow sinking* or type I, *fast-sinking* or type II, *extra-fast sinking* or type III, *high-density* or type IV, and *high-speed high-density* or type VI. Every line manufacturer has its own proprietary designations, but each produces lines in a variety of sink rates.

Knots are no different than for any similar system: Use a nail knot to attach leader to line, a blood or surgeon's knot for leader and tippet sections, and a Duncan or surgeon's loop to fix flies. Be sure to shorten the leader with the deeper systems. If you use a fast-sinking line and long leader, the nymph will tend to ride higher in the water than the line tip; 4- to 6-foot leaders keep the nymph at the same depth as the sinking line.

**Adjustments for conditions.** Focus your efforts on getting your nymph to the bottom and adjusting your rig to vary the depth to which your nymph is sinking. To accomplish this, select the right type of line—a wet-tip for small water, a wet-belly

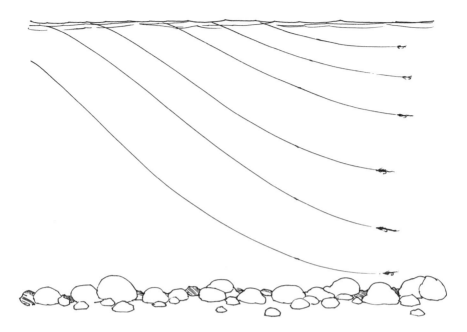

for bigger water, and a wet-head for rivers. You can also select a line type based on its sink rate—type I through type VI. Full-sinking lines come in the same set of sink rates, so your depth can be varied according to the type you choose. You can also vary the length of the leader, the amount of weight on the nymph, and the number of seconds you count the nymph down.

**Rules for the rig.** There are no rigid rules for sinking lines. Some folks prefer floating/sinking wet-tip/belly/head combination lines, others full-sinking line systems. You may have to experiment to find the type that suits you best and attains the depths you're seeking in the water you're fishing. Lines with floating running sections are easier to cast and control. Full-sink lines keep the nymph fishing longer at the desired depth.

**Appropriate flies.** Flies that imitate or at least approximate abundant naturals are certain to provide the most success. However, popular dressings, such as the

Gold-Ribbed Hare's Ear and Fox Squirrel Nymph (in standard and bead-head versions) look like a lot of trout foods and are always good bets if you aren't able to collect a sample to see what trout might be taking. Go smaller than you think appropriate. If you fish a big nymph, drop a smaller one off its stern.

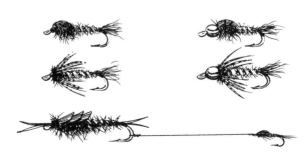

**RIG:** **WET-TIP/BELLY/HEAD OR FULL-SINK LINE SYSTEM**
**Method:** **Swinging nymphs deep**

**Situations to solve.** Sometimes you'll encounter trout water that is simply too big or too deep to bottom-nymph with the indicator-and-shot rig. Perhaps the reach of water is too broad to cover with indicator drifts from a safe wading position, but long casts cover the water on the swing from the same position. Or perhaps the water is too deep to reach bottom with a leader that can be controlled on a long cast, thus eliminating the indicator-and-shot method.

You might also want to imitate certain insects, such as big swimmer mayfly nymphs, that require an active retrieve rather than a dead drift.

**Tuning the rig.** Select the type of line that will get your nymph to the depth you want but still give you control over the swing. In most stream and river situations, you'll want to use a wet-tip, wet-belly, or wet-head line, because you can mend the running line, control the swing better, and in some cases attain greater depth. Sometimes it's surprising how shallow you're fishing when you think you're fishing deep. I once asked a guide to motor his boat with a depth finder over water that I'd thought was 20 feet deep. (I was using a depth-charge line to get down near the bottom.) At its deepest, it was 7 feet.

Shorten the leader when you go to a sinking line. Trout will not be shy of the line tip. Experiments with leaders as short as 1 or 2 feet have shown that trout will not back away from them, but it's wise to keep leaders to 4 or at most 6 feet long.

**Position and presentation.** Take your position toward the head, and off to the side, of the water you want to fish, usually a large pool or long, deep run. If you are fishing a pool with a current tongue entering into it, then position yourself high enough so that your initial swings will reach the highest water in the pool that might hold trout. Fishermen often wade in at the head of the pool and cast out as far as they can reach, which causes the first swing of the nymph to cross the middle of the pool, not the head. Instead, step in high, sometimes in the riffle upstream from the pool.

Make the first cast short—15 to 25 feet—and far enough upstream so the sinking portion of the line will have time to tug the nymph down. Let the nymph swing downstream, crossing the seam from the fast water outside of your position into the slower water on the inside, sometimes straight downstream. Make each cast a foot or two out from the first, continuing to place the nymph at an angle up and across the current. Once you've reached your comfortable casting limit, begin taking a single step downstream between casts. In this manner, you'll cover all the water from the head of the pool to the end of the water you believe might have potential to hold trout.

**Control of the drift.** After each cast lands at an angle upstream, let the line and nymph sink until they are at an angle just downstream from straight across the current. When the line draws tight, you can either let the nymph drift without any action or twitch the rod tip to animate it. On almost every cast, make nearly constant upstream mends from the time the line lands until the nymph crosses the seam from fast water to slow.

**On the water.** Although often considered more of a method for fishing either wet flies or streamers, a simple mended swing that fishes a nymph 1 or 2 feet deep through water that is full of trout can be surprisingly productive. With a wet-tip, wet-belly, or wet-head line, this method can be easy and even pleasant to execute. We often try too hard to please the trout by getting nymphs to tumble dead-drift along the bottom, but in difficult water, you can still catch many trout and thereby have lots of fun by swinging a nymph higher up in the water column. If it isn't going to work, you'll know quickly when the trout don't bite. Then you'll have to figure out another way to get your nymph down to them.

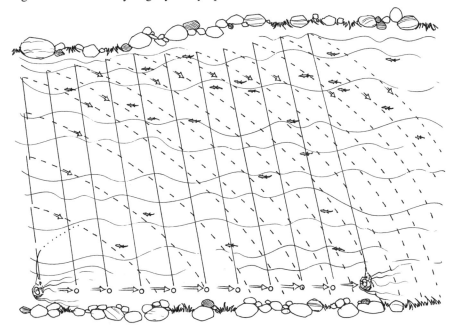

**The trout's point of view.** Whether you fish the nymph deep along the bottom or higher up in the water, it will arrive in front of trout tethered to a leader and looking as if it is swimming. As long as you mend your swing so the nymph does not race as nothing in nature might, the nymph looks alive. However, if your swing is too fast, you won't catch any trout.

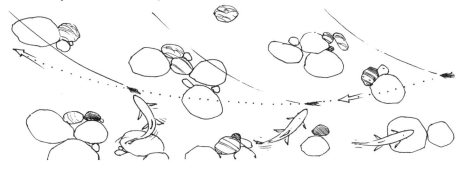

**Situations to solve.** Moving water tends to slow and pool when flows are low in late summer and early fall. What might have been riffles and runs in the earlier part of the season has become water too thin to hold trout in the late season; they have backed down into the depths of pools. While wet-tip, wet-belly, and wet-head lines work in succession on creeks, streams, and rivers of increasing size, full-sink lines work on some of the largest rivers with pools of the greatest depth.

Pooled water is common on tailwaters with dramatic differences between high and low flows. When the water is up, whether for daily power generation or seasonal irrigation, you'll find few pools and little opportunity to use a sinking line. When the water is down, because either power or irrigation needs are low, then riffles and runs diminish and water settles into pools. When the water is high, you'll do better with indicator-and-shot techniques, and when the water is low, then sinking lines can come into play.

**Tuning the rig.** Select the line type—wet-tip, -belly, -head, or full-sink—according to the size of the stream and the depth of its pools. In all but the largest, a wet-tip through wet-head will give you a bit more casting distance and line control than a full-sinking line.

One of the best ways to rig for this type of fishing and avoid snagging is with a short leader and buoyant nymph. Leave the lead wraps off your favorite nymph, and tie it with an underbody of foam. When the tip of the sinking line reaches bottom, the nymph will float just a few inches above it, in sight of trout and out of reach of bottom snags.

**Position and presentation.** If you're fishing a small stream with pools too small to allow standing at the side and casting across, take up your initial position at the downstream end of the pool, on the assumption that you're moving upstream. Make your casts upstream, give the nymph time to sink, and retrieve it slowly. Cover the water with a fan of casts that show the nymph to trout in all likely lies in the pool.

On larger waters, take up your initial position near the head of the pool, where the current, however strong or weak, enters and forms a tongue down the pool. Make your first cast the farthest upstream. If a substantial current enters the pool, then cast up into it, upstream from the head of the pool, so that the line will enter the pool already on or near the bottom. Let the line sink, and then begin your slow retrieve through the depths. Subsequent casts should be fanned out so that all the water you can reach from the first position is covered. Take subsequent positions in the middle and lower end of the pool, depending on its size, and cover all of the water. If the current is strong through the pool, revert to the previous method of swinging nymphs deep.

**Control of the drift.** If the water is slow, make an occasional upstream mend to control the drift while the line sinks. On the retrieve, use a handtwist, in which you gather line inches at a time by rolling your line hand over and over, or a very slow stripping retrieve. In pools, as in stillwaters, the old refrain *the slower the retrieve, the faster the fishing* usually applies.

**On the water.** Takes are almost always subtle when you fish the bottom with sinking lines. You'll have no strike indicator to tell you about them, so watch your line where it enters the water. If it suddenly shoots forward, twitches downward, or moves to one side or the other, set the hook quickly. If you feel the take, react quickly but not brutally; you don't want to yank one way against a big trout going the other. This will prove fatal, but not to the trout.

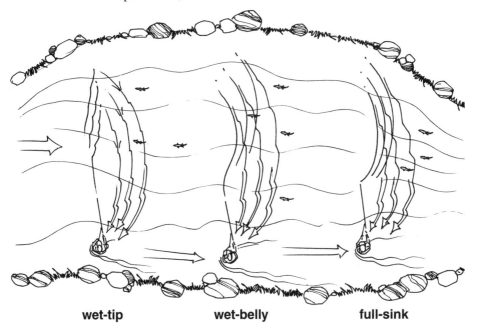

| wet-tip | wet-belly | full-sink |

**The trout's point of view.** A weighted nymph will scour the bottom, and that is often just what you want. If you get hung up, however, try the buoyant nymph method by showing the trout a nymph inching along just above the bottom. If snagging is not a problem, use the modestly weighted nymphs that are most common in your fly boxes.

**RIG:        WET-TIP/BELLY/HEAD OR FULL-SINK LINE SYSTEM**
**Method:     Strip tease**

**Situations to solve.** In his book *Nymphing,* Gary Borger described a method devised by Ed Mueller, who called it the *strip tease.* It's an excellent method to use for fishing deep pools when trout are feeding somewhat selectively on many types of insects and other organisms that alternately creep along, pause, and then dart a few inches. Try it with stonefly nymphs, swimmer mayfly nymphs, and crustaceans such as scuds. The method works best in creek, stream, and river situations where the water is slow to still, but it can also be applied to true stillwater situations—lakes and ponds.

**Tuning the rig.** The correct line should be chosen according to the speed and depth of the current you'll be fishing. Use a wet-tip for creeks and small streams, a wet-belly for medium-size streams, and a wet-head for large streams and rivers of all sizes. The line Borger mentions—with a floating tip and sinking running portion to keep the nymph down toward the bottom but riding just above it—is not available commercially, as far as I'm aware, though splicing one yourself is an option. You can get the same effect with a sinking-tip, -belly, or -head, or even a full-sink line, a short leader, and a buoyant nymph. Try your regular weighted imitations first. Then, if you get hung up, go to a nymph that rides above the bottom.

**Position and presentation.** Use the same position and presentation as described in the previous cast and countdown method. Fish from the foot of a small pool and positions at the head, middle, and tailout of a larger pool. The water should all be covered with a fan of casts from each position, and the size of a pool dictates the number of positions required to cover all of it. After each cast, give the line plenty of time to sink. Borger recommends a count of up to sixty seconds. Trout can take the nymph at any time during the sink, so watch for signs of a strike—usually no more than a sudden change in the movement of the line where it enters the water.

**Control of the drift.** The difference between the strip tease and the previous countdown and handtwist method is in the retrieve. First let the nymph reach fishing depth, usually either with the line right on the bottom or a few seconds' count short of the bottom—if you hang a fish repeat the count, if you bang the bottom shorten the count. Then lower your rod tip very close to the water, and begin with the same slow handtwist retrieve, rolling your line hand over and over to gather a few inches of line each time. This will cause the nymph to crawl along the bottom. After an interval, stop the retrieve and let the nymph rest. This pause is common behavior among many naturals. At the end of the rest, give a short strip with your line hand, anywhere from a short sharp tug to a foot-long steady strip, to cause the nymph to jump off the bottom, swim a short way, and then stop.

Continue interspersing handtwist, pauses, and strips throughout the retrieve. The strip tease is a patient way of fishing, but any successful method you use to fish the depths of pools will require you to wait out the sink and then be patient on the retrieve.

**On the water.** Some creek and small-stream pools can be covered with just a few casts. Pools in big rivers might be nearly the size of small ponds, and you should concentrate on them until you believe either you've covered them well or the trout have quit hitting. On some tailwaters, the strip tease method with a sinking line can be your best shot at hooking the kind of trophy you want to hang on your wall.

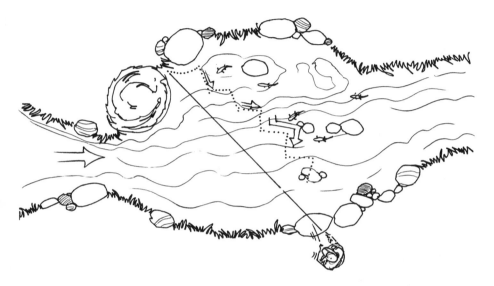

**The trout's point of view.** On the bottom of the pool, trout will see the nymph arriving into its view either on the crawl or in a burst of swimming. Either way, the fish will react by attacking at once or by swimming over to give the nymph a critical look. Keep varying the strip tease movement—crawl, pause, and swim—and the trout is likely to be satisfied with the nymph's activity at one point or other in the retrieve.

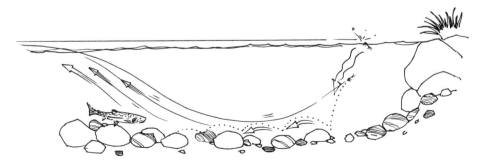

**RIG:          WET-TIP/BELLY/HEAD OR FULL-SINK LINE SYSTEM**
**Method:     Brooks method**

**Situations to solve.** The Brooks method, originated by the late Charles E. Brooks and described in his 1976 *Nymph Fishing for Larger Trout,* is designed to get big, heavily weighted nymphs to the bottom in strong, pushy water. Brooks confessed that not everyone would enjoy fishing with the heavy rods, lines, and flies required in the heavy currents that he preferred to fish. The method is best applied with modern extra-fast sinking or high-density wet-tip and wet-belly lines, though Brooks used the full-sink lines of his times. The shot-and-indicator rig was just coming into use when Brooks wrote his books. Because of the added control and the ease of detecting strikes, the shot-and-indicator method is used far more often today than the older Brooks method. However, you should know when and how to put the Brooks method into play.

**Tuning the rig.** Although Brooks used his method most often in big western streams and rivers that contained heavy currents and populations of giant salmon fly nymphs, it can be applied in any big and fast water with abundant large insects of any kind. The nymph should be heavily weighted. A properly tied Brooks Stone, when dropped just inches, will land in your hand with a thud. The leader should be stout and no more than 6 feet long. The line should be a fast-sinking wet-tip or, for very big water, a wet-belly. Because casts are most often short, the 10-foot wet-tip is almost always sufficient. The extra 10 feet of sinking line in a wet-belly can be a great disadvantage when it comes to line control and detecting takes. A heavy 7- or 8-weight line is best for this method, but if you're astream and armed with a 5- or 6-weight, it will work. The rod should be long, $8^1/2$ to $9^1/2$ feet, and balanced to cast the line.

**Position and presentation.** Take your initial position just upstream and inside from the suspected lie of the trout that is farthest upstream in the water you want to fish. Usually this puts you at the upstream end and inside edge of a long run of deep and powerful water. Make the first cast about 15 feet upstream and 6 feet out into the current. As the nymph and line tip plummet toward the bottom, lift the rod and gather slack formed by the downstream drift without hindering the sink of the nymph. The nymph should reach bottom in front of you, almost under the rod tip, and that is the point at which it becomes effective. Pivot to face the drift, and as the nymph tumbles downstream, lower the rod and keep the tip of the rod pointed over the entrance of the line into the water. Experience will help you achieve a balance between a line that is too tight, which lifts the nymph, and a line that is too slack, which will cause missed strikes.

At the end of each drift, give the current plenty of time to lift the nymph toward the surface. Water-load the line and make the next cast a foot or so out from the first. This method works better with short casts, so keep your casts to 30 or at most 40 feet. After you've fished the water you can comfortably reach from your first position, wade downstream a few feet, or a few feet out into the current, and begin again.

**Control of the drift.** To control the drift, lift the rod as the nymph plummets toward you, and then lower it after it passes your position. With a wet-tip or wet-belly line, you can make upstream mends to keep the line even with the nymph.

**On the water.** Although strikes will at times be felt, more often a strike is signaled by a stoppage of the line in the progress of its drift. Setting the hook will require taking out all slack between the rod tip and the trout. Brooks recommended throwing the rod tip over to one side and at the same time taking in a long strip of line with the line hand. If these movements do not succeed in moving the nymph, the hook will not be set. Such fishing, usually for big trout, can be brutal and require a stout leader.

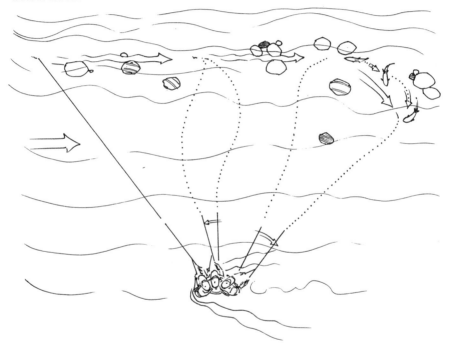

**The trout's point of view.** From the bottom, the trout see the nymph sink quickly, tumble, and roll along either on or near the rocks. At the end of the drift it lifts up toward the surface, as if it's a natural aquatic insect that has lost its moorings and is being buoyed up by the currents. Many meals arrive in front of trout this way in fast water.

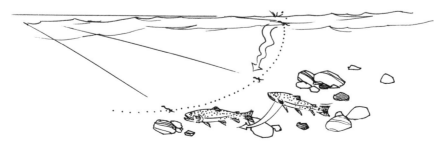

## RIG:         WET-TIP/BELLY/HEAD OR FULL-SINK LINE SYSTEM
## Method:      Pot-shooting

**Situations to solve.** Charles Brooks devised the pot-shooting method to take trout from what he described as brief pothole-type lies in rapids and cascades of mountain and foothill streams and rivers. He described the method in *Nymph Fishing for Larger Trout.* The water he used it in was big, fast, and interrupted by boulders, ledges, logs or rootwads, and slight trenches, all of which form breaks to the current and lies for big trout. Brooks also used the same method, under the same name, with floating lines and big, bushy dry flies, but he was known primarily as a nymph fisherman, and the method is most useful when employed with nymphs.

**Tuning the rig.** Brooks used flies size 2 to 6 based on naturals in the water he fished, in his case almost always salmon fly nymphs in big western rivers. He fished 7- and 8-weight full-sinking high-density lines, but the method is just as effective and a lot more pleasant if you use a fast-sinking wet-tip line. Since the pockets are short, the 10 feet of sinking line are sufficient in all but the biggest water. If you use lighter 5- and 6-weight lines, keep your flies toward size 6 and 8. The leader should be sized 1X down to what Brooks considered a light 3X.

You can downsize this method for use on creeks and small streams, which have plenty of the kind of small pothole lies Brooks fished, only on a smaller scale. Use a floating line, a leader no longer than 6 to 8 feet, and heavily weighted size 10 or 12 nymphs.

**Position and presentation.** Fish each short holding lie from one position with just a few casts. Move in close; never more than 20 feet, or between one and two rod lengths. The best position will vary from pothole to pocket, depending on the size and shape of the water around it. Your goal is to take a position that allows you to control the drift of the nymph through the edge and center of the pocket. Most often, that will be straight out to the side or just a few feet upstream or down from the suspected lie of the trout.

Make the first presentation just 2 to 4 feet upstream from the upper end of the inside edge of the pocket. End the cast with the rod tip low to the water and the line tight. Immediately steer the nymph through the line of drift you'd like it to take, following it with the rod tip and coaxing it along if it gets hung on the bottom. As soon as the nymph has passed the water you consider has potential to hold trout, lift it with a single backcast and pot-shoot it back to the water, but a little farther into the pocket. If you get no take, follow the drift and shoot again until you've covered the water thoroughly. In this type of fishing, things will most often happen quickly and violently, usually on the first or second cast, or not at all.

**Control of the drift.** Make sure you're close enough to the drift line of the heavy nymph to control it with little flick mends upstream or down. To give the nymph slack or lift if off the bottom, try lifting or lowering the rod or rolling a mend toward the nymph.

**On the water.** Hits in this type of fishing will be abrupt, brutal, and on a short line. Most will occur when your rod is pointed almost directly at the trout. Be sure your leader is strong enough to withstand the shock of a hit from the size trout you expect to catch. Frequently, you'll see the trout wallow on your nymph at the same time you feel the great yank, and almost as often, you'll see a trout leave a wake as it rushes out of the lie, frightened away by the big nymph. However, the largest trout will attack a lot more often than they'll flee.

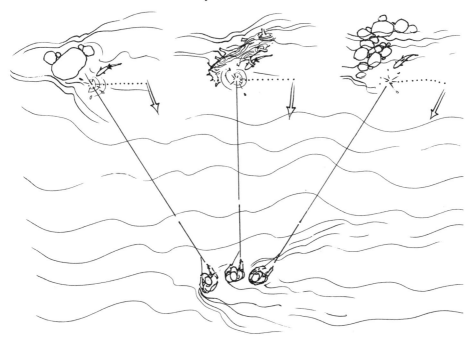

**The trout's point of view.** Holding in a short lie, surrounded by fast water, the trout either first spies the nymph as it lands with a whack on the water just upstream or sees it as it tumbles downstream, a grand bite arriving by surprise. Your goal is to show the nymph to the trout in the same manner a natural insect adrift on the same water might get bounced along.

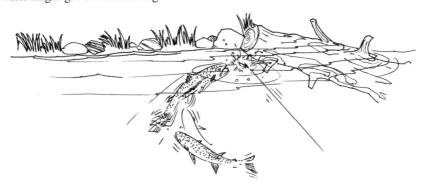

# CHAPTER 7

# Rigs and Methods for
# Wet Flies in Moving Water

If you believe that wet flies are out of fashion and no longer work, you need to disregard that old wisdom. Wet flies are the answer to many trout-fishing situations, including a few that can't be solved with dry flies, nymphs, or streamers. Wet flies are excellent for exploring unfamiliar water, especially if it's shallow, you want to cover it quickly, and you see no signs that trout might be willing to accept dry flies. When trout feed on drowned duns in the aftermath of a mayfly hatch or when they feed on pupae rising toward the surface in the blitz of a caddisfly emergence, wet flies become almost mandatory.

Many times trout seem bashful about the surface. They will rush to and perhaps even splash your dry fly but refuse to take it. The simple switch to a wet fly—which is fished with dry-fly rigging but inches deep rather than floating on top—can mean the difference between frustration and hooking trout after trout. At other times, when trout are willing to feed but are scattered and difficult to find, a wet fly, or pair of them, fished on the swing through all the water types the stream offers, is the fastest way to locate them and bring them into play.

**Selecting wet flies.** Most of the bright, gaudy wet flies of yesteryear were tied to catch unsophisticated trout. They worked wonders, but because they did, most of the foolish trout are gone now. Wet flies that work best today are based at least roughly on the natural insects that trout spend most of their time eating. If you fill a small box of wets in the range of insect sizes, say 12 to 16, and the most common insect colors—pale sulfurs, olives, browns, and blacks—you will find yourself falling back on that box to solve an increasing number of trout-fishing situations. Remember that wet flies represent both emerger and adult stages of many insects, so the sizes and colors should reflect adults as well as immatures.

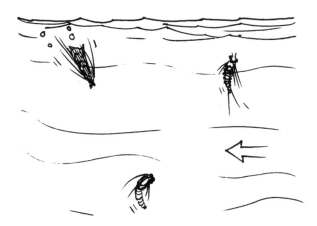

**Tying and fishing wet flies.** Trout feed on quite a variety of insects, from those passing up through the water column to emerge or down through the water to lay their eggs to others simply submerged and drifting along at the whim of the currents to deliver them down to death, usually in the open mouth of a trout. Trout that feed on such a variety are not often selective, but they do like flies that look alive, or at least lively. Select wet flies with lots of moving parts, as opposed to stiff and plastic appendages, so that your flies will look like they're alive, or at least have been recently. A couple of old styles of wet flies—the soft-hackle and flymph—are still commonly used by today's knowledgeable trout fishermen, who although employing a few traditional winged wet flies recognize that not many insects have stiff wings that cleave the water like the blade of a knife.

Tie or buy wet flies with rough-dubbed rather than tight bodies, with hackles of hen or game bird rather than stiffer rooster, and with stiff flight-feather wings only if the natural you're matching has prominent wings that trigger trout acceptance.

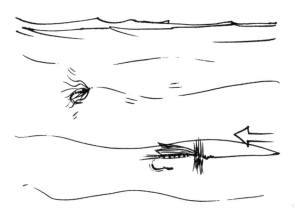

**The three types of wet flies.** There are three basic types of wet flies, though variations shade into each other: traditional winged wets, wingless wets, most often called "flymphs," and soft-hackled wets. Traditional wets, which are usually winged with stiff quill from mallard, pheasant, and other bird wings, fish well when trout are feeding on drowned adult caddis and clumsy alderflies. Flymphs are tied with rough bodies and hen hackle, often wound over the front half of the body, and look a lot like tangled emerging mayflies. They can be fished either in the surface film or tugged under just beneath it. Soft-hackles are tied with bodies of floss or tying silk and one or two turns of land-bird hackle, which collapses around the body. The body becomes an under-color to the kicking and pulsing hackle fibers, making the soft-hackles come alive and looking like a wide variety of things that trout eat.

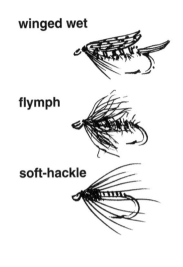

**winged wet**

**flymph**

**soft-hackle**

**Two-fly rigs.** It's very common to fish two wet flies on the same cast, especially if you're exploring and trying to find the trout and a fly they will take. If you use a brace of wet flies, be sure they give trout a choice. Don't tie two of the same dressing to the leader, in the same size, in the hope that you'll catch two trout on the same cast. That's not the objective. Instead, try one fly that is large, say size 12, and another small, size 16. One might be dark, the other light, one winged, the other a flymph or soft-hackle. If you observe more than one natural insect in the air or the water, choose a fly to imitate each to see which the trout prefer.

Whenever you establish that trout want one wet fly over the other, nip off the one that is not producing. An extra fly dangling around could rehook the trout just when you think you have released it, or could lodge a hook in your own hand while you're trying to remove the fly that fooled the fish.

## RIG:        FLOATING LINE AND STANDARD LEADER

**Purpose.** The basic wet-fly rig conveniently uses the same floating line you would use for all of your dry-fly fishing and, with the advent of the shot-and-indicator nymphing rig, for almost all of your nymphing. Most of the experienced trout fishermen I go on trips with use the floating line at least 90 percent of the time on moving water. A wet fly fished on a floating line, with a standard leader the length of the rod or a bit longer, will sink just a few inches to a foot or more, especially when cast so it swings on the current. In this upper part of the water column, trout take many emergers and pupae, failed emergers, drowned duns and spinners, adult caddis swimming toward the bottom to lay their eggs, and even stonefly adults and unlucky terrestrial insects that fall in the water.

Because trout see a wide variety of food forms adrift in the top foot or so of the water column, they are almost always primed to dash up there and take whatever drifts by. They're rarely selective about their feeding unless a certain stage of a single insect species overwhelms all others. The standard wet-fly rig will help you fish a lifelike fly in the top few inches of the water column.

**History/origins.** Sunk flies have been fished in shallow depths since the days of greenheart rods and horsehair lines. As the materials used in rods, lines, leaders, and flies have changed, so have the tactics—reels and better lines allow casts much longer than a rod length. However, the basic fly-fishing concept of a floating line, leader the length of the rod, and wet fly or brace of them works as well now as it did when it was first introduced.

**Knots and notes.** The leader should be tapered and, before the tippet is added, about the length of the rod. I buy $7^1/_2$-foot base leaders in 4X for creeks and small streams, 9- or 10-foot base leaders in 4X for typical streams and rivers. I add tippet if necessary, and the leader is automatically adjusted for the size water and the size fly I'm fishing.

Leader and tippet sections should be tied together with the blood knot or surgeon's knot. Attach the fly with the improved clinch knot, though if you need more freedom in the drift or swing, try a Duncan loop. If a dropper fly is used, leave the stiffer tag end of your tippet knot long and uncut, and tie the dropper to it. If you add a point fly, tie the 12- to 20-inch point tippet to the hook bend with an improved clinch knot, and then the fly to the tippet with the improved clinch or Duncan loop. Make sure the tippet to the point fly is one size finer than the leader to the main fly.

If you want to get the fly down into the water a bit, usually because the current is too fast to allow an unweighted wet fly to break through the surface, then add a split shot between the flies. Some purists would say you are no longer wet-fly fishing, but these decisions are always personal and can be influenced heavily by one's desire to catch trout as opposed to just fish for them.

**Adjustments for conditions.** The length of the leader should be adjusted to suit the size water you're on, a problem solved already if you use leaders about the length of the rod plus the tippet. The strength of the tippet should suit the fly size

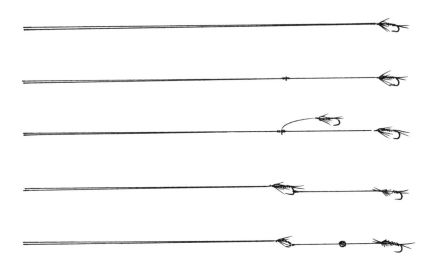

you're casting (see chart on page 78) and the size trout you expect to catch. Trout are rarely leader-shy when you're fishing wets, unless the trout are selectively feeding on insects. In that case, you'll want to be as astute about your tippet as you are when fishing a dry fly.

**Rules for the rig.** If you're fishing a dry fly and find that rising trout refuse it, try nipping off the dry and tying on a wet the same size and color as the insect you're imitating. You'll be rigged just right and will be surprised when you begin catching trout after trout.

If you're exploring by searching the water for scattered trout, try two flies of different sizes, colors, and styles. Let trout choose which they like, and then get the other one off your leader.

Whenever you fish wet flies on the swing, do not let them break through the surface and swim with little wakes trailing behind them. Although on rare occasions you'll catch trout on a waking fly, it won't happen often.

**Appropriate flies.** All three wet-fly types work with the standard wet-fly rig. Be sure that the flies, whether you tie them yourself or buy them, are tied on heavy-wire hooks. In recent years, some have experimented with adding beads to wet flies of all styles. Although this goes against tradition, beads almost always add to the fly's effectiveness, if for no other reason than that they weigh it down enough to get the fly through the surface to sink a foot or so.

**Situations to solve.** The standard wet-fly swing is an excellent method for exploring all of the water in a stream of medium size. You can cover it from side to side, letting your fly swing through the water and thereby finding trout that are holding where you wouldn't expect them. Take a step or so downstream between casts, as you continually show the fly to new water and new trout.

On most creeks and the smallest streams, this method won't work as well because the waters are not wide enough to allow setting up and casting across. You either fish them upstream or down. But on many small streams, you can creep into a single position at the head of a pool, riffle, or run and fish a short first cast and then one a foot or two longer, continuing to extend casts until you've covered all of the water you can reach.

On large streams and rivers, the water must be fished a piece at a time, usually as a swath of a riffle, run, or pool. I especially like to use the wet-fly method when faced with big expanses of riffle or choppy run or even a bumpy flat, when trout are scattered and rising only occasionally. Trout always seem susceptible to wet flies when they are feeding so randomly.

**Tuning the rig.** Generally, the leader that works with dry flies will work just as well with the wet-fly swing. The tippet should be about 2 feet long. Often the best way to achieve that length is to tie a size 12 or 14 wet fly to a $7^1/_2$- or 9-foot 4X base leader and then add 2 feet of 5X tippet and tie a contrasting size 16 or 18 wet to the point.

**Position and presentation.** Take your initial position 10 to 20 feet upstream from the highest water through which you want to swing your wet fly. Many anglers make the mistake of wading in at the corner of a riffle and making their first cast 40 or 50 feet out from there. The best lie might be right in the corner at your feet, and you'll be swinging your fly in an arc the length of your cast downstream from the water with the best potential to hold trout.

Make your initial cast short, one to at most two rod lengths. Let the fly swing down and around on the current, making sure that it crosses that seam between fast water on the outside and slower water on the inside. Lengthen each subsequent cast a foot or two until you have reached the extent of a comfortable cast, typically between 45 and 60 feet for most folks. Don't forget that shorter casts allow you to get the hook home so that you're taking trout more consistently.

The angle of your cast across the stream depends on the speed of the current. You want the fly to swim slowly down and around. If the water is fast, cast farther downstream than across. The swing, though shorter, will be at the correct speed. If the water is slow, cast higher up into the current for a longer swing at the same correct speed.

**Control of the drift.** Because the current will get a better bite on the thicker line than it does on the line tip or leader, the resulting downstream belly will speed the swing of the fly. When the wet fly is moving more slowly, you'll almost always have faster fishing. Make upstream mends, from two to as many as eight or ten per swing, to keep the fly swimming at an appropriate speed. You'll learn quickly how fast the fly is moving. The speed at which you get most of your hits is the speed you should try to attain.

**On the water.** Sometimes trout will take a swung wet fly with a thud. If that occurs, you must raise your rod to engage the fish while resisting the urge to thump it back. If you do that and the fish has any size, you'll instantly be separated from it. Because trout often take wets by trying to inhale them, and the fly is on a tight line, you'll feel only a slowly increasing tension on the line. If you yank, you'll pull the fly away. Discipline yourself to wait until you feel weight, and then raise the rod to engage the trout.

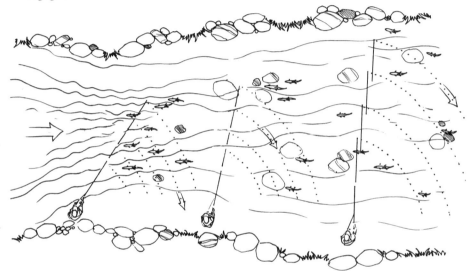

**The trout's point of view.** Trout often turn to follow a wet fly through at least part of its swing before deciding to take it. You'll get most of your takes as your fly crosses the current seam below you, but the trout might have followed the fly from farther out in the current. Make your casts as long as you comfortably can so that you cover as much water as possible.

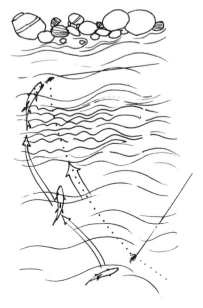

**RIG:        FLOATING LINE AND STANDARD LEADER**
**Method:    Bergman natural drift (greased line)**

**Situations to solve.** Many times, when trout are taking insects that have drowned and are drifting on the current a few inches deep, or when they're not taking anything visibly and you can't coax them to wet flies fished on the swing, then try fishing with the same wet fly, or pair of them, without any animation from the line and leader. Essentially you are making the same choice as you would when deciding whether to fish a dry fly with or without drag, the difference being that drag often animates a wet fly and makes it more enticing to trout.

Ray Bergman wrote about this method in his wonderful 1938 book, *Trout.* The method is very similar to A. H. E. Woods's greased line tactic, recorded in Jock Scott's 1935 book, *Greased Line Fishing for Salmon.* Both Woods and Bergman wanted to present their flies as if they were unattached to the line and leader, drifting downstream as freely as a leaf might, showing themselves to fish sideways in the current.

**Tuning the rig.** The only tuning you might do to make the rig suitable for the natural drift is to extend the tippet to 3 feet or so and make it as fine as you dare to turn over the size fly, or flies, you plan to cast and to handle the size trout you hope to catch. That might mean 5X or even 6X, whereas you would fish 4X or 5X with the standard swing.

**Position and presentation.** Take your initial position straight across from the highest water in the riffle, run, pool, or flat you want to fish with this method. You would, therefore, be straight across from the highest place you expect trout to hold.

Make your first cast short and place it at about a 45-degree angle upstream and across the current. The fly will have time to sink, but it will begin fishing the moment it touches down. The fly is fished on a free drift until it reaches a position directly across the current from your position. Then you begin to turn and follow it, feeding line into the drift to keep the fly moving straight downstream. When the fly has reached the limit of your ability to keep it drifting freely, draw the line tight and let the fly fish down and around below you on the swing.

Lengthen subsequent casts a foot or two, at the same angle upstream, until you've reached a distance that is comfortable to you. After that, take a step downstream between casts, and fish through the length of the water you want to cover.

**Control of the drift.** The key to this method lies in line control, not casting prowess. As the line begins to drift downstream toward you, gather slack as it forms, and toss upstream mends as a belly begins to assert itself. By the time the fly is directly across the current from you, you'll have to mend almost constantly. As the fly drifts downstream a few feet from straight across, continue to mend and begin feeding slack back into the drift. You might be able to fish a free drift from 45 degrees upstream to 45 degrees downstream. At that point, let the fly move into its swing, but continue mending to slow it to a natural swimming speed.

**On the water.** Takes might come at any point during the drift and swing. When the fly is on the swing, you should feel the fish. On the upper end of the presentation, however, when the fly is drifting freely, you'll have to watch carefully for signs of line or leader movement contrary to the current. Often you'll feel a slow and slight uptake of pressure transmitted to the rod tip, in which case you'll want to be patient until you feel the weight of the fish and then set the hook.

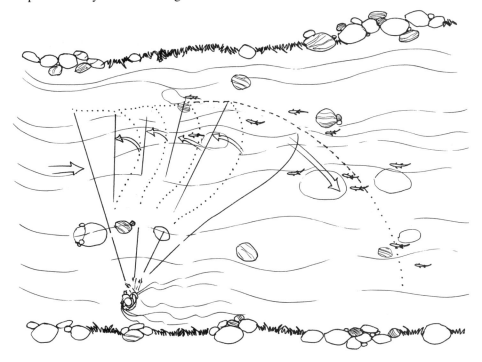

**The trout's point of view.** The trout will see the fly as a drifting natural in the upper part of the drift and as a swinging, animated insect in the lower part. This method is an excellent way to cover the water as it offers the trout their choice of presentations on a single cast.

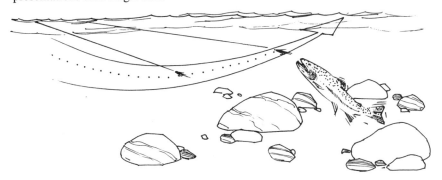

**RIG:**        FLOATING LINE AND STANDARD LEADER
**Method:**     Leisenring lift

**Situations to solve.** The Leisenring lift, detailed in James Leisenring and V. S. "Pete" Hidy's 1941 book, *The Art of Tying the Wet Fly,* is one of the best-known wet-fly fishing methods, and yet Hidy told me that it was a peripheral method that the famous Leisenring used only rarely. Since the lift was the only method recorded in their little but valuable book, everybody got the idea it was the only method Leisenring used. The lift is designed to solve a narrow situation—when you find a visible fish, or an obvious lie, in water no more than 3 feet deep with an even set of currents delivering food downstream to it—but it can produce big trout for you. Because the method depends on sinking an unweighted wet fly to the depth of the trout's lie, the area of unobstructed water upstream must be from 5 to 15 or even 20 feet long.

The Leisenring lift is similar to the Sawyer-induced take nymph method except that the Sawyer trout is suspended and feeding during a hatch, while the Leisenring trout is holding along the bottom and feeding on the drift.

**Tuning the rig.** For maximum sink rate, select a wet fly tied sparsely on a heavy hook. Though Leisenring never weighted his flies, he probably wouldn't object to placing a small tungsten bead on the body of one of his wets. Such experiments have decreased the length of smooth water needed to sink the fly and thus made the lift more deadly by opening up the number of situations the method solves. Lengthen your leader with a 3-foot tippet of the finest material you dare to use against the size trout you've either spotted or suspect is in the lie you're fishing.

**Position and presentation.** Take up your position at a 30- to 60-degree angle off to the side of the trout and upstream from it. Because the water you're fishing will tend to be smooth rather than rough, move into this position carefully to avoid pushing wading waves over the lie or the trout. If a trout becomes aware of your presence, it might not move, but it most likely will not come to your fly.

Calculate the distance upstream required to sink the fly to the trout's level by the time it reaches the trout's position, and make your presentation there. How far you place your fly above the trout will depend on the sink rate of the fly, the speed of the current, and the depth of the lie. The slower the sink and the faster and deeper the water, the farther upstream you must cast. The faster the sink and the slower and shallower the water, the closer you can place your fly to the trout. The most common placement is 5 to 15 feet upstream from the trout

**Control of the drift.** Allow the fly to sink for almost the entire range of its drift. Follow the line, leader, and fly downstream with your rod tip. If your line begins to belly, make upstream mends to keep it from lifting the fly prematurely. When you either sense or see that the fly has reached the position of the fish, stop the rod and lift the tip a foot or two. The fly will move right in front of the nose of the trout. If you see the trout take it, see the trout move, or notice the white flash of the trout's open mouth, set the hook.

**On the water.** The Leisenring lift is generally considered a one-shot method to be used on visible trout. But if you mistake the sink rate of the fly on the first cast, you'll have to cast again and again until you get the fly to the precise depth at the exact right moment. This method can also be used to fish blind to an obvious lie or down the length of a flat with smooth currents and shallow lies. Start at the upper end, and work your way down, executing lifts as you go and taking a step after each presentation.

**The trout's point of view.** The trout, holding along the bottom and feeding on the drift, will observe lots of items entering its view: leaves, watersoaked twigs, and other detritus. If your fly suddenly takes life and lifts toward the surface in front of the fish, the trout's reaction is almost certain to be a take.

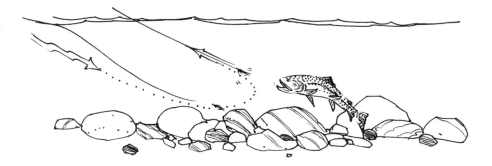

**Situations to solve.** Pete Hidy described his subsurface swing to me in person and touched on it in his notes in the 1971 second edition of *The Art of Tying the Wet Fly and Fishing the Flymph.* I combined what he told me and what he wrote in a detailed description of the method in my 1995 book, *Wet Flies.* The subsurface swing, which Hidy used more often than the more famous Leisenring lift, works well during hatches.

The subsurface swing is useful when you encounter trout working caddis pupae or adults, mayfly emergers, or ovipositing stonefly adults in relatively smooth water, whether it's spring creek and tailwater flats or the calm stretches of freestone streams. You'll almost always see insects in the air and on the water, and the trout will be taking naturals so close to the surface that it appears they're taking floating naturals. If you observe a few insects floating safely through the rises, you'll know the trout are feeding subsurface. Use the subsurface swing to single out a trout and bring it to your wet fly.

**Tuning the rig.** Your rig for the subsurface swing should be exactly what you would use to fish a dry fly over rising trout on the same smooth water. That's fortunate since you will almost always resort to this method after you've tried dry flies and been snubbed. Nip off the dry and tie on a flymph—a wingless wet fly—that is close in size and color to the naturals on the water, and you're tuned.

**Position and presentation.** Take up your position 30 to 50 feet upstream from the trout you've singled out, and 10 to 20 feet off to one side, for a casting angle that is more downstream than across. If you're working a pod of trout, begin with a cast at the upper end and inside edge of the pod to avoid spooking the other fish with your presentation.

Make your cast 3 to 5 feet to the far side of the trout and a foot or two upstream from it. The fibrous flymph will almost always float; give it a sharp tug the instant it lands to pull it under the water. Then follow the line and fly with your rod tip, allowing the fly to swing slowly in front of the fish. Usually you'll see a bulging rise and feel the take at the same instant. If the fish does not take, make the next cast the same distance to the far side of it, but a foot or so downstream closer to it. If you fish out several casts without a take, move on to another trout, or experiment with smaller and drabber wet flies until you find one the trout will accept. If you can capture a specimen of what is on the water, choose a fly closer to its size and color.

**Control of the drift.** Your position and presentation will control your initial short swing. If a pod of trout is feeding consistently, you might want to pick out a single fish and direct your cast to it and then fish out the rest of the drift and swing through the pod if the first fish refuses. Your target fish might fail to notice the fly or be busy taking a natural when your wet swings by, so fishing out the swing might bring a different trout to the fly and will keep you from lifting the fly over the head of another trout, thereby spooking the entire pod.

**On the water.** Be careful not to send wading waves over the trout you're approaching, and do not line it or place the fly onto the water so close to the fish that when you tug your fly under the surface it might spook the trout. When you hook a trout at the edge of a pod, try to coax it gently away from the rest of the fish before you engage it with the butt of the rod. You might be able to catch two or three trout before the pod ceases feeding, and you'll either have to rest the pod for half an hour or so or go and find another.

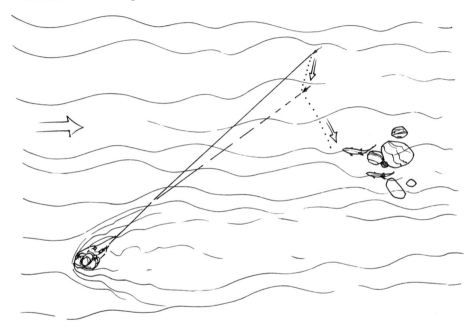

**The trout's point of view.** The fly swings slowly downstream and across, into the sight of the feeding trout. Choose your position and casting angle so that the swim of the fly is at about the same speed that a natural would move. If your wet fly dashes into the trout's area of vision like a minnow might, it's more likely to frighten the trout than fool it.

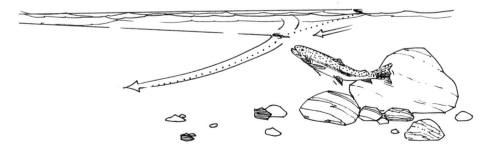

**RIG:      FLOATING LINE AND STANDARD LEADER**
**Method:   Upstream soft-hackle to small pools**

**Situations to solve.** Often on stairstep mountain and foothill creeks and small streams, trout are hungry but bashful about rising to the surface to take dry flies. On bright days when sunshine strikes down into the pools, trout rush to your standard drys with splashy rises but turn away at the last instant. You set the hook, but the fly blows over your shoulder. You think you've been too slow or too fast, but it's not your fault: The trout has changed its mind.

On such days, the simple switch to a soft-hackled wet fly—which might as easily be a lightly weighted nymph—fished exactly as you would a dry fly, will solve the situation. I enjoy this method most on water where pools alternate with plunges, sometimes so steeply that when you fish out one pool and move up, your head and shoulders are level with the next pool. The method, which originated on Scottish streams with small riffles or broken, boulder-studded runs, is effective on streams of just that sort.

**Tuning the rig.** The leader should be just longer than the 7- to 8-foot rod you would already be using on your favorite small stream. I usually use a 7 1/2-foot base leader in 4X, and add 2 feet of 5X. If you expect larger trout, stick to a 3X base leader and 4X tippet. Use size 10 to 14 soft-hackled wet flies tied on dry-fly hooks. You don't want them to sink more than a few inches. My favorite is a size 10 Partridge & Yellow; its size and brightness allow me to see it on short casts, which means I'll see the trout rush and strike it. You can't beat the excitement. Other soft-hackles, such as the Partridge & Orange or March Brown Spider, will take as many trout, but I can't see them as well in the water.

**Position and presentation.** Creep into position at the lower end of the pool you want to fish. Use boulders for concealment, stoop, or stay on your knees. Don't stand in plain sight, and don't wear bright clothes or a flashy hat. Make your first cast with just a rod length of line. You'll find that the tailout of a tiny pool almost always holds a trout or two. You won't see them until your bright fly drifts toward them just inches deep, but one will materialize, lift up, and intercept the fly. Small-stream soft-hackling on bright days is the most visible of all fishing. When you set the hook, watch for the shock of surprise it sends the trout.

As you work your casts farther up into the pool, you might see clouds of trout dashing out of their hidden lies to compete for your fly. Many times, the largest trout will get there first. If it doesn't, and you refrain from setting the hook, that big one might take the fly after a smaller trout has spit it out. You'll be able to cover most pools from one position. If the pool is too long to cover with 20- to at most 30-foot casts, move up rather than casting farther than you're able to follow the fly's drift.

**Control of the drift.** Gather slack as the line drifts toward you, just as you would when fishing a dry fly. Watch your line or leader tip where it enters the water. If it twitches or darts, set the hook. You have a trout.

**On the water.** The original soft-hackle anglers, on Yorkshire border streams between England and Scotland, used two-fly, three-fly, and even gang setups to take more than one trout on a cast. Hooking multiple fish with this method is more than possible on mountain creeks and small foothill streams. If you ever want to see what it feels like to play two or three trout at once, this method is your best opportunity.

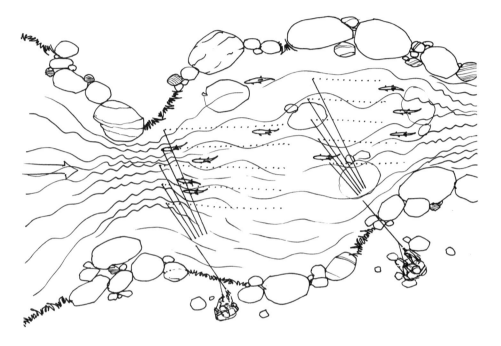

**The trout's point of view.** The trout sees the soft-hackle drifting along naturally at the same speed as the current, sometimes upright and looking like a mushroom or opened umbrella, but always with its long and soft fibers working in the water. To a trout, the soft-hackle looks alive and safe to eat.

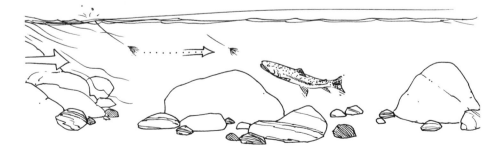

| RIG: | FLOATING LINE AND STANDARD LEADER |
|------|-----------------------------------|
| Method: | Soft-hackling eddies |

**Situations to solve.** On large streams and small to large rivers, you'll find eddies wherever a point juts out into the current and the flow reverses itself to fill the void. Eddies are gathering places for an abundance of insects of all sorts: Mayflies, caddis, stoneflies, terrestrials, emergers, and adults will be trapped on the surface or just beneath it, twirled endlessly around, often with foam and bits of leaves, twigs, and other detritus. Trout gather in these eddies and feed at complete leisure on whatever is trapped there, whether it's on the surface or sunk.

Because your cast invariably must cross at least two or three currents of different speeds, the currents will tug the line and leader in separate directions. Since it's almost impossible to get a drag-free drift with a dry fly in such places, try using small to tiny soft-hackled wets, which resemble a lot of what's rotating around that smorgasbord. Small amounts of drag, far from killing your chances, can animate the wet fly and make it look alive and enticing to trout in an eddy.

**Tuning the rig.** Rig as you would to fish a dry fly in a similar situation. The leader should be the length of a long rod plus 3 to 4 feet of fine tippet; 5X is the standard in eddies, and 6X is useful if the trout are spooky and the insects tiny. Your flies should be size 16 to 20. If a natural insect, such as a blue-wing olive or black caddis, is dominant, then use a soft-hackle the same size and color. If not, then a Hare's Ear soft-hackle or a darker Starling and Herl might work well. If you'd like, try them both on the same tippet.

**Position and presentation.** The shape of the eddy will determine what position you can take to place yourself within casting distance of the trout. You'll increase your chances if you can get within 20 to 30 feet of the fish, but stay low and keep your rod movements low to the water. If you have options, then choose a position that places you behind the working trout to reduce the chance that they will spot you.

If you can see the trout working the eddy, make your cast so the currents will deliver the fly to them just as it would with a dry fly. Single out a trout—perhaps the largest!—and direct your casts and drifts to it, rather than to the pod at random. At the last moment before you cast, try wetting the fly and a couple of feet of tippet to be sure they sink rather than get stranded on the surface. Place your cast within 2 to 5 feet of the trout, depending on the amount of seething in the upwelling. Fish the soft-hackle to the trout and then through the eddy on a slow and natural drift, letting the current animate it and move it slightly but never fast. If you get drag that is dramatically fast, lift the fly and present it again.

**Control of the drift.** Most of your control comes from the cast. But by lifting or lowering your rod, you might be able to delay drag or add movement to the fly just when you think a trout might see it. If the current catches your line and begins to belly it, lift it up into a mend, whichever way the confusing eddy directs you to do it. You can also feed line to get a longer drift.

**On the water.** When you hook a trout and cannot quickly coax it out of its pod, it will spook the rest of the fish in the eddy. Sometimes you can let the fish respond to the sting of the hook and dash out of the eddy at its own discretion, before you engage it with any strength. If this happens, you can play it away from the others, and you might be able to catch two or even three fish before you have to rest the eddy or move on to another.

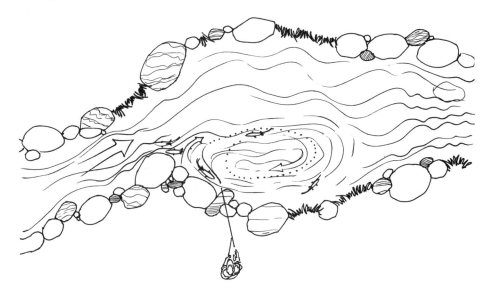

**The trout's point of view.** As all of the other bits of food are moving around in its view, the trout must see the fly swirling around the eddy and being slightly animated. The soft-hackle will help you avoid the problems of drag that plague the dry fly, but you still have to keep drag to a minimum.

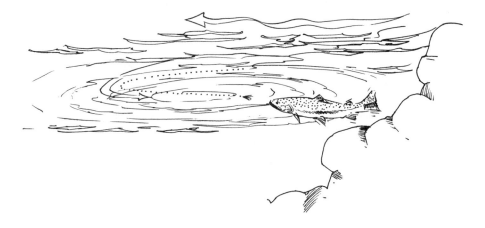

## RIG:  WET-TIP/BELLY/HEAD OR FULL-SINK LINE

**Purpose.** This rig, much like the similar wet-tip, wet-belly, wet-head, or full-sink line system for nymphing, is designed to get a fly down in the water column farther than would be possible with a floating line. The line you choose, and the method you use to fish it, dictates that depth, whether it's a couple of feet beneath the surface or right along the bottom. Any of the sinking lines, from the wet-tip to the fastest full-sink, serves the purpose of getting a wet fly, or pair of them, through the surface and sunk a few inches in fast water, so that the fly will fish without riding on top and creating a wake.

Most of the time, your goal will be to get your flies into the upper couple of feet of the water column or the 1 or 2 feet just up from the bottom. Trout spend most of their time either near the surface, where they feed on all sorts of mayfly, midge, and caddis emergers on their way to the top, or near the bottom, where they feed on insects staging for their trip to the top and bottom-dwelling insects that lose their grip and get caught in the natural drift.

**History/origins.** You could go back in time and discover that this rig might have been the earliest trout-fishing rig. Wet flies clearly came before dries, and the earliest braided horsehair lines, which were later replaced by silk lines, were likely similar to today's intermediate lines or slow-sinkers. Anyone old enough to remember the first coated lines will recall how difficult it was to keep them afloat when fishing dry flies. If they were not constantly dressed, they would become the sorts of lines at the shallow end of the types used for the rig we're discussing at the moment.

**Knots and notes.** The leader is best built around a 7½-foot tapered base leader, either left at its original length for shallow work with slow-sinking lines or cut back as short as 4 or 5 feet for deeper sinking lines, with an appropriate tippet added. Leader and tippet sections should be tied together with blood or surgeon's knots. If you're cutting your leader short and adding tippet, and the sizes are more than 1 or 2X separate in diameter, then always use the surgeon's knot. Tie the fly or flies on with the improved clinch or Duncan loop. If you use a dropper, either leave the stouter tag of your tippet knot long enough or tie the point tippet directly to the hook bend of the dropper fly.

**Adjustments for conditions.** Almost all of your adjustments will come in the line you choose. When fishing lakes from a boat or other floating device, it's easy to carry a set of spools with spare lines ready to go, but on a stream or river, where you normally leave the vehicle behind and go forth with everything in a vest, a set of spare spools would overload you. Typically the only option you'll carry, unless you're on a familiar bit of water and know you need a specific sinking line, will be a fast-sinking 10-foot wet-tip line. In a perfect world, you would adjust for conditions by choosing from an array of all sinking line types. But in reality, you will choose between sticking with your floating line or switching to your wet-tip.

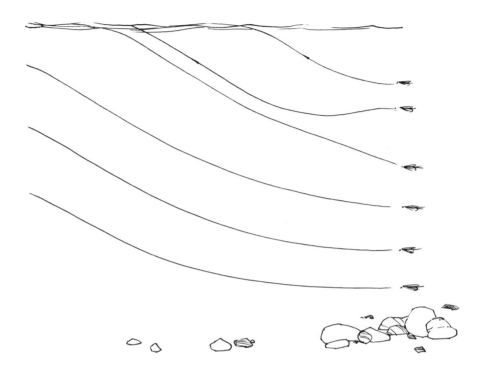

**Rules for the rig.** The only rule for the rig is to shorten your leader as you go to faster sinking lines. With a wet-tip or slow-sinker, use the full 7$\frac{1}{2}$-foot base leader. With a wet-belly, wet-head, or extra-fast full-sink line, shorten the leader to between 5 and 6 feet.

**Appropriate flies.** All sorts of wet flies are appropriate for sinking lines: winged wets, flymphs, soft-hackles, and grand old Woolly Worms. The rig can be used with nymphs as well as wets. The difference is that with nymphs you'll try to find the bottom and fish your fly or flies either handtwisted in slow water or tumbled along the bottom in faster water, while the goal with wets is to fish them on the swing.

## RIG:       WET-TIP/BELLY/HEAD OR FULL-SINK LINE
## Method:    Mended middepths swing

**Situations to solve.** Use a sinking line rig to fish wet flies whenever you encounter water that is faster and/or deeper than you can cover well with wets fished on a floating line. Although that will almost always occur on a large stream or small to large river, the defining factor is not the size of the water, but the need to get your wet fly deeper in its swing. Sometimes you'll want to make sure it penetrates the film and doesn't ride on the surface where it would leave a wake. A sinking line can also solve situations in which you want to fish your wet fly, or pair of them, deeper in the water column, most likely near the bottom.

**Tuning the rig.** Choose the wet-tip, wet-belly, wet-head, or full-sinking line in a sink rate that will deliver your wets to where you want them in the water you're fishing. If it's a foothill stream or river with a modest current, and you want your flies 1 foot or at most 2 feet deep, then the wet-tip, wet-belly, or full-sink line in a slow sink rate will do. If the water is 4 to 6 feet deep, and you want your fly all the way down to the bottom, then a wet-head or full-sink line in an extra-fast sink rate might be necessary. But such bottom fishing falls more in the realm of indicator and shot nymphing than it does the wet fly.

As you go to longer heads and faster sink rates, shorten your leader from 8 feet or so to between 4 and 6 feet.

**Position and presentation.** Usually, your goal will be to cast out into fairly fast water and fish your wet fly or flies on the swing through the fast water and across the seam between fast and slow water. Because trout hang out in the highest soft water that they can find in the length of a riffle or run, you want your fly to fish the upper end of the corner where the water type forms. Take your initial position upstream from that corner the distance of a short cast; if you take your position right at the corner, then your first swings will be downstream from the most promising water.

Make your first casts short, down and across the current, and at an angle determined by the speed of the current: the faster the water, the farther downstream; the slower the water, the farther upstream. Let your fly swing down and around, across the seam between fast water and slow, and even hang in the slow water for a moment downstream from you. Don't make the mistake of lifting for the next cast just because the swing has slowed; that is the moment you're most likely to get a hit.

Lengthen each subsequent cast a foot or two, until you've reached the distance you can handle with comfort. Then after fishing out each swing, begin taking a step downstream to fish the next sweep of water until you've covered the length of the water you hope holds trout.

**Control of the drift.** Much of your control depends on choosing the correct angle of your cast. After the line lands, throw an upstream mend at once. Obviously, wet-tip or wet-belly line allows you to do this much more effectively than a wet-head or full-sink line. When using lines with floating running portions, make almost constant mends throughout the swing. With full-sinking lines, once you make that first mend and the line sinks, you can only follow the swing of the line and fly with your rod tip.

**On the water.** Get into the rhythm of the stepping and casting routine. It can be quite pleasant, especially if it is interrupted now and then by a trout swatting your fly. Takes will vary from resounding thuds to sullen pulls to the slow and relentless uptaking of pressure on the line. Your instinct will be to set the hook with a wallop, but refrain from doing so. If a large trout has taken solidly, you might smash your tippet. If the trout has taken with uncertainty, you will pull the fly away from it. Be patient and let most trout hook themselves.

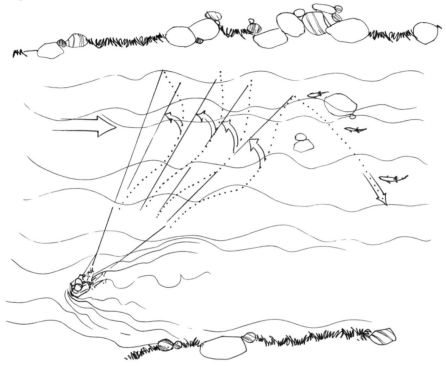

**The trout's point of view.** If you've chosen the right line and the correct casting angle and have mended as much as your line allows you, then your fly should swim into the trout's sight much as a natural might, whether it's in the subsurface zone or along the bottom. The fly should be moving slowly, tethered to the leader and line, rather than racing at an unnatural speed.

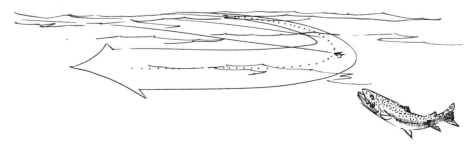

**Situations to solve.** The up-and-across cast, used with a sinking-line rig, solves situations in which you wish to fish wet flies on the bottom of the stream. It can be seen as a continuation of the previous method used to fish wet flies on the down-and-across swing and is also closely related to the Bergman natural drift described for floating lines. The method calls for a relatively broad reach of water 3 to 6 feet deep, with fairly constant currents from side to side, fast but not boisterous. You'll find this method most useful on broad, open riffles, runs, and flats of medium to large trout streams and small rivers. It's less useful on creeks, small streams, and big rivers, and won't work at all in swift water or in currents broken by boulders that could interrupt the sink of the line.

**Tuning the rig.** Select your line sink rate based on the depth and speed of the water you're planning to fish. Because the method depends on almost constant mending and tending of the line, it is easiest to apply with wet-tips and wet-bellies, more difficult with wet-heads, and very difficult with full-sink lines. Shorten the leader to between 4 and 6 feet to keep your wet flies down near the end of the line tip.

**Position and presentation.** Take your initial position at the upper end of the reach of water you want to fish. If the reach has a corner at its head, position yourself so your first casts allow your fly to cross the seam in that corner, not downstream from it. Envision the sweep of water in front of you as bisected by three lines: one at a 90-degree angle straight across the current, another at a 45-degree angle upstream, and the third at a 45-degree angle downstream. Make your cast across the current at the upstream angle, and allow the fly to sink until it is straight across from your casting position. Turn and follow the drift until the line cuts downstream at the lower angle. Then begin coaxing the fly into its swing across the current until it crosses the seam between fast and slow water downstream from your position.

Vary your casting angles depending on the way your fly fishes. Sometimes you'll have to cast higher than 45-degrees up into the current or lower toward that 90-degree angle across it. Fish out each cast, and take a single step downstream before making the next cast until you cover the length of water you believe might hold trout.

**Control of the drift.** Make mends and lift your rod during the drift from the upstream cast to the angle straight across. At this point, presume the fly has reached the bottom. Lower the rod, follow the fly, and feed slack through the drift to the downstream 45-degree angle. Extend this effective portion of the drift as far as you can, and once you can no longer extend it, let the line draw the fly into a swing across the current, following it the entire way with your rod tip.

**On the water.** Your goal is to get the fly, or brace of them, on the bottom or as near to it as possible. In truth, the most dense sinking line will not get your unweighted wet flies much deeper than 6 feet before you lose control fishing with them. This wet-fly method is best reserved for modest depths of 2 to 4 feet. Beyond that depth, apply nymph or streamer methods. Fishing should be pleasant, and though you might gain a few fish, you won't gain much pleasure trying to fish wet flies deeper than they're designed to be used.

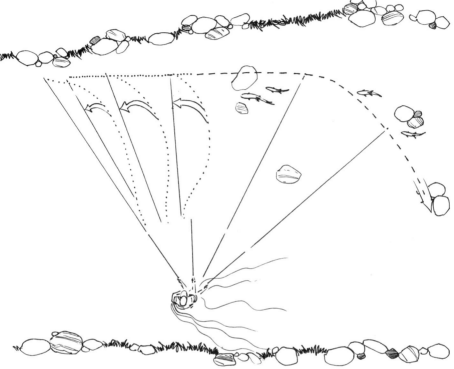

**The trout's point of view.** Your flies should come swimming along on the current into a trout's view, just inches above the bottom, perhaps alternately swirling aimlessly and then animated by the pressure of the line tip and leader. They should look alive to trout but should not be swimming with greater agility and strength than a natural insect would.

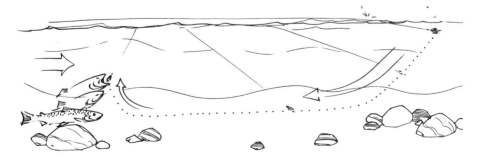

# CHAPTER 8

# Rigs and Methods for Streamers in Moving Water

The use of streamers has been narrowed in recent years to a couple of classic situations: fishing in waters roiled by spring runoff and pounding the banks of big rivers from a boat, usually for big trout. Although excellent ways to fish streamers, restricting their use to these situations unnecessarily limits the other ways that streamers can help you catch more, and very often larger, trout. Small streamers, for example, are effective in low, clear water, especially when trout are prowling to hunt or just hanging along thin edges and on tailouts, waiting for luckless baitfish and sculpins to make mistakes. Larger streamers can be used to probe the depths of big runs and pools, whether the water is dirty or not. A heavily weighted streamer, smacked into pools on small to medium-size streams, can startle trout into attacking at any time of year and in any set of water conditions.

**Selecting streamers.** The first consideration in deciding which streamer to fish is its size. Streamers range from the size of bats and mice, 1/0 and 2/0, through the more normal size range for sculpins and baitfish, size 2 to 8, down to the less common but surprisingly useful fry and tadpole types the size of wet flies, 10 to 14. Choose the size based on the size trout you expect to be in the water you're on, the size naturals that trout eat in that water, and, perhaps to the greatest extent, the size outfit you're armed with to propel the streamers.

If you're on a small to medium-size stream and expect trout of modest size, use smaller streamers, since that's the size bites such trout are most accustomed to eating. If you're on big water, full of big trout that have become piscivorous—fish making a living eating other fish—then try streamers in the largest sizes. If you're in any doubt, go smaller than you think you should, and you'll have it about right.

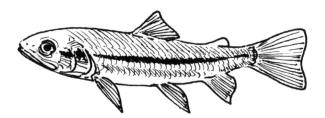

The second consideration is the amount of weight on the streamer. Weight is dictated by the depths you want to attain or the speed with which you want to get the streamer down. If you're fishing shallow water, just a few turns of lead on the hook shank will help the streamer break through the surface and begin fishing right away. If you're trying for the bottom in deep or fast water, you'll need a layer and perhaps a second deck of lead wraps on the shank. When you're fishing sharply dug banks from a passing boat, then you need a conehead or lead-eye streamer to pitch down at once.

The third consideration for selecting a streamer is the abundance or lack of a predominant food form in the water. If sculpins or mad-toms are thick, use a Muddler Minnow or Marabou Muddler. If dace and minnows are more abundant, try a hairwing or featherwing imitation. Use a Woolly Bugger streamer if leeches or pollywogs are most common. If trout are onto chubs, suckers, and other big fare, try something like the Zonker.

**Choosing tackle.** The size of the fly, the amount of weight on it, and the size and depth of the water you want to fish all add up to dictate what tackle you select. If you're planning to use big, heavily weighted streamers on big water, you need a 7- or 8-weight rod and line to propel them. If you're going to use the more normal run of streamers on streams and small rivers, you will be able to use a 5- or 6-weight outfit. If you're like most of us, and go astream armed with only a single light rod, generally in the 4- to 5-weight range, then your streamer box should be filled with small to medium-size streamers.

When fishing from a boat, keep a spare rod rigged just for streamers. Your boat bag can contain the wide array of lines, floating and all sorts of sinking lines and perhaps a range of shooting heads. When my friends and I float big rivers, we typically keep a single streamer rod rigged with a wet-tip or wet-head line. Then we take turns rowing and banging banks and probing riffle corners. At anchorings, we get out to wade and fish with our smaller outfits.

**Types of streamers.** Streamers come in a wide range of sizes, but think of them in a narrow set of styles. The Muddler and related Marabou Muddler have thick hair heads that displace water and make noise as they swim. They are excellent sculpin imitations and attractors. Hairwing and featherwing streamers have a much more slender profile and make good minnow and dace imitations. Woolly Buggers, with their marabou tails, look like leeches and pollywogs on the gallop, but they also incite trout into striking because they look like something alive and escaping. Such heavy streamers as the Zonker get down to the farthest depths and look like a variety of foods trout find down there.

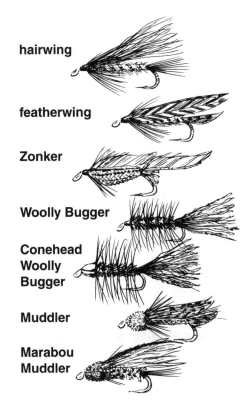

hairwing

featherwing

Zonker

Woolly Bugger

Conehead Woolly Bugger

Muddler

Marabou Muddler

## RIG: FLOATING, WET-TIP/BELLY/HEAD, AND FULL-SINK LINES

**Purpose.** A range of lines allows you to fish your streamers at any depth, and this rig takes into account the full range of standard fly lines for fishing streamers. The floating line is fine for fishing streamers shallow, and it can be used to fish heavily weighted streamers deep in slow water. It is also the standard choice for casting streamers to the banks from a moving boat; the floating line lets you lift the fly quickly and place your next cast without hesitation.

The wet-tip (10-feet), wet-belly (20-feet), and wet-head (30-feet) all have sinking front ends with floating running line. Each type comes in slow-sinking through extra-fast sinking. The fastest sinking wet-tip takes the fly down quickly, but the wet-belly and wet-head are also most useful when you want to have the fastest sink rate you can find. If you can use one of these sinking/floating combination lines to solve a situation, you'll find you have far more control than a full-sink line, because you can mend the combination line.

Full-sink lines come in a variety of sink rates. They are best on waters where you are casting over a broad expanse of currents flowing at the same speed, and therefore they can eliminate the need for mending.

**History/origins.** The history of the full range of streamer fishing tactics is tied together with the development of the full range of sinking line types. Few books have been written about streamer fishing. Joe Bates's 1950 *Streamer Fly Tying and Fishing* has little reference to any but floating lines, and John Merwin's 1991 *Streamer-Fly Fishing* contains detailed information on all line types. All of the progress in lines as applied to streamer fishing is encapsulated in those two books. Both are classics; Bates's is an excellent history, Merwin's the more useful primer.

**Knots and notes.** When streamer fishing, the first decision is choosing an appropriate line for the depth you'd like to fish your streamer. Select a line type and sink rate that gets your streamer down to where you want it and lets you fish it with the amount of control, mostly mending, that you need.

Use the blood knot or surgeon's knot to fasten leader and tippet sections together. If you're connecting sections with more than .002-inch difference in diameter, use the surgeon's knot. Either the improved clinch knot or Duncan loop can be used to attach the fly to the tippet. If you'd like the fly to have a bit more freedom in its drift, then use the loop knot. If you'll be fishing the fly on a tight line, then the improved clinch is a good choice.

**Adjustments for conditions.** After selecting the most appropriate line for the water you're fishing, you then must decide on the amount of weight on the fly and the length of the leader based on the conditions. Determine the amount of weight according to the depth you'd like to attain and the speed with which you'd like the fly to sink. Shortening the leader as you go toward faster sinking lines keeps your streamer from riding up above the line and thus defeating the purpose of a line that plummets.

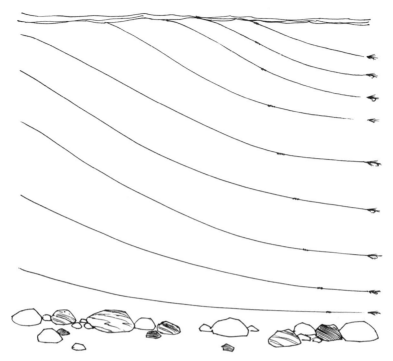

**Rules for the rig.** Streamer fishing can be looked at from two directions, both correct. In the first direction, you choose the streamer and amount of weight on it to suit the water size and depth and the size trout you expect to catch. Then you must choose the line type to reach that depth and finally a rod to propel the weight of the line and fly you've decided upon. From the second direction, you are already armed in a stream when you reach the conclusion that you need to fish a streamer. Be sure to choose a fly size and weight that the outfit you're holding will handle. If not, you're in for a long, uncomfortable day. No matter which way you approach your decision, a long rod, $8^1/2$ to $9^1/2$ feet, will be better than a short one.

**Appropriate flies.** You'll want a broad range of lines to cover fishing the full spectrum of streamer types. Think in terms of lightly weighted Muddler types for fishing shallow; moderately weighted Woolly Buggers for fishing water in the medium range of depths of, say, 2 to 4 feet; and Zonker types for fishing deep. But this is a generalization, and any streamer, when placed on the appropriate line, can be fished at any depth. If a natural food is abundant in the water you're fishing, then choose a streamer that at least roughly resembles it.

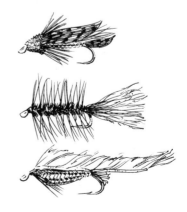

**Situations to solve.** This standard streamer method works best in medium-size streams to the largest rivers. Because the method calls for cross-stream casts, it does not work well on creeks and small streams where upstream or downstream casts are standard. One way to apply this method is to work from one side of the head of a small pool and drop a short cast to the other side across the entering current, which delivers the streamer downstream a short way before tightening the line and causing the streamer to swing across. However, the most common way to use this method is to take a position next to a fairly broad sweep of current, cast across it, and fish the streamer on a swing down and around below you.

The method is excellent on all larger water types, from riffles and runs to the current tongues of pools. Use it to explore all the water down the length of a stream or river, when you don't know where trout might be holding. You can fish from just subsurface to down near the bottom, though the deeper you get a streamer, the more often you'll draw trout to it.

**Tuning the rig.** When tuning your rig for this method, you'll often be limited to the floating line and wet-tip that you carry on a spare spool. The floating/sinking wet-tip will almost always be your best bct, except on the shallowest water. If you have a full range of sinking line types available, choose the one that gives you the right sink rate and the amount of control over the line that you need. Be sure to shorten your leader as you go to faster sinking lines.

**Position and presentation.** Your position for this method is the same as it would be to fish nymphs or wet flies on the swing: a few feet upstream from the highest water that you want your streamer to fish through. You probably will have to step in at the edge of the riffle upstream from the corner it forms when it plunges into a pool downstream.

Make your initial casts short and at an appropriate angle to give you the sink time and swing that you desire. Most of the time your cast will be at an angle from almost straight across the stream in slow water to just a few feet out from straight downstream in very fast water. If you are trying to reach the bottom, you might lay your casts up and across the current to give it 10 to 30 feet of sinking drift, before it reaches the depth you want. When it does, it's time to bring the line tight to the fly and coax the streamer into its swing.

Lengthen your casts by a foot or two until you've reached the distance you can cover comfortably; then begin taking a step between casts. On pools of modest size, it might be better to fish all the water that you can from the first position and then move downstream to a new position and cover all the water you can from there.

**Control of the drift.** During the swing, if you feel the streamer is moving too fast, mend the line to slow it. Experiment between the standard swing and staccato swing. On one cast, let the streamer swing without action. On the next cast, use a 6- to 12-inch rhythmic pulsing of your rod tip to give the fly a jerky, staccato swim across the current. If trout prefer one swing over the other, stick to it and forget the other.

**On the water.** Be sure your streamer swings out of the fast water, through the seam at its edge, and into the slower water downstream from you. Many of your hits will come as the fly crosses that seam. If you feel a pluck—this is true whether you're fishing a streamer, wet fly, or nymph on the swing—repeat the cast two or three more times, throw in a mend to slow the fly right where you felt the tap, and show the opposite action, staccato or standard swing, before taking that next step downstream. Trout will often come back.

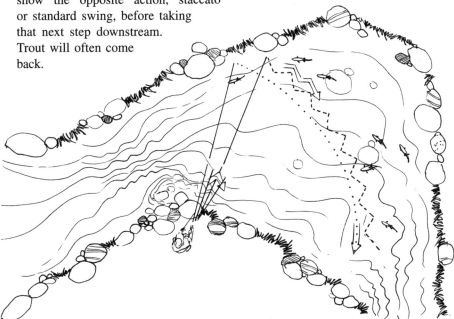

**The trout's point of view.** The streamer should swim into the trout's view temptingly, one time without hesitation, the next time in a series of starts and stops. It should be moving as fast as a natural baitfish would swim. If standard retrieves don't stir the trout, try using a stripping retrieve to race it.

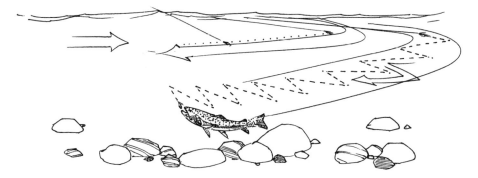

**RIG:**     **FLOATING, WET-TIP/BELLY/HEAD, AND FULL-SINK LINES**
**Method: Upstream streamer**

**Situations to solve.** Most of the time, you'll use the upstream streamer method on creeks and small streams, where because of their narrowness, they resist the standard cross-stream swing. On this type of water, baitfish, displaced by predators or more aggressive members of their own kind, often flee downstream, and trout are accustomed to seeing them rushing in that direction. Injured baitfish also tumble downstream with the current into the sight of hungry trout. Although the upstream streamer method can be effective in water of almost any size, it's easiest to apply, and most useful, on smaller waters rather than larger rivers.

The method is also effective in small to medium-size runs with protruding or submerged boulders, where the currents glance and are redirected downstream but are not fast enough to form surging pocket water. Because trout hang around the boulders, it's productive to work your way upstream, casting streamers up and allowing them to swim and stumble back downstream toward you among the obvious holding lies.

**Tuning the rig.** On creeks and the smallest streams, a floating line and leader the length of the rod, or even a bit longer, will work fine with a weighted streamer. On medium-size and larger streams, your wet-tip line will almost always be better, except where the water spreads out and remains as shallow as it might be in a creek. On small rivers and the shallow parts of large ones, a wet-belly line might help you achieve the depth you want, but usually the wet-tip line will be all you need to provide the control you want over the downstream progress of your streamer.

**Position and presentation.** Take your initial position at the downstream end of the pool, riffle, run, or whatever sort of water you're fishing. In a typical situation, you work your way upstream with 30- to 45-foot casts, rarely longer, probing readable lies and fishing most of the water between them. You might have to shift positions from side to side to cover all of the water surrounding a protruding boulder. Don't forget that one of the most likely lies is directly in front of the boulder, in the soft water deflected upward by its leading edge. Your streamer should swim or tumble down the length of the current seam behind a boulder, fish along each side of it, and drift or swim downstream into the sight of any trout holding in front of the boulder.

If you're fishing upstream through unfeatured water, then you'll want to cover the water with a fan of casts, working from one bank to the other if the water is narrow or covering all of the water you can reach if the water is wide.

**Control of the drift.** There are two ways to fish out an upstream streamer cast: either faster than the current, using a downstream retrieve that makes the fly appear to be swimming, or the same speed as the current, with the fly tumbling along on or just above the bottom. You won't know which is most effective until you've tried them both. To accomplish the swim, give the fly a few feet to sink, then keep your rod tip low to the water, and retrieve using strips with your line hand. For the tumbled streamer, merely gather slack as it forms, and slowly raise your rod tip as the fly approaches your position.

**On the water.** If you're retrieving your streamer downstream, you'll have no trouble knowing when you've had a take: You will feel a thump. If you're letting your streamer tumble downstream, more or less on a free drift, you won't always feel when a trout hits. Watch your line tip if you're fishing a floater, or observe the point where your line enters the water if you're fishing a wet-tip or wet-belly line. If the line tip darts or you see any signs of a stoppage in the drift of the line, raise your rod and set the hook. Often the downstream pressure of the line will hold the streamer in a trout's mouth long enough for you to pull the hook home.

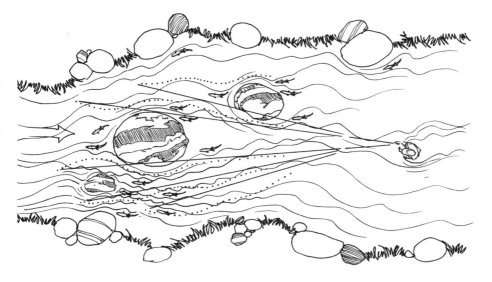

**The trout's point of view.** Your streamer either swims into the trout's field of view, looking like a sculpin or baitfish displaced from upstream and fleeing downstream in a frantic search for a new hiding place, or it stumbles along the bottom, looking like a sculpin or baitfish that has been injured upstream and is tumbling toward its fate downstream.

**RIG:      FLOATING, WET-TIP/BELLY/HEAD, AND FULL-SINK LINES**
**Method:  High-sticking plunge pools and pockets**

**Situations to solve.** High-sticking streamers is effective on any size water, from stairstep mountain creeks and small streams to high-gradient sections of mountain and foothill streams and rivers. It is more effective the farther you go toward the headwaters of any river system, but even mature rivers in flat country have sections that tilt down or cut through lava flows and boulder gardens, forming pocket water. In most turbulent water, it's not difficult to read the more promising lies, but it is difficult to fish them.

To fish streamers effectively in such water, whether it's large or small, you need to get in close, cast short with a heavily weighted fly, and let it plunge close to the bottom. Then steer it, coax it, and otherwise lead it through a drift where bottom-hugging trout can see it.

**Tuning the rig.** You'll want a long rod, $8^1/2$ to $9^1/2$ feet, and preferably at least 6- or 7-weight, but your standard stream 4- or 5-weight will work if you're careful to keep your casting loops open. The line for smaller water should be a floater, with a leader the length of the rod or a bit shorter. If you're fishing a creek or small stream with a short rod, use size 8 or 10 flies and a short and stout leader. On larger water, a wet-tip line of the heaviest density will work best, though even on some large streams the pockets will be shallow enough to fish with a floating line. A good rule would be to start with the floater and go to the wet-tip if you feel it's necessary, but shorten your leader to around 6 feet if you do. Larger lead-eyed and conehead streamers are excellent for big water.

**Position and presentation.** Move in as near to a lie as you can. On a small stream, cast your fly into the riffle feeding a pool, and let it wash down into the depths. Once it is in the pool, animate it, leading it across the pool. On the first cast, try to fish it from one corner pocket to the other. Each subsequent cast should fish the fly through the pool, directly under the current tongue, a foot or two farther downstream.

On larger water, take a position a rod length or at most two from the prospective pocket water lie, off to one side, and closer to the head than to the lower end. Pitch your fly—it's hard to call this casting!—to the water from 2 to 6 feet upstream from where you'd like it to begin fishing. Let it sink freely. When it reaches the water you suspect to hold trout, lift your rod to make a connection from the rod tip through the line and leader to the streamer. Fish out the drift; then pick up and cast again either in the same line or a foot or so farther out. Give the trout several chances to get a look at your streamer. In such rough water, they might not see it on the first pass.

**Control of the drift.** After making connection with the streamer, lift and lower your rod to raise and lower the fly, but do not lift it more than what you think would be a foot off the bottom. If it's not getting down there, it's not fishing. Use small twitch mends upstream and down to reposition the line and redirect the drift of the streamer. Draw the rod tip in the direction you want to coax the fly. In essence, you are steering it through its drift, which is why you often fish it almost directly under your rod tip.

**On the water.** Never try to fish plunge pools and pocket water when you're out of position by using your casting to compensate. Instead, do everything you can to get into the precise spot from which you want to place your cast and direct the drift of your streamer. Wade from position to position to cover each lie, rather than planting yourself in one place and covering all of the water you can from there. At times, in brutal water, you'll be constrained and will have to make a long cast to cover a somewhat distant lie, but realize that your chances of taking trout at that distance are diminished.

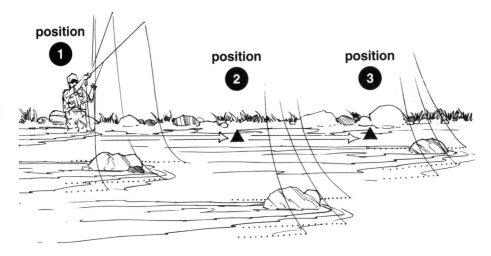

**The trout's point of view.** Your heavy streamer should come darting, tumbling, and swimming amid and beneath the turbulence that surrounds the trout and its somewhat peaceful lie. If you can envision the lie as a big bubble and get your fly to swim into that bubble, you'll catch a trout if one is there. You can bet that if there is such a bubble of comfortable water, a trout will be in it.

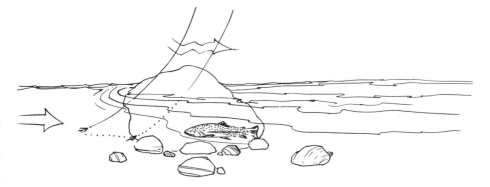

**Situations to solve.** Bank water is known to hold many of the best trout, and a streamer poked into that water is one of the best ways to force them out. Fishing the banks while wading, instead of from a boat, requires a certain set of circumstances. First, you must be able to move freely along the stream, sometimes wading upstream, but more often working your way down. Second, the stream has to be wide enough to cast across—this eliminates creeks and the smallest streams—but not too wide to cast to the far bank from the one you're wading—this eliminates wide and deep rivers. Third, the stream or river must have the type of bank water that holds trout. Such water is earmarked by a modest current to deliver food, moderate depths to provide protection from predation, and shelter—boulders or indentations—where trout can lie without fighting the current.

**Tuning the rig.** Your floating line will be fine for almost all but the steepest banks, and a wet-tip will do for those. You will not need the longer sinking-tips or full-sink lines. On small water, the fly should be weighted enough to penetrate at once and sink a few inches. On larger streams, a heavily weighted fly will get down quicker and bring trout out from some of the dark holes into which they tuck themselves for ambush. Your leader should always be stout, both to land big trout and to tear free from grass and brush. But even with heavy tippets, you'll lose flies in this type of fishing.

**Position and presentation.** Your position should be at almost any angle to the far bank. Make your casts quartering across and down if you're wading downstream, and across and up if you're wading upstream. On most streams and small rivers, take a position that will allow you to work your fly past overhanging branches, bunchgrass clumps, and any other obstructions into the backs of the pockets you want to cover. Your fly should land inches, not feet, from the bank.

As you move, make casts to every 3 to 5 feet of bank water, because it's not always possible to tell exactly where a trout will hold. You might be surprised to find trout, often big ones, over gravel so thin it seems no smart trout would ever expose itself in such a place. Other lies will be obvious, such as backeddies, rootwads, and undercut banks. Hit these carefully on the first cast, and follow up with a few extra casts.

On some streams, you might be able to wade into position out toward the center, and cast to both banks. Although rare, it's fun when you can do it. On most streams, you'll fish outside bends from inside shallows, cross at tailouts where the stream turns, and reposition yourself to fish the next outside bend, where the current tends to be pushiest, the water deepest, the sheltering lies most numerous, and the trout biggest.

**Control of the drift.** Fish out just the first 5 to 10, or at most 20, feet of each cast. Lay the streamer against the bank, and let it sink a second or two. Then draw the line tight and begin stripping the fly out from the bank. If you have no hit—you feel no thump or see no follow—pick up and cast again, either to the same spot if it looks prime or 2 to 5 feet down the bank. If you see a follow, stop the fly and then lift the rod to see if the trout has attacked the streamer while it's sinking.

**On the water.** If the stream you're on holds brown trout, then look for pockets of foam at the edges. These soft spots in the current collect food, are protected from overhead predation, and are excellent ambush points for trout. Smack your streamer right into the foam. If you get a hit, it will be almost instant. On rainbow and cutthroat streams, the fish are more likely to hold in clear currents flowing a foot or two deep along bouldered or undercut banks. Browns will hold there as well.

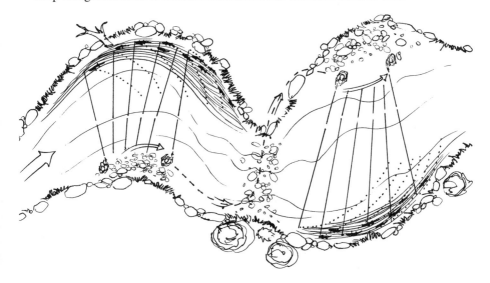

**The trout's point of view.** Your fly will hit the water, sink a bit, and then almost instantly be animated by your retrieve. The trout sees it falling in as if from shore, diving for cover, and then racing away in panic. Hits will come on that initial drop as often as they will on the retrieve. As soon as you get control of your line and take up the slack after a cast, be prepared for a trout to be there fighting the fly.

**RIG:**     **FLOATING, WET-TIP/BELLY/HEAD, AND
FULL-SINK LINES**
**Method:**  **Fishing a streamer from a boat**

**Situations to solve.** When you're floating a river with a guide or friend at the oars, you can fish streamers either as the prime method or as something to keep yourself occupied during floats between places where you anchor and get out to wade and fish. Many rivers are at their best when fished from a boat with either streamers or heavily weighted nymphs, and the situations and methods used to fish the two types of flies are similar. The most productive rivers for fishing streamers from a boat have heavy flows, brushy banks that restrict wading, and currents that dig right into banks that drop off rather steeply. Because dams regulate flows and tend to cause stable banks where brush can grow over eroded undercuts, tailwaters are often the best streamer rivers. But any stream or river big enough to float a boat will have riffle corner, bank, and boulder lies that can be fished with streamers.

**Tuning the rig.** Almost all streamer fishing from a boat can be done with a floating line or fast-sinking wet-tip, preferably 6- to 8-weight. For the floater, the leader should be the length of the rod, the tippet 0 to 3X, and the fly heavily weighted. If you're using the wet-tip, try a moderate to heavy fly, and shorten the stout leader to around 6 feet. A long and slow rod is always best; you don't want to cast tight loops with heavily weighted flies of any kind. If you find yourself fishing streamers with a little less control than you'd like, try overlining your rod one or even two weights. Not only will the extra weight slow down the rod, but it might make a rod you already own perfect for fishing streamers from a boat.

**Position and presentation.** Most of the positioning is done by the rower. An expert will keep the boat offshore at the distance of a moderate cast, typically 40 to 60 feet, with the boat canted at an angle to keep the backcast from going over his own head, so the caster can face the bank water he wants to fish.

The boat will be in the faster central currents. Fish riffle corners by casting to the soft and shallow side of the seam that forms the corner. Swim the fly out of the soft water, through the seam, and a few feet into the faster and deeper water. Then lift it quickly and cast again a few feet downstream from the first cast, again across the seam.

You can hit bank lies by casting at an angle either ahead of or behind the boat. If you cast ahead, let the current belly your line a bit while the fly sinks, and then begin your retrieve out for 5 to 15 or at most 20 feet before lifting for the next cast. If you cast behind the boat, let the fly sink the same short time, and then draw out any slack and begin your retrieve for the same few feet. If you have a follow, drop the rod to stop the fly.

When the boat approaches a midstream boulder lie, place your cast 5 to 15 feet upstream from it and 5 to 10 feet beyond it. Let the fly sink until it is just upstream from the boulder; then swim the fly as near to the boulder and the bottom as you can, trying for the trout that is tucked into the bubble of easy water just in front of the boulder. You'll get just one shot, so make it good. If no trout hits, place the next cast at the downstream edge of the boulder and retrieve it down the length of the eddy.

**Control of the drift.** On each cast, give the fly a few seconds to sink, and then begin a stripping retrieve that moves it fairly fast. If you're not having any luck, vary your retrieve with pauses, pulses of the rod tip, and short and long strips with the line hand.

**On the water.** As you float, you must mind the cast you're making and at the same time watch ahead for the next likely place that holds trout. Your ability to catch trout with this method hinges on being able to read lies in a hurry and cast to them quickly but accurately. The method requires a sort of schizophrenic split in your focus, but try placing each cast carefully before shifting your eyes to reading the water. Fish out each cast almost by feel while you watch for the precise location to place the next cast.

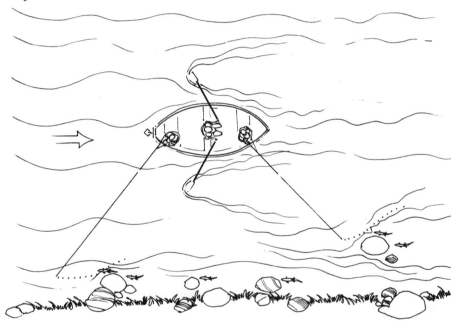

**The trout's point of view.** The streamer enters the sight of the trout, sometimes with a smack, sinks as if stunned, and then suddenly gets its legs under it and takes off screaming. Most trout will hit it instantly or chase it down within 5 feet or so. You only have to fish out the first few feet of each cast before lifting the fly and placing it to the next likely lie.

**RIG:     SHOOTING HEAD SYSTEM**

**Purpose.** Shooting heads allow you to cast long and fish deep in big and sometimes fast water. Since a shooting head system is stored in coils, usually in a wallet, it allows you to carry a set of lines for all depths without the need to carry a vest full of spare spools. Because the short head is backed by thin running line, or more often monofilament, there is less to hinder its sinking, and you can attain greater depths more abruptly.

Exploring the full range of depths is more important in stillwater trout fishing than it is on moving water, so you'll find more applications for this system on lakes and ponds than you will on streams and rivers. However, a few situations, such as big rivers where trout move out of reservoirs to spawn, can be solved with a shooting head. They're most useful against the largest trout.

**History/origins.** Shooting heads were first designed and used by steelhead fishermen who wanted to get down to the bottom in broad sweeps of big rivers. Individuals experimented with them in the 1960s and '70s, and line companies incorporated them into their catalogs by the 1970s and '80s. As soon as they became available, trout fishermen began applying them to specific situations, most notably big western tailwaters during fall spawning runs of brown trout and spring runs of rainbow trout.

**Knots and notes.** The running line should be 100 to 150 feet of thin fly line or heavy monofilament. Amnesia, a flat monofilament designed specifically for shooting, is less prone to tangling than standard mono, and therefore is recommended if you plan to get serious with shooting heads. Attach the heads to the running line and the leader butt with a loop-to-loop connection system that allows for fast changes. All heads and many leaders are now available with loops already spliced or tied in. Be sure to test all factory splices before using them. I've had them open up and release not only big trout, but the leader and sometimes the whole head, depending on which loop gives away. I prefer my own splices, made by stripping the end of the line, twirling a bobbin loaded with fly tying thread around and around the splice, and covering it with flexible cement when finished.

Heads vary in length from 20 to 35 feet, depending on the amount of weight needed to balance the rod for which they're designed. They come in sink rates from intermediate through slow-, fast-, and extra-fast sinking, to high-density and even lead-core heads. Always try a head, or better yet a manufacturer's system of them, on the rod you plan to use before you buy them. Some 6-weight heads require a 7-weight rod, others a 5-weight, and most rarely, it seems, the 6-weight for which they are rated.

**Adjustments for conditions.** When using a head system, the main adjustment will be to choose a faster sink-rate shooting head for deeper or faster water. The faster the sink rate, the shorter your leader. The larger the streamers you intend to cast, the heavier the outfit you'll need to cast them. For streamers up to size 6, a 6-weight system and appropriate rod will be fine. For streamers in the size 6 to 2

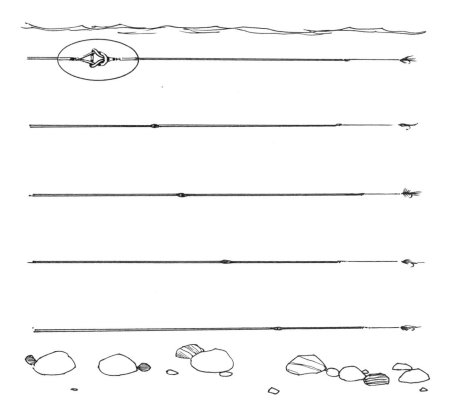

range, a 7-weight system will be better. For larger streamers, an 8- or 9-weight out-fit might be necessary.

**Rules for the rig.** A long rod, 9 to 9½ feet, will help you loft a shooting head when you're wading deep. The rod should be at least somewhat slow. Because line control is next to impossible with thin running lines, your control almost always comes through your choice of casting position and angle of attack on the current.

Once the cast is launched, wait until the fly sinks to the bottom; then coax it into a swing, either with or without action added by your retrieve.

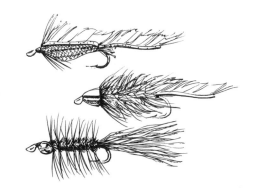

**Appropriate flies.** All streamers are appropriate for shooting head systems, but the situations in which you'll want to use a head usually call for streamers at the large and heavy end of the range. Egg-Sucking Leeches, Zonkers, Rabbit Strip Streamers, and other heavily weighted streamers will all work well.

**RIG:** SHOOTING HEAD SYSTEM
**Method:** Bouncing bottom

**Situations to solve.** Usually a shooting head system is used on big, broad reaches of small to large rivers. The water will commonly be deep and difficult to wade, with a pushy current that can't be too swift or it would sweep you away. The depth will be somewhat even, shallower where you're wading and sloping off in front of you, usually not very steeply, but into depths that are not easy to plumb with standard sinking lines. The currents should be even from side to side; it's difficult, though not impossible, to fish a shooting head system or any other sinking line system over a lot of conflicting and seething currents.

This type of fishing is out of the comfort zone of many anglers, but the trout that hang out in this water, especially if they're on spawning missions out of reservoirs or natural lakes, might be worth the fight.

**Tuning the rig.** The most critical part of tuning is choosing a line weight suitable to the size flies you'll be casting and then a line sink rate appropriate for the depth and speed of the water over which you'll be casting them. If you fish for some time without ever touching the bottom or being touched by a trout, it's quite likely that you're not nearly as close to the bottom as you think. It might be better to start with your heaviest head, and go to lighter ones until you're no longer thudding onto the bottom, rather than starting with a light head and going to heavier ones. You'll find your depth faster, and you'll be surprised at how fast-sinking the head must be to get to the bottom.

**Position and presentation.** If you fish a long reach of water, begin at the head of it so that you can let the current ease you downstream rather than fighting your way upstream against it. Make your first cast short and at an angle upstream into the current from 20 to about 50 degrees, depending on its depth and speed. The nearer you can cast to straight across the stream and still get your line and streamer to the bottom, the better control you'll have over the swing of your fly.

Extend each cast a couple of feet, and fish out each swing to cover water in a sweep down and around, until you've found a comfortable casting distance. Never strain yourself; instead, extend your casts patiently and gracefully over time, rather than forcing a long cast, which will result in more tangles than trout. After you've reached your comfortable casting range, begin letting the current push you downstream a step at the end of each swing before you make your next cast.

**Control of the drift.** As soon as your line lands upstream across the current, lift your rod as high as you can and do what you can to mend your running line upstream. You'll get only one mend, and although it won't be that effective with thin fly line or mono, it will help get your line and rod tip pointing upstream from the fly. Follow the line as it plummets until you feel the line has reached the bottom or is near it, usually anywhere from straight across the stream to 45 degrees downstream. It's far more critical to get a short swing along the bottom than to get a long swing somewhere above it. Ideally, your streamer would bounce along the bottom for a portion of each drift. Then move into a swing when the line comes tight against it.

**On the water.** As you move downstream through a riffle, run, or pool, you probably will have to change the angle at which you cast up and across the current and the distance you give your fly to sink. These adjustments in angle are equivalent to the changes in depth you make by adding split shot and moving your indicator up and down the leader in nymph fishing. If you still don't get your fly to the bottom, then go to a faster sinking head. Try to start out fishing a piece of water with the right head; it's not easy to change shooting heads in midstream.

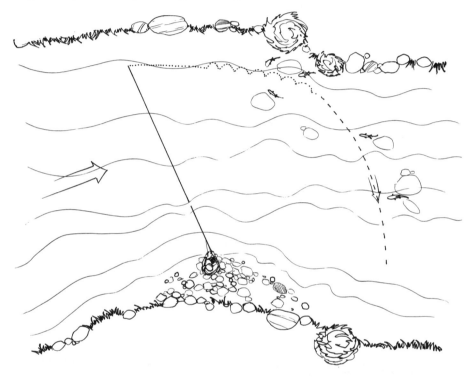

**The trout's point of view.** To the trout, your streamer should come bouncing, swimming, stuttering, starting, and stopping along the bottom, more like an injured baitfish than a healthy one. If your shooting head is too light, the fly will amble along far above the trout and not be noticed.

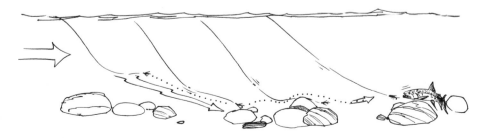

**RIG: SHOOTING HEAD SYSTEM**
**Method: Counting down in pools**

**Situations to solve.** The depths of big pools often hold the largest trout in any stream or river. Although smaller and shallower pools can usually be fished well with wet-tip, wet-belly, wet-head, or full-sinking lines, the broadest and deepest pools can only be plumbed with shooting heads that sink more abruptly because the thin running line does not hinder them. These deep pools usually balloon out from a necklike head, where the riffle from above enters through a broad center portion into the stricture of the tailout. Often the deepest water is backed against a bend or cliff on the outside, with a shallow gravel bar on the inside that makes an ideal platform for wading and from which to launch long casts. To take the trout such pools hold, you have to get a streamer far down into their depths.

**Tuning the rig.** Because the current in a deep pool is slower than that in a riffle or run, you might be able to fish with a slower sink-rate shooting head. Make sure, however, you're fishing deep enough to touch bottom during the retrieve. Choose a line that gets your streamer to the bottom with a count somewhat short of sixty seconds, or you probably won't let it attain the depths you need.

**Position and presentation.** You'll usually fish big pools from at least three positions: one at the head, another off the gravel bar in the center, and the last just upstream from the tailout. If the pool is long, try taking several positions along the gravel bar, or step and cast down the length of it.

Begin at the upper end of the pool, and make your first cast across the current tongue entering it. Work your casts out to a comfortable distance; then cover the water with a fan of casts as you move down the current tongue, covering all the water you can from the head of the pool.

Take your second position at the downstream end of the first fan, so that the fan of casts you make from the gravel bar overlaps with those made from the head. Make your initial casts upstream, and place each cast 2 to 4 feet downstream from the one before it. Again, either fan your casts across a short pool or step and cast down the length of a long pool.

When you reach the tailout, the water will become shallower and will gather speed. Your fishing at this point will slowly switch from casting and counting the streamer down and then retrieving it, to casting it across the accelerating current, giving it a few seconds to sink, and fishing it on the swing across the tailout.

**Control of the drift.** Each cast will require a hazy calculation of the speed of the current and the depth of the water. Toward the head and tail, you'll give your fly some time to sink and then fish it out on a combination of swing and retrieve. In the slower, deeper center of the pool, you'll count your fly down, usually between fifteen and forty-five seconds and then begin a stripping retrieve through the depths. Every cast in a typical pool will require a bit of adjustment to the sink time, retrieve, and swing.

**On the water.** Trout are territorial. The faster the water, the more scattered their lies, and the more fierce they are about defending them. The slower the water, the more they gather up. In pools, they often hold in pods. If you hook one trout with the shooting head rig and countdown method, rest that water for a few minutes and then repeat the cast. You might be able to catch more than one trout from the same lie.

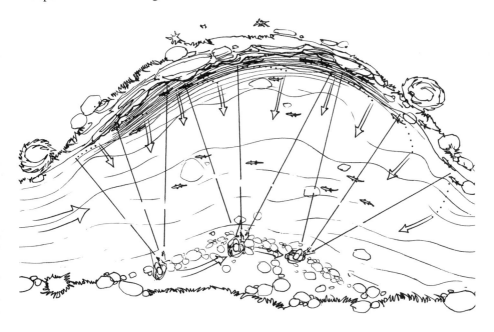

**The trout's point of view.** Your streamer, fished through a pool with the countdown method, should swim along near the bottom, perhaps bouncing into it once in a while. If it moves erratically, like it's been injured, a big trout will think it's easy prey and try to convert it into a meal.

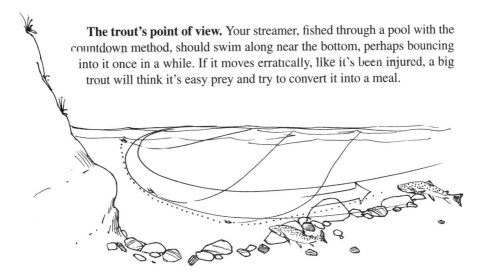

# CHAPTER 9

# Dry Fly and Dropper

A dry fly was the original strike indicator during the earliest nymph and indicator fishing. The prescription was to use a big, bright, and high-floating dry fly, but it probably didn't take long for some astute angler to realize that he could double his chances of catching fish with a dry fly that could fool trout but still be big enough to suspend the nymph and be visible throughout its float. The strike indicator almost completely replaced the dry fly when shot-and-indicator nymphing became popular in the 1960s and '70s. I cannot recall, in any of my early nymph fishing, whether I realized that I could use a dry fly as a way to fish a nymph.

The concept of fishing the two together seemed to seep into the average angler's consciousness in the 1980s. Through the 1990s up to today, a dry and dropper rig, usually a combination of a heavily hackled dry fly and a standard or beadhead nymph, has become the common way to explore water when it is unknown whether one type of fly, dry or nymph, would work better than another.

**Exploring.** The primary use for the dry and dropper is to scout out water and situations in which you know there are trout and suspect they'll be willing to take a fly but you have no clue what type of fly they might want. By rigging with two flies of such separate sorts, you offer them a choice and greatly increase your chance of discovering what they might prefer. This technique is an effective way to fish small streams, especially if you've started with a dry fly but either haven't drawn many trout to it or have seen only splashy refusals. Trout that rush at but refuse a dry will often accept a nymph suspended just beneath it.

The dry-and-dropper rig is among the most efficient ways to search for trout on almost any water that is somewhat rough: riffles and corners, broken runs, brisk bank water, stairsteps and benches of mountain and foothill waters, and any other water where you do not believe that trout are feeding selectively. In short, try fishing the dry-and-dropper rig upstream whenever you're on anything but smooth water and have no idea what might be happening with the trout.

**Working feeding fish.** During a hatch of mayflies, caddisflies, or midges, you may discover visible feeding trout but not be able to tell precisely what stage of the insect they're taking—whether it's an adult on the surface or an emerger just beneath it. You've made frantic attempts to bring them to an array of floating imitations, but all have failed. You could take time to rerig to fish an emerger, but it's far easier to tie 2 feet of fine tippet to the hook bend of the dry fly you're already casting, add an emerger for the same insect over which you're already fishing, and give the trout a choice between the two. Almost certainly, if they've already refused the dry, they'll continue to do so and accept the sunk fly. But since you have a strike indicator built in, you'll know your emerger is fishing just inches deep, where the trout are working. In any pod of feeding trout, some will be taking emergers, others adults. With the dry and dropper, you'll be able to take both kinds of trout.

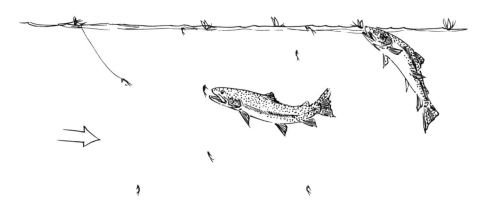

**Dry fly and floating dropper.** The dry-and-dropper rig does not always have to be a combination of dry fly and sunk fly. At times you'll get into situations where you need to fish a dry fly that is so small and floats so flush in the surface film that you're unable to see it on the water. Usually this happens during an emergence of midges or small mayflies. One solution is to tie a small yarn indicator into the leader. Another is to use a small dry imitation as your indicator, which will have some chance on its own of fooling trout.

**Landing trout.** Landing a trout on a two-fly setup can be awkward. If the fish takes the point fly, then you have to draw the leader tight and unpin the fish without hooking yourself, or rehooking the trout, on the dropper fly. If it takes the dropper, then the point fly will swing dangerously and usually almost invisibly at the end of its fine tippet, and if the trout thrashes, you're both in danger. With no clear solution to this, you may have to play the trout so near to exhaustion that it might die after you release it. It helps to use a tippet to the point fly that is longer than any trout you

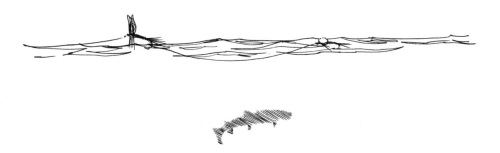

could possibly catch in the water you're fishing. That usually, though not always, puts the dangerous dangler beyond the trout's tail and reduces the chance it will hook the fish.

If you use a landing net, the odd fly out will almost always catch in the meshes, making it safer to release the fish. You'll probably have to untangle both flies from the net when the excitement is over. I rarely carry a net on moving water. The one sure solution is to get rid of the fly that is not working as soon as you determine which fly the trout prefer.

## RIG:         DRY FLY AND DROPPER

**Purpose.** The main purpose of the dry-and-dropper rig is to give trout a choice, usually between a high-floating dry fly and a standard or beadhead nymph, to see which type of fly they prefer. Such a rig is almost always used on water that is at least somewhat rough. By fishing a floating imitation and a subsurface emerger through trout feeding selectively during a hatch, you can also use the rig to determine which stage of insect those trout are taking. Typically this would be a smooth-water situation, though trout also can get selective on water that is a bit bouncy if enough of a specific natural insect are around to cause them to narrow their focus. Another use of the rig is to fish a tiny, almost invisible, floating fly behind one that is not large and is quite possibly an imitation of the insect that is hatching. The larger fly should be visible enough that you can follow it through its float and thus mark the position of the smaller fly floating near it.

**History/origins.** Although fishing two-fly tandems has a longer history than we'd like to credit, its common usage is fairly recent, within the last ten to fifteen years. It's quite likely that the rig is overused by many anglers. A dry and dropper should be used to figure out which type of fly, or which specific imitation, trout prefer on a given bit of water at a moment in time. But keep in mind that it does put the trout in some danger, so the second fly should be dispensed with as soon as you've determined which fly the trout prefer. If it's the dry, nip off the trailing tippet. If it's the nymph or other point fly, cut out the dry fly and either replace it with a yarn indicator, or retie your tippet knot and insert an indicator higher up the leader.

**Knots and notes.** Rig the dry fly with a leader appropriate for conditions. If you're on a creek or small stream, use a leader the length of your 7- to $7^1/_2$-foot rod. If you're on bigger freestone waters, your searching leader should be the length of your longer rod. If you're fishing a hatch on smooth water, then keep your leader as long and fine as the hatch and the trout require. Rig the dry-and-dropper combination with your leader and dry fly already adjusted to the water and conditions you'll be fishing. Tie the trailing tippet to the hook bend with an improved clinch knot, and the point fly to the tippet with a Duncan or surgeon's loop knot.

The most common dry-and-dropper rigs combine a high-floating dry such as an Elk Hair Caddis or Royal Wulff with a Gold-Ribbed Hare's Ear or Fox Squirrel Nymph, often beadhead versions. Other rigs combine a similar dry with a soft-hackled wet fly, an imitative dry fly with a subsurface emerger, or an imitative dry fly with a floating emerger that is difficult to see on the water.

**Adjustments for conditions.** Adjust the leader to the dry fly for the type of fishing you're doing before you rig the dropper. The length of the trailing tippet will depend on the size trout you're after and the type of water you're fishing. The tippet should be at least a few inches longer than the biggest trout you suspect you'll catch. For most of us, that means an 18- to 24-inch dropper. If you want to get your nymph deeper, go to 3 to 4 feet. A dropper tippet any longer than that gets unwieldy; instead switch to the shot and indicator rig. If you're fishing a dry followed by a sunk emerger or flush-floating dry, then the fine point tippet should be 3 to 5 feet long.

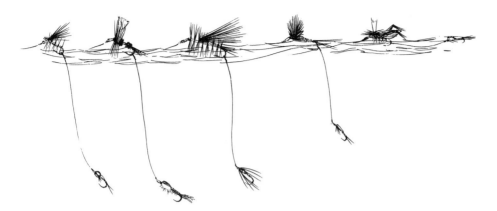

**Rules for the rig.** Your dry fly should be able to support the sunk fly you're fishing beneath it. As a general rule, keep the dry at least one size, and often two sizes, larger than the nymph. You won't be able to fish a weighted or beadheaded nymph under a low-floating imitative dry fly. If your dry is not heavily hackled, try unweighted or very lightly weighted nymphs and emergers as point flies.

Your point tippet should always be one X size finer than the tippet to the dry fly, for the simple reason that if you snag the nymph, or break it off on a trout, you don't want the dry fly to go with it.

**Appropriate flies.** Some favorite combinations often take trout in quite an array of situations. Try a Stimulator over a Beadhead Gold-Ribbed Hare's Ear in spring, an Elk Hair or Deer Hair Caddis over an Olive Beadhead in early to midsummer, a Parachute Hopper above a Beadhead Fox Squirrel in late summer and early fall, or a Blue-winged Olive Parachute over a Pheasant Tail Flashback during *Baetis* hatches at any time of year.

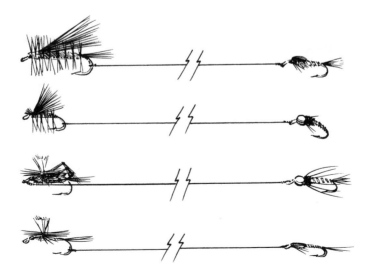

**RIG:          DRY FLY AND DROPPER**
**Method:       Exploring moving water**

**Situations to solve.** When you want to explore a creek, stream, or river with a dry-and-dropper rig, look for two sets of conditions: first, seasonal weather that makes you think trout will be looking up and are willing to move at least partway to the surface, and second, somewhat rough or at least brisk water. Don't try to draw up trout to a dry fly or the dropper fished just beneath it on bitter cold days, brutally hot days, or any other time when you suspect the fish to be holding the bottom and reluctant to leave it. And when trout are feeding selectively in smooth water, don't try a brushy dry-and-dropper combination as your typical exploring rig.

Instead, try exploring with the dry-and-dropper rig on all sorts of riffles, from small and shallow on creeks and streams to big and bouncy on the largest rivers. A nymph dropped off the stern of a brushy dry fly is one of the most likely combinations for finding trout holding in riffle corners. The same rig will be effective in broken runs and along brisk bank water, especially if no specific hatch is occurring.

**Tuning the rig.** Always adjust the length of the leader to suit the size water you're on. Usually this means a base leader the same length as the rod to the dry fly and an 18- to 24-inch tippet to the dropper fly. The dry fly should have plenty of hackle and be around size 12 to 14; the nymph should be either a beadhead or slightly weighted, a size or two smaller than the dry at size 14 or 16. The dropper tippet should be one X size finer than the base tippet.

**Position and presentation.** You'll almost always want to fish upstream when you're exploring somewhat rough water with dry-and-dropper rigs. In fact, you'll find little difference in the way you fish the combination rig and the way you would fish a dry fly on the same type of water. In unfeatured riffles and runs, you will have to pattern the water to cover it all. Fish current seams in broken water and the downstream, sides, and upstream lies around boulders. Probe up into the shallows of riffle corners, and fish bank water from a few inches to just 2 to 5 feet out. Cast parallel to the bank whenever you can, so the dry and sunk fly land in the same line of drift. If you cast at a dramatic angle to the bank, the dry fly will land 1 to 2 feet outside of the nymph and pull it out of the water you'd like it to fish.

**Control of the drift.** Control the drift precisely as you would the float of a dry fly on the same water. Gather slack as the fly moves toward you. Make any mends necessary to keep conflicting currents from causing drag. If the dry fly does drag, your chances on that cast are not necessarily at an end. Fish out the cast. Trout often notice the dragging dry, investigate it, and then after refusing it, take the nymph as an afterthought.

**On the water.** Always watch your dry fly for indications of takes to the sunk fly beneath it. I find it easy to forget that the sudden disappearance of my dry fly means something has happened to my trailer. I'll watch the dry fly shoot under and, rather than set the hook, will wonder what is going on with it. If at any time during the drift of your dry fly your attention wanders for a moment before retuning to search for the dry, lift the rod to make sure that it has not been taken under by a trout striking the trailer.

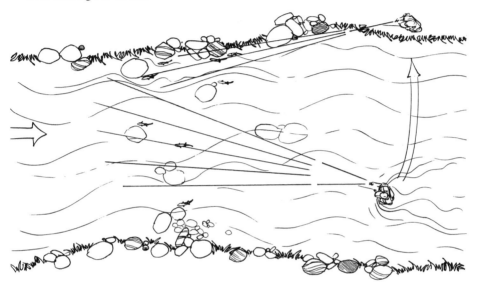

**The trout's point of view.** As the dry fly rides high into the trout's sight, it often triggers a strike. But just as often, the dry attracts the attention of an uninterested trout that then notices the trailer and rises up to accept it, perhaps because the subsurface take appears to pose less risk of predation than a rise closer to the surface.

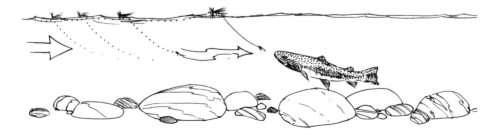

**RIG:          DRY FLY AND DROPPER**
**Method:      Fishing to working, feeding fish**

**Situations to solve.** You might spot trout feeding but won't be able to tell if they're feeding on floating adults, surface film emergers, or subsurface emergers. Sometimes a few trout in a pod will be feeding on adults, while others are feeding on emergers. At other times, you might notice fish feeding on either adults or emergers in the surface film, and your imitation is so small that you need some sort of unobtrusive indicator near it to follow its float and tell you when a trout has taken it.

You'll be fishing at least fairly smooth water most of the time when you get into such situations. Your drys will float without much hackle and should be imitative. Your dropper should be unweighted, or weighted at most with either a small beadhead or just enough turns of lead wire to ensure it penetrates the surface film.

**Tuning the rig.** On the type of water where you want to fish a dry-and-dropper rig over feeding trout, you'll usually already be armed with a long and light rod. Your base leader should be the length of the rod, with the addition of a 2- to 4-foot tippet to the dry fly. The dropper should be tied to a 2- to 5-foot tippet one X size finer than that to the dry.

**Position and presentation.** When you cast to feeding trout on smooth water, the upstream presentation will work as long as you're careful not to line your fish. It's always best to move slightly off to one side or the other, so that your casts do not send the line and leader over the head of the trout to land right on top of it.

Take a position farther off to one side or the other from the trout, or working pod of them, and use some form of reach cast that allows you to show the dry and dropper flies to the trout without alarming them with the line and leader. A disadvantage to this presentation is that the dropper will land beyond the dry, but with a few feet of sink time, it will realign itself under the dry. Cast at least 3 to 6 feet upstream from the rising trout to give the dropper fly time to sink.

In slick-water situations on spring creeks and tailwaters, you might find a downstream wiggle cast to be useful. With this presentation, the dropper will arrive in front of the trout first; the dry fly that follows will serve more as a marker of the nymph's drift position and as a strike indicator rather than a potential killer. Still, make sure the fly is at least a reasonable imitation of the adult insect over which you're fishing, since some trout might pass on the dropper and accept the dry fly.

**Control of the drift.** Fish each type of presentation as if you were casting a dry fly without a dropper. If your cast is upstream, gather slack as the dry fly and dropper drift toward you. If your cast is a reach across the currents, then follow the drift with your rod tip, and lean into the downstream end to extend the drift. For a downstream cast, feed slack to extend the drift. In all cases, watch the dry fly to make sure that it floats with a drag-free drift; any unnatural movement is likely to put trout off both flies.

**On the water.** Always be alert for any rises. Keep an eye on the entire area in a circle the diameter of your tippet length around the dry fly. If you're fishing a 3- to 5-foot dropper, especially with a trailing fly that floats flush in the surface film, you might see rises that you believe to be unassociated with your fly. That's a mistake. If you see a rise anywhere near the fly, raise the rod gently to set the hook. If a trout has taken the dropper, you'll seat the tiny hook firmly into its lip. If you miss, the gentle hook set will just slide your flies out of there.

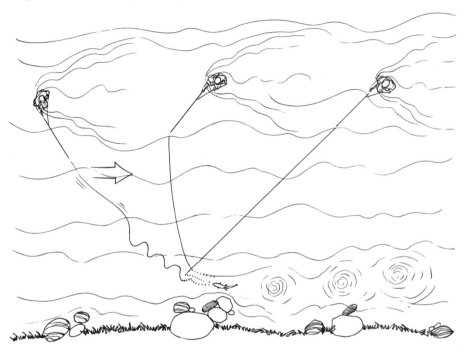

**The trout's point of view.** The dry and dropper come to the trout more or less as unrelated bits of food, one of which the trout might find appealing, the other perhaps a little less so. As long as the rejected fly does not frighten the trout, you'll have an excellent chance of taking it on the other.

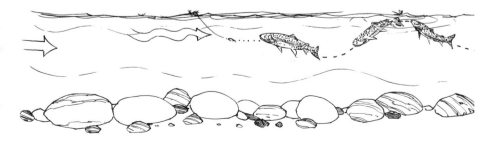

# PART 3

# Lakes and Ponds

# CHAPTER 10

# Tackle for Stillwaters

When choosing tackle for lakes and ponds, you'll have to solve some problems that are different from those you encounter on moving waters. That is not to say that you must go out and buy everything new to fish stillwaters. Most of the tackle you use on streams and rivers will be useful on lakes and ponds as well, but you might also need a few items that you, or at least I, use rarely except on stillwaters. For example, a float tube will get you around a lake or pond, and a landing net, which I almost never use on moving water, is a requirement on stillwaters.

On lakes, you'll have to cast long more often than short, and in wind as often as not, so you will need a rod 8½ to 9½ feet long and usually balanced to a 5-, 6-, or even 7-weight line. You'll want to explore a full range of depths, from the surface to 30 or 40 feet down, so you'll need some sort of sinking line system.

Although you can fish stillwaters from shore, you'll infinitely increase your chances of catching trout if you provide yourself with some manner of aquatic transportation. A float tube is a wiser, and possibly a bit cheaper, purchase than a new fly rod designed specifically for fishing stillwaters. If you're able to peddle out close to the fish in your new tube, your stream rod will fish fine. You will need a fly box designed specifically for stillwater food forms. Many things that trout eat in lakes and ponds are similar to what's found in streams and rivers, but a few, such as dragonfly and damselfly nymphs, become important fish food in lakes and ponds. Carry your stream boxes—they'll often contain just the fly that you need—but make sure you include these flies you won't find in those moving-water fly boxes.

**Rods and reels for stillwaters.** Distance casting, rather than delicate presentation, is common when you're fishing lakes and ponds. Usually the trout will be in a small radius around you, so the farther beyond that radius you can reach, the more undisturbed trout that will see your fly. Trout in stillwaters cruise rather than hold stations as they do in moving water, so you have to be able to reach out with a quick and long cast. Your rod should be long, and its action fast. If you're fishing from a boat, an $8^1/2$- to 9-footer will work fine. Many rods designed specifically for float tubes are between 10 and 11 feet long. In almost all lake and pond situations, the long and stout nymph and streamer rod that you already own, balanced to a 5-, 6-, or 7-weight line, will be all you need. Your basic floating line for stillwaters should be a weight-forward taper, rather than the double-taper that is standard on streams.

Because trout grow large in stillwaters, they will test your reel's drag system more often than trout in streams do. The only requirements for a reel are an adjustable drag and a size that allows you to wind 100 yards of 20- or 30-pound-test backing line behind your fly line. An inexpensive reel with at least a couple of interchangeable spools will be all you need.

Many serious stillwater fly fishers prefer to keep more than one rod rigged, especially when fishing from a boat. The first should be strung with a floating line. The second should be armed with a clear intermediate line for fishing the subsurface and the shallows. The third, if you have room for it, can be rigged with backing and running line and a spliced loop that allows you to change through the various sink rates in your shooting head system to explore the rest of the depths.

**Lines for stillwaters.** Your basic line, whether your fishing dry flies, wet flies and streamers in the shallows, or nymphs from shallow to some substantial depths, should be a weight-forward floater. The second most important line is a clear intermediate for fishing shallow water and for trolling. If you don't own one, a fast-sinking wet-tip, wet-belly, or wet-head sinking line system for moving waters will also work on lakes. Keep at least one or two density-compensated full-sinking lines on spare spools. These lines sink and ride through a retrieve with the entire line at the same depth, rather than sinking faster at the thicker portion and riding up at the tip.

If you are like most anglers and do 90 percent of your stream fishing with a floating line, then you might be starting from scratch when setting up a lake line system. In that case, I recommend you use your floater, buy a clear intermediate, and then get shooting heads in various sinking rates to plumb the rest of the depths. Many manufacturers sell them in sets, all of the same weight to cast with the same rod but each with a different sink rate. These shooting heads can be backed with floating running line or with flat monofilament Amnesia shooting line—I prefer the latter. They load a rod quickly, shoot to long distances, and sink from slowly to abruptly, depending on the head you choose.

**Leaders for stillwaters.** The rules for leaders are relatively simple. Use leaders the length you would on smooth water for dry flies, 10 to 14 feet long. Use extra-long leaders, 15 to 25 feet, to fish the depths with a floating line and weighted nymphs. Cut your leader back as you go deeper, as short as 4 feet, when using sinking lines. I use fluorocarbon leaders for sunk flies on stillwaters, but I do not use them for dry flies or on moving waters because they sink, are less visible, and tug dry flies under.

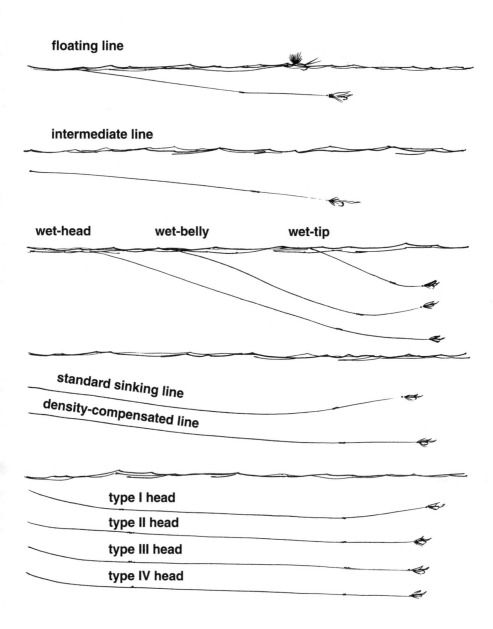

floating line

intermediate line

wet-head    wet-belly    wet-tip

standard sinking line
density-compensated line

type I head
type II head
type III head
type IV head

**Boats, float tubes, and pontoon boats.** You're going to want a vessel to get you away from shore when you're fishing on stillwaters, especially those choked with brush or swampy around the edges. A float tube is a good beginning; they are inexpensive and easy to store, and with light fins and breathable waders, they can easily fit into a backpack. The most common kind are circular, but U-shaped tubes let you get in and out more easily. You might need a foot pump, but the U-tube I own can be pumped sufficiently with lung power, and I use it on many hike-in waters.

A pontoon boat is the next step up from the float tube. With the use of oars, you can cover more water as you explore the shoreline in the chase for trout. Not only do you sit higher in a pontoon boat than you would in a tube, you can easily strap a second and even third rod to a pontoon. Although easier on the legs when you want to troll, pontoon boats are difficult to carry more than 100 yards to water.

If you're serious about lake fishing, a hard boat is the best way to go. On smaller waters, consider a pram, which has a fairly flat bottom that allows you to stand and cast. I like prams and how they can be tied to the top of my rig in a hurry. A canoe might be the most pleasant craft for exploring, but it can be too tippy for standing in, especially if you don't have good sea legs. On large lakes, a boat with a motor will let you move from place to place without wasting time, and it becomes the most stable casting platform when you get there. Be sure to rig your boat with anchors at both ends to hold you stationary against wind. Also keep clutter inside the boat quelled, or it will catch your line.

No matter what kind of craft you use, don't forget to bring along your life vest and whistle. Carry water, fly boxes, rain gear, and camera in a waterproof boat bag, which can be kept packed, ready to grab and go. Keep a landing net tied by a short cord to the side of your tube or pontoon boat or in your pram, canoe, or motorboat.

**A stillwater fly box.** Many food forms that either exist in small populations or are not found at all in moving waters become important in lakes and ponds. Your stream fly boxes will contain many flies that work on lakes, but they won't cover the basic diet of the trout. You need flies that will do that if you want to catch trout consistently.

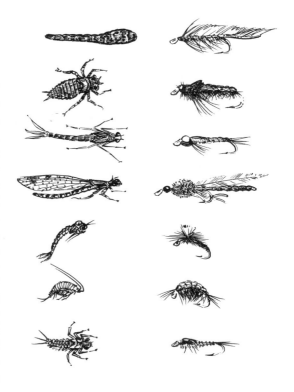

*Leeches* live in nearly all stillwaters. Though you'll see leeches up to 4 inches long and fat, it's rare to find them that size in trout stomach samples. You'll have better luck if you imitate them at an inch or two long and slender. Size 8 to 12 black, olive, and brown Woolly Buggers will do the job, but specific leech imitations, such as the Rabbit Strip Leech, in the same sizes and colors will do it even better.

*Dragonfly nymphs* are a staple on lakes and ponds. They are large and hourglass-shaped, and swim fairly fast when disturbed, as when they're chased by trout. To imitate them, try pinching half the tail off a size 8 or 10 Woolly Bugger or using specific flies such as the Lake Dragon.

*Damselfly nymphs* are prolific in stillwaters. They're long and slender and have tail gills shaped like willow leaves. When choosing a fly based on this insect, you must imitate its sinewy swimming motion as much as its shape. Try the Green Damsel in size 10 or 12 or a beadhead and wisp of olive marabou on a size 14 or 16 hook. Adult damselflies require specific imitations such as Andy Burk's Damsel.

*Midge pupae* suspend along the bottom, rise slowly to the surface, then suspend again just under the surface. Trout take them at all levels, so you will need red, tan, and black Midge Pupae to fish deep and on the rise and Klinkhamer Specials in the same colors to fish as surface film emergers.

*Scuds* swim like animated little sticks in and around weedbeds at all levels in lakes and ponds. They are available to trout all year long and are so abundant that trout are always willing to eat them or their imitations. Try size 12 to 16 Shellback Scuds in olive and gray.

*Lake mayfly nymphs*, usually *Callibaetis,* are swimmers, darting in and around vegetation or along the bottom. Even when they emerge into adult mayflies and you see duns sitting on the surface, trout continue to feed on the nymphs, taking as many as ten or twelve beneath the surface for every floating insect. Be sure to carry Flashback Pheasant Tail nymphs in size 12 to 16 in your lake fly box.

# CHAPTER 11

# Reading Stillwaters

A nglers often lament that lakes and ponds are blank slates, impossible to read. The surface is flat, gives little hint of what lies below it, and therefore provides few clues about where you might find trout. In reality, though, that is true about very few lakes and ponds. Almost all stillwaters reveal their structures if you know what to look for, the first being the trout themselves and the second the shape of the land around it, which will tell you a lot about the shape of the lake bottom. Most are far from blank slates.

**Visible fish.** If you spot rises, or the trout themselves, then you know precisely where to fish for them. Whenever you arrive at a stillwater, whether you've fished it before or not, take time to climb to a higher elevation and look around as you scan for rises and search the water for cruising trout. Use binoculars and wear Polaroid sunglasses. Be patient, and try to see as much of the lake or pond as you can. If it's a windless day and the sun strikes down through clear water, the conditions are perfect to see cruising trout. If you find them, you can eliminate most of the lake and direct your fishing time to areas you know hold trout. If conditions for spotting fish are poor—it's a cloudy or windy day, or the water has little clarity—spend less time trying to spot trout from a distance. Instead, get saddled up in whatever craft you've chosen to take you out onto the water, and look for them up close.

Once you start fishing, continue to look for rises and trout. As you move along, whether you're casting or trolling, a hatch might start, or you might enter an area, possibly when nosing into a shallow cove or over a weedbed, where insects are already hatching and trout are rising. You might also find a lee area where the surface is suddenly calm and you're able to peer down into the water. If you see trout, start fishing.

When looking for trout, focus on water shallow enough that your sight can penetrate if not to the bottom, then at least close to it. Watch along the edges of the lake or pond and in the shallows near shore. Weedbeds often show as no more than dark patches on the surface, as if they're the shadows of passing clouds. Watch such areas for signs of cruisers. If you can discern a drop-off, usually revealed by water that turns from light to dark, then watch for trout moving up and down the length of it.

**Likely lies.** In the absence of visible trout, try reading the water for the most likely places to hold them. If a lake is entirely featureless, you might have to begin by trolling, using your fly as a way to explore. But in most cases, you'll be able to read several of the following features. Concentrate your fishing on them.

1. *Edges, structure, and points.* Look for rocky points, fallen trees, reed and cattail beds, lily pad flats, and shallow coves. Trout find cover and food there.

2. *Extensive shallows.* Vegetation grows wherever sunlight penetrates to the bottom. Shallow vegetation produces abundant insects, and they attract trout.

3. *Weedbeds.* Submerged weedbeds at any depth will furnish food and hold trout. You'll need the right line to reach the correct level to fish them.

4. *Drop-offs.* Trout cruise drop-offs to intercept insects and other foods migrating up out of the depths, toward the shallows, or to shore for emergence.

5. *Shoals.* If you find shallow, weedy water surrounded by depths, you might find trout moving up to feed there for at least a part of every day.

6. *Inlet and outlet streams.* The inlet delivers insects from the moving water upstream, and the outlet gathers and funnels insects that hatch or fall to the lake surface.

7. *Spring seeps.* Wherever cool water wells up into the lake, trout find a haven from the warm water of summer and the bitter water of winter.

8. *Submerged streambeds.* Try to locate the depths of an old streambed, especially in a shallow impoundment, and you might find a line running the length of the stillwater, holding trout from end to end.

**Annual trout movements.** From early spring—ice-out if your lake freezes over—until early summer, trout can be found in relatively shallow water, actively feeding and doing their best to thrive and put on weight. When insects are hatching, they'll be rising to them, and when there is no hatch, they'll be cruising, looking for food. If you fail to find trout in shallow water, look in waters from 5 to around 25 feet deep, depths conveniently fished with flies.

In the heat of midsummer, a typical lake stratifies, with a layer of warm water suspended over a layer of cooler, deoxygenated water, at around 20 to 40 feet, depending on the depth of the lake and wind-mixing of the water. When a lake is stratified, you'll find trout, which need oxygen, above the deoxygenated water but

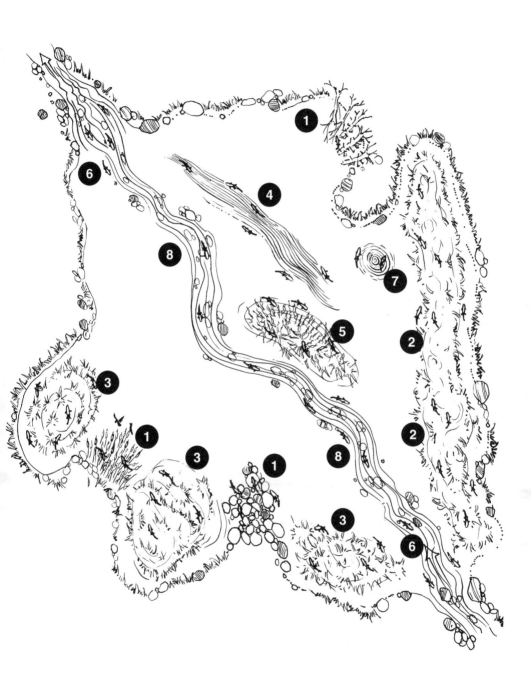

near the dividing line for its coolness. You'll have to go deep for them, but be careful not to go below them. In hot weather, trout are lethargic, so you'll have to retrieve slowly to take them.

In fall, the stratification is broken up, and trout once again will be up and feeding when insects are active and down and cruising at fly-fishing depths when nothing is happening. They'll be hungry and eager to take flies. In winter, trout will move back into the depths and become lethargic once more. Again, you'll have to fish deep and slowly for them.

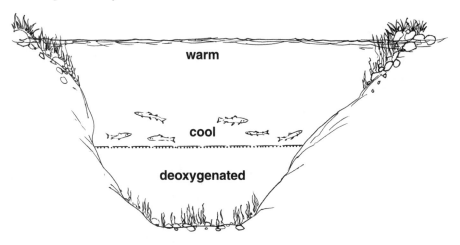

**Daily trout movements.** Aquatic insects tend to hatch in the warmth of midday in spring and fall, and that's when both trout and insects are most active. Look for hatches and rising trout from just before noon until 3 or 4 P.M. (A). The rest of the day they tend to be either on the bottom in relatively shallow water—5 to 15 feet deep—or hanging around submerged vegetation, where they look for scuds, leeches, and all sorts of nymphs and larvae to prey upon (B). Any time you're fish-

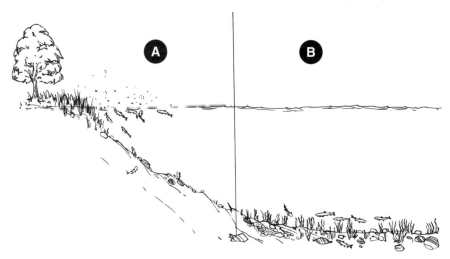

ing a stillwater and know the water is neither stratified in midsummer nor chilled in midwinter, yet you see no trout rising, they might be feeding on the bottom in somewhat shallow water. Find an area where vegetation is suspended from 10 to 25 feet down, choose a fly line that will get your fly to that depth, and cast or troll until you find trout.

In summer when the lake is stratified, trout will stay in their depths during the heat of the day, but they might make forays into the shallows to feed on hatches in the cool of early morning and late evening. In winter, it's unlikely that they will make any daily movement at all, unless a hatch of midges stirs the trout. Any time insects become available, trout will violate all the rules of annual and daily movements and go on the feed.

**Finding fish.** When trying to find trout, first look over the lake or pond for visible evidence of their presence: either rises or cruisers that you can spot. Climb some elevation to get an overall look, and sit next to the bank and peer into the water near you. In lakes where the edge breaks off abruptly into deep water, trout will often cruise up and down the shoreline, a foot or two out and a foot or two deep, in a pattern that makes it easy to set a fly in front of them and wait for their next arrival. If you see no signs of trout, begin fishing the types of lies outlined earlier in this chapter.

A depth finder is a valuable fish-finding tool on stillwaters. It shows the structure of the bottom, and to a certain extent its composition, whether soft or hard. Not only does it reveal the location of any weedbeds beyond depths at which you're able to see them, but it shows trout. Mount a depth finder on your boat, or strap a portable model to the chambers of a float tube or pontoon boat. If you fish lakes more than a few days each season, a depth finder will

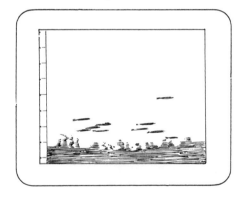

add up to a tremendous advantage, saving you time in figuring out the lake and enabling you to find and engage trout. Use it to find all sorts of structures, and the trout lurking within and above those structures.

**Algal Blooms.** Many productive lakes suffer algal blooms each year, which cause the water to become so opaque that it appears to be unfishable. When fishing looks hopeless, consider that a typical bloom does not go all the way to the bottom, stopping instead between 15 and 20 feet down. Any water deeper than that will be clear beneath the bloom, and trout will be down there and able to see your flies. The secret is to find the depth of the bottom and then to rig to fish just above it. If trout are present and this lower water is clear, it won't take long to find them.

You can read the depths of an algal bloom on the screen of a depth finder. If you fish without one, measure depths until you find water around 20 feet deep; then fish at about 18 feet. To find the depth quickly, snap a hemostat onto your fly or tie a heavy sinker to your leader and drop it overboard until it hits bottom. Then measure the amount of line you bring in.

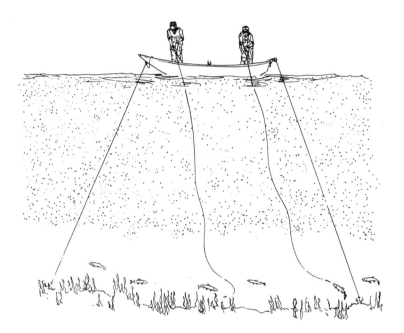

# CHAPTER 12

# Rigs and Methods for Dry Flies on Stillwaters

Y ou'll usually fish dry flies on lakes and ponds when you see trout rising to work a hatch of aquatic insects, a fall of terrestrial insects, or a flight of returning aquatic insects. Such feeding is usually localized, often over a shallow weedbed or near a stand of shoreside trees. The trout will often feed in pods, a loose gathering of trout that either remains in a specific area or cruises slowly through an area much as a single trout might move.

You'll fish dry flies less often to sporadic, occasional, and scattered rises, which indicate that no hatch, terrestrial feeding, or spinner fall is happening and that just a few cruising trout are finding a few insects on the surface. A searching situation, when no trout are rising but conditions give you hope that you might bring some trout to the surface, might be worth trying with a dry fly, but you'll have more success in streams than in stillwaters. Unlike in a stream, where an insect on the surface is usually within sight and striking distance of trout at the bottom, trout holding on a lake bottom are not likely to go to the top to take a single insect, or your fly.

**Rising, feeding fish.** When you find rising trout, avoid rushing out into the middle of them and thrashing around with whatever fly you already have tied to your leader. Instead, back away from them and spend some time watching to see what they're taking, and whether their movements have a pattern. Then follow a specific set of steps to catch them.

First, collect a natural insect without disturbing the feeding fish. Use an aquarium net, your landing net, or whatever else you can to lift a specimen off the surface. Observe it nose-close, the way a trout does just before it sips it. Notice its size, shape, and color. A trout sees the insect's underside; tip it up and look at it from that direction. The color will usually be different on the belly, which is the side you want to match, than on the back.

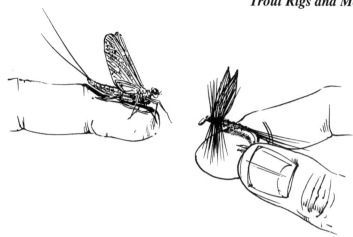

Second, choose a fly that is at least roughly the same size, shape, and color as the natural you're holding in your hand. Hold them side-by-side, and make sure your fly is at least somewhat close in size, shape, and color.

Third, rig properly to fish the fly. The rig can be as simple as a floating line, a leader 2 to 4 feet longer than your rod, and a 3-foot tippet the right diameter to balance the size fly you've chosen. In wind, you'll want a shorter, stouter leader, and on glassy water you might need to go longer and finer.

Fourth, move into position to fish over the rises with a controlled cast, but without putting the trout down. Your ability to cast long can confer an advantage here, but you don't want to move out so far that you're crashing your casts onto the heads of trout. If you have an anchor and the trout are not moving, fix your position before you begin fishing.

Finally, begin placing casts over rises. Get the fly as near to the rise as quickly as you can, and let it sit for at least a minute or two. Resist the temptation to frantically paste the fly into every rise-ring. If trout are moving, one will find it.

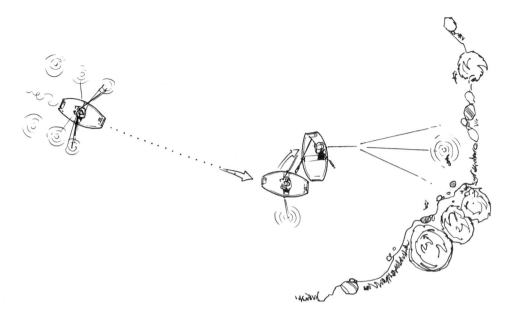

**Scattered rises.** When rises are occasional and one occurs near enough that you can move to it, do so as quickly as you can so you can get your fly onto the water close to the fish. Let it sit for quite some time. If no trout takes it, then pattern the area with casts placed 10 to 15 feet apart. Let each sit. Be patient; you know at least one active trout is in the area, so don't chase distant rises until you've fished the targeted area with at least a few casts. However, if you can pattern a moving trout, then chase it and get into position ahead of it. If you can place your fly where you might expect its next rise, you'll have an excellent chance to catch it.

**Absence of rises.** If no trout are rising but the weather is mild and you see a few insects in the air, then why not see if the trout might respond to a dry fly? Choose a generic fly; a size 12 or 14 Adams resembles many mayflies, midges, and even buzzing caddis. Fish the shoreline, especially along reed and cattail edges, and any structure over shallow water, such as downed trees, rocky points, and lily pad flats. Set your fly over shallow shoreline vegetation or weedbeds, and let it rest. Fish the slight currents of inlets and outlets.

If you fail to catch fish, don't persist too much longer with the dry, unless you're a dry-fly purist. If trout are not feeding visibly on the surface of a stillwater, you'll usually just waste time trying to get them to come up and feed there. Instead, switch to a nymph, streamer, or wet fly, and rig to fish it near the bottom.

## RIG:      FLOATING LINE AND STANDARD STILLWATER LEADER

**Purpose.** This is the standard rig for fishing floating flies on stillwaters, and it's similar to the rig you would use for drys on moving water. Recall that a leader for the smoothest spring creek and tailwater flows and rising trout is extended to a fine tippet. When you fish dry flies on a lake or pond, the water will be as flat as any you encounter on a stream, so your requirements begin just about where the moving water requirements end.

Trout in rich lakes and ponds grow portly and strong. Very often, while stillwater fly fishing, you'll encounter the conundrum that makes a tippet that is fine enough to fool the trout too weak to hold it. Keep that balance in mind, and try to choose a tippet that gives you some hope of hooking trout and landing them.

**History/origins.** The history of dry flies on lakes reaches back to the days when gut leaders were used. Silkworm gut could only be extruded to about 14 inches, so that became the maximum length available for tippet. Gut of 4X was fine, but 5X was fragile at best and undependable on average. Monofilament, once it became available, allowed for the extension of leaders, and as quality improved over the years, so did the strength and dependability of tippets.

**Knots and notes.** The rig begins with a weight-forward floating line in a minimum 4-weight and more often 5- or 6-weight. The base leader should be a tapered 3X, 9- or 10-footer. You can add a 3- or 4-foot, 4X tippet, or 1-foot tapering sections and finer tippet. If the water surface is glassy and the insect you're matching small, you might extend your leader out 15 to 18 feet. The average length for lake fishing with drys would be between 12 and 14 feet. Although often an advantage, fluorocarbon pulls small drys under and therefore is not useful with any drys lacking flotation.

Use blood or surgeon's knots to connect tapering and tippet sections. Fix conventional dry flies to the tippet with the improved clinch knot. If you're using surface-film emergers, or drys such as Klinkhamer Specials that suspend from a parachute hackle, use the Duncan or surgeon's loop to let the fly dangle properly.

As you would on moving waters, you can add either floating emergers or nymphs beneath your drys. The sunk fly should be a size smaller than the dry, and the tippet one diameter finer than the tippet to the dry.

**Adjustments for conditions.** The only adjustments that should be made to the rig when dry-fly fishing are extending the tippet when conditions are calm and trout are snotty and reducing the length of the leader when wind is a factor. Fortunately, a wind that makes presentation difficult with a long and fine leader also roughens the water and makes the long, fine leader less necessary.

**Rules for the rig.** The outfit and leader you use should always be light enough so that your fly lands lightly on the water. If your line tip, leader, and fly crash in, back away and rerig, trying a lighter rod and line if you have one. On the other hand, the outfit should be heavy enough to cast in the conditions under which you fish. If the wind is up, you will be glad you have your 6-weight. If your leader is

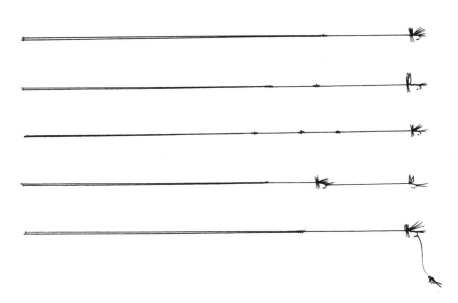

tapered correctly and your casting careful enough, this rod can be delicate enough for almost all stillwater situations.

The leader must be able to turn over the flies you're casting. At times, you might find trout feeding on large drys and demanding fine tippets, but that is rare. Be sure that your leader always turns over, extends, and sets the fly down gently. The pile cast works over moving currents on streams, but it's fatal on lakes.

One final rule: Don't let your tippet get much shorter than a couple of feet. If repeated fly changes shorten it, clip it off and tie on a new 3- to 4-foot tippet.

**Appropriate flies.** Most dry flies you use to fish stillwaters will imitate something trout are eating at that moment. Because you will want to collect a specimen and match it as closely as you can, your stillwater fly box should contain imitations of mayflies, caddis, midges, damselfly adults, and terrestrials such as beetles and ants. In addition, carry emergers for mayflies and midges, because trout feeding on those two groups often focus on individuals stuck in the surface film.

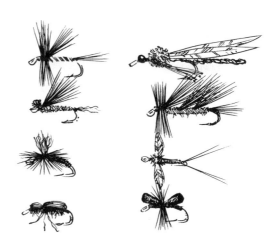

**RIG:   FLOATING LINE AND STANDARD
        STILLWATER LEADER
Method: Covering water**

**Situations to solve.** When you want to catch trout on dry flies but either no trout are rising or only a few scattered fish are working, you have no choice but to go looking for trout and try to drum them up. To use a dry, conditions should be favorable. You want a day with some warmth to it, but it should not be the heat of midsummer or the dead of winter when trout are down and the dry fly is hopeless. You also are looking for some insects to be out and, if not in the air, at least on shoreside vegetation. You want shallow edge water with such features as rocky points, downed trees, and reed or cattail forests. You need some hint that a dry fly will at least have a chance. A recent hatch, which might have the trout up and still looking at the surface, can be sufficient. Even better is the presence of sporadic rises that let you know at least a few trout are cruising and willing to feed on top, though they might be too scattered to be worth chasing.

**Tuning the rig.** Try to match any insects you see that are abundant in the air or on lakeside vegetation, even if trout are not rising to feed on them. Even if the insects are not on the water at the moment, trout are on the lookout for them. If you see no signs of insects, try a generic dry fly such as the Adams or Elk Hair Caddis. Once you've chosen your fly, then balance your leader to turn it over, with an appropriate diameter tippet about 3 feet long. Your leader need not be any longer than the stillwater average, 12 to 14 feet.

**Position and presentation.** If you're fishing from shore or wading the edges, cover the water you can reach with a fan of casts. Make your first cast short and along the shoreline, and extend it half a leader length at a time. Cover the shore first in both directions. If you wallop your first cast out as far as you can right along the shoreline, you'll line any fish between you and where your fly lands. Work subsequent flies in an arc over the open water around you.

If you're afloat, keep your boat or tube a medium to long cast out from shore. The less you disturb the trout by sending waves washing over them, the more likely you'll catch them. If the wind is blowing, or conditions along the shore make you think you should cover the water thoroughly, anchor both ends of your craft, if you can, and cover the edge water from a stationary position. Again, use a fan of casts that places your fly no more than 2 to 3 feet out from the shoreline. Use extra casts to place the fly on all sides of any cover, such as rocks, downed trees, and shallow weedbeds.

If the wind is light or nonexistent, you can drift and cover the shoreline as you move along it. If you are fishing with a buddy, take turns rowing the boat and covering the shoreline. A boat with an electric motor will let you go it alone. You just need to position and move the boat, tube, or pontoon boat parallel to the shore so you can remain an easy cast away from it.

**Control of the drift.** Normally when fishing drys on stillwaters, you do not control the drift at all. You are merely placing the fly in a likely place, letting it sit half a minute to a minute, and then lifting it off to present it a few feet down the shore to a different bit of cover. If you're fishing a caddis dry fly, then try skittering it a few feet from shore or cover before picking it up for the next cast. This technique will rarely be effective, however, on lakes that lack hatches of traveling sedges.

**On the water.** I don't often fish dry flies on stillwaters when I don't see any rising trout. When I do, it will almost always be along a shoreline with downed trees, rocky points, reed and cattail edges, shallow weedbeds, or some other cover that makes me think that trout not actively feeding might move to the surface. I don't give the dry fly much time, a half hour to an hour at most, to prove itself before switching to a sunk fly that allows me to retrieve and therefore cover the water much more efficiently.

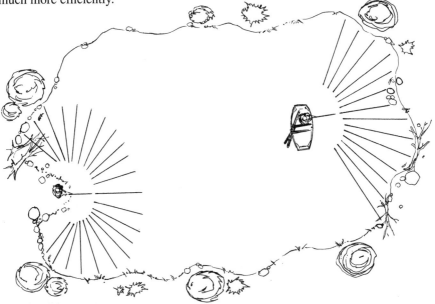

**The trout's point of view.** When a trout is not feeding on the surface, it is usually at the edge or near the bottom either cruising or holding under some sort of cover. If it's cruising, it is likely feeding or willing to feed. If the water is shallow enough, say 3 to 5 or 6 feet deep, the trout often moves to a dry fly that arrives suddenly in its sight on the surface.

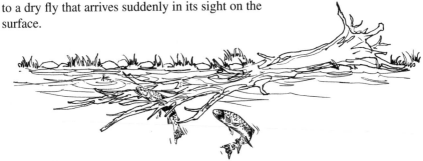

**RIG:**      **FLOATING LINE AND STANDARD STILLWATER LEADER**
**Method:**  **Dry and/or emerger to rises**

     **Situations to solve.** Trout rise to take naturals, either in pods or as individuals. They either feed in a rough area or move slowly as they feed. It's not unusual for a single trout, and at times for small pods of them, to cruise and feed in consistent 20- to 40-foot ovals, as if confined to a racetrack. When trout feed consistently in a defined area, they almost always are selective, though at times when a variety of windblown insects fall onto the water, they will accept almost any dry fly. Most of the time, you should collect what they're focused on and match it.

     **Tuning the rig.** If you're not sure what trout are taking or you think they might be feeding just subsurface, try rigging a dry with an emerger or nymph trailer on a 2- to 4-foot tippet. Such a rig will be almost necessary during the most common lake and pond mayfly hatches *(Callibaetis)*. You might catch some trout on duns, but you'll do much better on emergers such as the Quigley Cripple since trout take nymphs about ten to one over duns. If spinners are in the air and on the water, you'll want a spent-wing dressing that floats flush in the surface film.

     **Position and presentation.** If you're rooted to shore, take whatever position you can to place a cast over trout. If you're wading, be careful not to send waves over the feeding trout. If you're afloat and the trout are not moving, anchor if you can, but be sure to drop the hook quietly. If the trout are moving slowly through a limited area, keep the anchor up and follow them, although this depends on wind as well. A float tube is the perfect craft to fish a pod of rising trout, because you can position yourself with your fins, while both hands are free for the rod and line.

     When casting to a pod of trout, first place your fly over those closest to you. If you cast over the pod to reach one on the far side, you might spook the others away. When casting to an individual trout or to a trout on your side of a pod, wait for a rise to locate the fish, then place your fly to the near edge of the rise-ring as quickly as you can. Let it sit for a half minute to a minute. If the trout are in a pod, let it sit even longer, rather than lifting it to cast to another rise. After the fly has had its chance on that initial cast, pick it up and place it 5 to 10 feet to one side of the rise. Let it sit another half minute, then cast it the same distance to the other side of the rise. A trout is always moving when it rises, and targeting your fly around a rise gives you a chance to intercept it.

     If another trout rises nearby, you might calculate that it is better to cast to the new rise rather than continue casting to one side and the other of the first rise. I agree.

**Control of the drift.** You will have to control the drift less than you must control your patience to pick the fly up and paste it into every rise-ring in a 60-foot circle around you. The longer you let the fly sit, when you're working over a pod of trout, the more likely a trout will come along and whack it. Of course, your attention span will play a part in your success. If you're like me, and your fly is on the water very long, you'll be gazing at the distant scenery when a trout sips your fly. Try to keep your eye on the fly, and recast it if your attention begins to wander away from it.

**On the water.** When trout are feeding on an abundance of insects on the surface, you can often mark a first and second rise and predict almost precisely where the trout will rise for the third time. Place your fly there well ahead of the anticipated rise time, and you should have your fish. Of course, the trout could change its mind and its direction, or you could have the wrong fly, or a natural nearby could win out and get eaten instead of your fly. If that happens, try again.

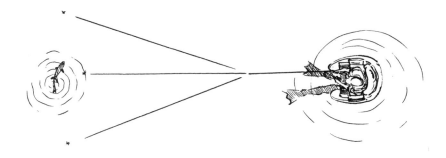

**The trout's point of view.** The trout should see one of two things: either a dry fly that lands at the edge of its rise-ring just after it's taken a natural, in which case it will usually turn back and take the fly, or a fly that is on the sit in its projected path, so that all the fish has to do is tip up and take it.

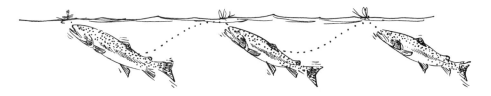

**RIG:      FLOATING LINE AND STANDARD STILLWATER LEADER**
**Method:  Skittered dry fly**

**Situations to solve.** Many lakes have traveling sedge—caddis—hatches. Though most famous in Canadian lakes, especially the Kamloops region, they are widespread but often go unnoticed. I fish a lake in Oregon's Cascade Range where the common knowledge among fly fishermen is that you don't have to be on the water before 9 A.M. I row my pram out at dawn and by the time I come in at nine for a late breakfast, I have enjoyed three early hours of excellent fishing over a traveling sedge hatch that nobody else seems to know about.

Most traveling sedges are large, sizes 8 and 10, though I've seen travelers as small as size 14. They emerge in open water most often during the middle of the day; sometimes earlier, sometimes later. Rather than taking wing, the adults motor around on the surface like little speedboats. Trout key in on the movement more than the exact shape and size of the insect and take the naturals with explosive rises. You should have no trouble knowing when to use a traveling sedge.

The same flies and skittering method can be useful for exploring shoreline waters. Try it any time of day or season. If it works, the violent takes you get from the trout will be worth the patience you've shown.

**Tuning the rig.** Not only must your fly float well, but it should skate across the surface rather than dive beneath it when retrieved. Special flies such as the Mikulak Sedge have been created specifically for the hatch. The pattern has an elk-hair tail, elk-hair wing tied in two or three sections, and heavy hackle up front. It trots along the water and leaves a wake. If you lack anything else, you can skate a heavily hackled Elk Hair Caddis, or try a stonefly pattern such as the Stimulator, which will float rather than dive.

Your leader should be of normal stillwater length, 2 to 3 feet longer than your rod. The tippet should be somewhat stout, 3X and certainly no finer than 4X, both to turn over the large flies and to withstand the brutal takes you'll get.

**Position and presentation.** Your position will be dictated most often by the location of rising trout. Since you'll almost always be in a boat or tube, move into position on a rise—they'll often be scattered—to cover the water in the area. Often you'll be positioned 100 to 150 feet from shore and casting toward it. If trout are rising over a weedbed out in open water, then position yourself to fish for them there. If you know traveling sedges have been hatching in the last few days, but they are absent when you're on the water, try one anyway, the trout are likely to remember it. Either cast the fly toward shore and retrieve it out, or let a slight wind nudge your boat along while you cover all kinds of water.

**Control of the drift.** Make your cast long. Let the fly sit for a period to give the trout time to settle from the landing of the line and a chance to take the fly on the sit. Then give the fly a long tug, anywhere from half to the full length of your leader. Let the fly sit again; then skitter it the same amount. If you see signs of trout in the area, continue alternating sitting and skittering as you pull your fly all the way to the boat.

**On the water.** If you see a wake building up behind your fly, resist the temptation to drop your rod tip and stop the fly. The trout will stop, too. Natural, traveling caddis don't stop to rest when trout are on their trails. If you suddenly stop your fly, a chasing trout will commonly turn away. Keep your retrieve going, and get ready for a jolting take; just don't jolt back.

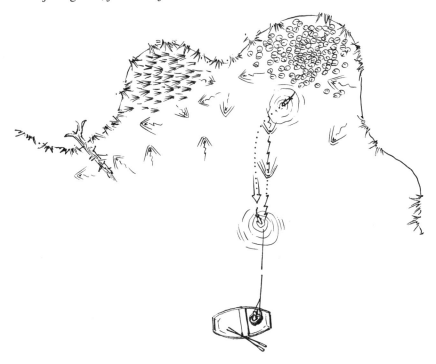

**The trout's point of view.** The wake of a caddis scooting across the surface will attract a trout to a traveling sedge. The trout will come gunning up in a hurry, perhaps because it knows the caddis might take wing, but more likely because it suspects another trout might get to the insect first. Takes are often violent.

## RIG: FLOATING LINE AND STANDARD STILLWATER LEADER
## Method: Intercepting bank feeders

**Situations to solve.** Trout, often outsized ones, cruise along certain types of banks watching for insects that have fallen to the water. The bank is a transition line between the aquatic and terrestrial worlds: Aquatic insects migrate there to emerge, while terrestrial insects moving across land often find their progress interrupted when they encounter water and fall in. By feeding there, trout double their chances to be well-fed.

The right type of bank water for fishing these situations has some depth to it, falling away abruptly to at least 2 to 4 feet. Water that slopes off from shore and is only inches deep at the edge will lack cruising trout. The best banks have some vegetative growth on shore, but none so thick that it prevents you from taking an ambush position and either making a short cast or snaking your rod out to dap the fly.

**Tuning the rig.** Most of the insects that drop in from shore will be tiny beetles and ants, which are good to imitate when you can't find any specific food form either on the water or visibly eaten by trout. If an aquatic insect is present in any numbers, then match it. Otherwise, try a size 16 or smaller Foam Beetle or Foam Ant. Your leader should be the standard length for a stillwater, 12 to 14 feet, and tapered to a 3- to 4-foot tippet of 4, 5, or even 6X. Recall that damnable conundrum: A leader fine enough to fool a stillwater trout is often too light to handle it.

**Position and presentation.** Take up an ambush position at the edge, not more than a rod length back from the bank. You have to dap your fly, dropping it to the surface rather than casting it to a trout. Tuck yourself out of sight, but where you can see the water. Don't move, and don't wear bright clothing. Next, put on Polaroids and spend some time watching for trout. If they're cruising the bank, you'll find them usually in singles or twos or at most threes, and they'll pass every few minutes, at times on a clockwork schedule. The most common scenario is for one or two trout to cruise 20 to 50 feet of bank in one direction, reverse course, and cover it again, a sort of patient marching up and down as they tip up every few feet to examine or take something from the surface.

Once you've located a trout and patterned it, place your fly where you know it will show up next. Don't paste your dry fly onto the water right in front of a trout. Instead, place it several feet ahead, or if you can time a trout, set the fly in its known circuit, and then wait for it to arrive. Never wave your rod in sight of a bank-cruising trout, because in shallow water they are susceptible to overhead predation and will be easily spooked.

**Control of the drift.** Don't try to control the drift when intercepting bank cruisers with dry flies; simply let the fly sit. If a trout fails to notice your fly or tips up to examine it but refuses it, don't lift up the fly and cast again in front of the trout. Instead, allow the trout to pass out of sight; then make a choice: Either let the fly sit, and then bring it in and cast again when the trout is due to arrive, or bring it in and change flies to try to find one that hasn't been refused. It's often a good idea to change flies. The rule is to go smaller on a tippet that is finer.

**On the water.** Become a patient predator. Retune your thinking away from searching and pursuing trout to watching and waiting for them instead. Because it's a bank show, you'll do poorly if you try to fish from a boat or tube; most likely you'll send out waves that alert the trout. During hatches of small midges, however, you may want to cast a tiny Foam Midge Pupa near a reed or cattail edge and then remain perfectly still in your float tube, pontoon boat, pram, or anchored motorboat.

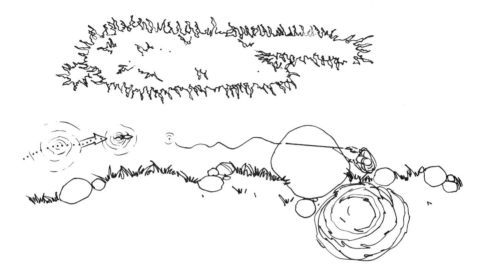

**The trout's point of view.** The fly should always be sitting on the water or, better yet, impressed into the surface film. That's why foam flies work so well for this method. Even with the gentlest presentation, the fly should not arrive in sight of the cruising trout, unless it is directly in the line of travel, head-on, with the leader leading away from the trout.

# CHAPTER 13

# Rigs and Methods for Sunk Flies on Stillwaters

S unk flies come in three varieties: wet flies, nymphs, and streamers. Although they are usually fished differently, each can be fished with the same set of rigs. For that reason, and the avoidance of abundant repetition, they're covered together in this chapter.

*Wet flies,* most often of the winged variety on stillwaters, are usually fished in the presence of a swimming type of mayfly nymph, an emergence of caddis pupae, or a fall of winged adults such as alderflies or flying ants that sink. Wet flies are almost always fished in the top few inches of the water column and can be used effectively to search shallow water when no other type of fly seems to work better. They also are effective when cast to rising trout.

*Nymphs* are often imitations of particular forms of lake food: mayfly nymphs, caddis or midge larvae or pupae, damselfly and dragonfly nymphs, and crustaceans such as scuds. They can be fished at any level in the water column, from the shallows to the deepest depths, depending on the level at which trout are feeding on naturals. Use nymphs either to imitate a specific food on which trout are focused and feeding or to search for trout. The nymphs you select for your stillwater fly box should be based on the common food forms prevalent in all stillwaters.

*Streamers* imitate such trout foods as pollywogs, leeches, and baitfish. Like nymphs, they can be effective at any depth and used as either imitations or searching flies. Pollywogs are at best scattered, and baitfish are absent from many lakes. Leeches are almost universal. For that reason, use streamers that look at least a little like leeches, when you have no indication that a different dressing would work better.

Before selecting a sunk fly type and specific pattern, try to collect naturals, and imitate those that are most abundant. In some lakes, this will be mayflies; in others it will be scuds, midges, leeches, or caddis. If you're unable to collect, or if you do so and find no prevalent natural, then base your fly selection on local knowledge—

talk to employees at fly shops—or on common patterns that resemble the most abundant food forms in all lakes.

**Collecting.** You can go to a scientific supply house or on the Internet to buy a collecting net made specifically for aquatic insects. You also can make one by sawing the handle off an old broom and lashing a kitchen strainer to it. To collect insects, run the net through weedy shallows, bang it against the submerged stems of reeds and cattails, and lift it up to see what's wriggling in it. A good way to collect in the depths out of reach of such a strainer is to drop your anchor, tug it through weeds until it's covered, then hoist it up quickly. A lot of food types will escape, but some will get stuck in the weeds, and you can imitate them.

**Choosing a rig and a method for the depths.** When you see no signs of feeding trout on the surface, you might decide to use a sunk fly on a stillwater, but how do you arrive at a rig to use and a method with which to use it? First, you can focus on one of the specific water types where trout are found most often: the shoreline, the shallows, a drop-off, or a weedbed. Once you've chosen the type of water you want to fish, next determine its depth and choose a line type that gets you down there and a method that keeps the fly in the zone you want to probe. Your rig and method will vary more according to the depth you desire to fish than it will by the type of structure over which you're fishing.

Second, you might decide that you want to explore the lake and not restrict yourself to one water type, a wise decision the first time you arrive at new water. Again, choose a line that lets you get your fly or pair of flies—my favorite exploring tandem is a size 10 or 12 black or olive Woolly Bugger trailed by a size 14 or 16 Olive Scud or TDC Midge—to the depth you want. Make one cast off the stern of your transportation; then begin rowing or finning slowly, watching while you troll for signs that you should do something else.

Fluorocarbon leader has a place in stillwater fishing with sunk flies. It sinks and is less visible than regular monofilament tippet. Guides have told me that it increases their subsurface stillwater catch rate four- to five-fold.

**Finding the depth.** If you don't have an electronic depth finder, the quickest way to find the depth of the water is to snap your hemostat onto the end of your leader, drop it overboard and let it settle to the bottom, and then measure the line you bring in. You can do the same with your anchor, though it's slightly more difficult to lift.

## RIG:      FLOATING LINE AND STANDARD STILLWATER LEADER

**Purpose.** This basic rig has three purposes. First, you'll use it to fish sunk flies to trout that are rising visibly but are either not taking floating naturals or refusing your imitations of them. You'll also cast sunk flies to fish that are cruising and feeding high in the water column but not on the surface.

The rig's second purpose is to fish shorelines, shallows, and even some modestly deep weedbeds and other types of habitat. To use the rig shallow, cast weighted or unweighted flies, begin your retrieve right away, and keep your fly moving along. To fish from 5 to 15 feet down, cast weighted flies, count them down to the limits of your patience, and use a slow handtwist retrieve.

The third purpose of the rig is to suspend a weighted fly, usually a midge pupa pattern, from a foot beneath the surface to as deep as 20 or even 25 feet. These depths require an extremely long tippet, perhaps some putty weight above the fly, a patient count, and a retrieve that keeps you in touch with the almost idle fly.

**History/origins.** This rig arrived on the heels of the development of adequate floating lines. In the days of silk lines, lake anglers likely started the day with a dried, dressed, and floating line and ended the day with a line that had soaked up enough water that it closely resembled today's slow-sinking intermediate. A line that floats has a visible tip, which tells you about a take when it darts forward or downward.

**Knots and notes.** The leader, depending on its purpose, can vary from short and stout for probing bank water with large streamers to a length a few feet longer than the rod and fine for fishing small wet flies and nymphs to rising trout. To suspend a nymph just inches beneath the surface, the leader can even be dressed with line dressing or fly floatant to within a few inches of the fly. The longest leaders are used to suspend midge pupae as deep as 20 feet or more, though it's a method that has largely been supplanted by the use of indicators on stillwaters. If you fish with a 10- to 20-foot leader and want a quicker sink, then use a base leader a bit longer than your rod, one or two tapering sections at most, and add a single diameter tippet all the way out to the fly.

Two-fly rigs are appropriate, and the normal knots—blood, surgeon's, improved clinch, and Duncan loop—are used to attach tippet sections and flies.

**Adjustments for conditions.** You will adjust your rig based on the different depths you're fishing. Use weighted or unweighted flies, add weight to the leader, and then add or subtract small shot or bits of putty weight. You can also adjust the length of the tippet—the longer and finer, the deeper your fly will sink—and the duration of the count while the fly sinks.

**Rules for the rig.** Only use the floating line and standard leader rig on stillwaters when trout are shallow or you have a specific reason to attempt the depths with a floating line, such as suspending a midge pupa. Another valid reason for using the rig is to fish a weighted nymph in the shallows or over shoals or high weedbeds,

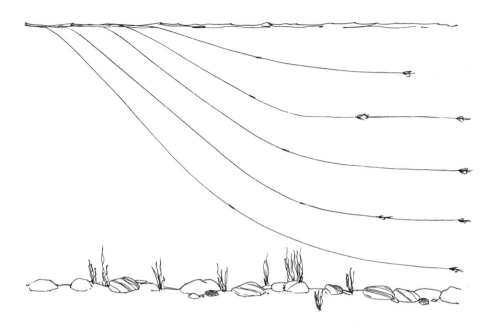

especially if you want to use a slow retrieve and would like a floating line tip to tell you about takes.

If you want to fish moderate to profundal depths, you almost always should use an appropriate sinking line and shorter leader rather than the floater and a longer leader. It will take less time to get your fly down, the fly will stay in the strike zone longer, and you can retrieve at a constant depth, rather than retrieving upward as you would with a floating line.

**Appropriate flies.** You can fish all kinds of sunk flies with the floating line rig, including winged wets and soft-hackled wets, imitative nymphs for mayflies, dragon- and damselflies, midge and caddis larvae and pupae, and scuds. Try the rig with Woolly Buggers in waters with leeches, featherwing streamers in waters with baitfish.

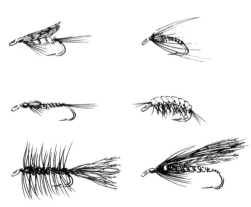

**Situations to solve.** Quite often trout will feed so near the surface that each take sends rise-rings to the top. It appears the trout are taking insects off the surface, but they're not. If you try to fish such situations with a dry fly, your attempts will be fruitless. Even if trout might be feeding on the surface, you're not always going to hook them with dry flies. Sometimes it's because you either don't recognize the right fly or don't own one. Other times, trout are taking a dozen or so nymphs subsurface for every adult they take off the surface, but this behavior is difficult to notice.

Whatever the reason, if you are surrounded by rising trout but can't bring them to a dry, switch to a nymph, a wet fly, or in desperation even a streamer, and see if they'll respond to that. If you can recognize the adult and extrapolate to the nymph—for example, trying a Flashback Pheasant Tail nymph when *Callibaetis* mayfly duns are on the water—then you're likely to solve the problem. But any sunk fly can instill greed in feeding trout at times and solve the situation just as well as an exact imitation.

If trout are cruising visibly but not feeding on the surface, then you should begin fishing with a sunk fly tied to your tippet instead of a dry fly.

**Tuning the rig.** If you're switching to a sunk fly after trying a dry, simply nip off the dry and tie on the wet, nymph, or streamer. If you arrive at the water, see working or cruising trout, and want to try a sunk fly first, then use a base leader the length of the rod and a 3- to 4-foot tippet in a diameter appropriate for the fly size you have chosen. If you want to suspend a nymph pattern inches deep, usually during a midge hatch, then dress the leader and tippet to within about a foot of the fly.

**Position and presentation.** Move onto rising trout the same way you would if you were planning to fish a dry fly. Approach the edge of a pod, but don't move so close that you frighten trout on the periphery. Anchor if the wind is brisk; otherwise, position yourself and drift, if you're in a boat or pontoon boat, or use your feet and fins to move if you're in a tube. Rather than crashing the leader and fly across the rise-rings, cast to trout at the edge of the pod, and place the first cast to the near side of any rise. Subsequent casts should be placed to the right and left, in hopes of intercepting the moving trout.

If trout are cruising and you can calculate their course, then place the fly well ahead of them, and animate it when one comes into sight of the fly. Otherwise, move to the edge of the area where they're working and cover all of the water you can reach with casts that form an arc.

**Control of the drift.** No matter what type of fly you use, allow it to sink for at least a few seconds after each cast. Trout often will take a sunk fly either on the sit or on the sink. Trout seem to favor wet flies without any retrieve, although nymphs and streamers can also be effective without any animation from the rod. Fish nymphs with a handtwist or slow strip, and retrieve wets with a slow to moderate strip. Streamers should be fished with a modest to the fastest strip you can achieve.

**On the water.** If you see your line tip dart, especially when your fly is on the sink or you're using a handtwist retrieve, lift the rod to draw out any slack line and to set the hook. Stillwater takes can be subtle at times. Trout often take a leech by slipping up behind it and flaring their gills to inhale it. If it's your fly a trout is trying to take, it will be tethered to your leader and might not enter the trout's mouth. You'll feel a tap. Often the trout will circle and take again. If you feel a tap, drop your rod, wait a moment, and then lift the rod tip again. You'll be surprised how often you have a trout on.

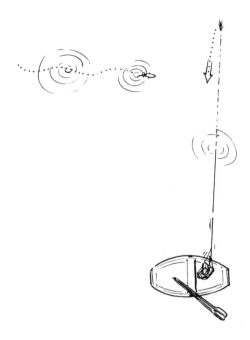

**The trout's point of view.** A feeding or cruising trout sees something—your nymph, wet fly, or streamer—creeping, swimming, or galloping away, and unless it's frightened by it, the fish will usually rush to take it before another trout can get to it.

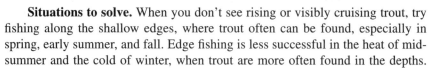

**Situations to solve.** When you don't see rising or visibly cruising trout, try fishing along the shallow edges, where trout often can be found, especially in spring, early summer, and fall. Edge fishing is less successful in the heat of midsummer and the cold of winter, when trout are more often found in the depths.

When I fish any new stillwater, I first look for rising or cruising fish from a high vantage point as soon as I arrive. If I see none, then I launch myself and begin a circuit of the shoreline if the lake is small enough to cover in less than a day. If the lake is vast, I'll begin by trolling, which allows me to see more water. In either case, my goal is to fish while seeing all the water I can. I hope to catch a few trout as I go, but more than that, I want to discover the type of water that trout are using, and within that, find rising or cruising fish sometime during my explorations.

You can also use the same rig and method you employ while in a float tube or boat casting *toward* shore that you use to cast *from* shore.

**Tuning the rig.** The most useful rig has a normal base leader, the length of the rod, plus a tippet of 2 to 4 feet, its diameter tuned to the size fly you want to turn over. My most common combination for exploring shorelines and cover has become a 3 or 4X tippet and a size 10 or 12 black or olive Woolly Bugger. Another favorite is a 4 or 5X tippet and a winged wet fly such as an Alder or Blue Quill. I also like a 4X tippet to a size 12 or 14 Olive Scud trailed by a 5X tippet to a size 16 or 18 Black Midge Pupa. Each combination is fished differently, which allows me to give trout a choice if I'm not doing well.

**Position and presentation.** If you're fishing from shore, cover all the water you can reach from one position with a fan of casts; then move to another position and repeat the process. On ponds and lakes with open shorelines and no brush behind, you can cover water almost as effectively from foot as from a boat.

If you're afloat, move along the shoreline and place casts 3 to 5 feet apart. Cast to any associated cover, including overhanging tree branches, fallen logs, boulders, reed patches, cattail edges, and lily pad flats. If the wind is strong, and you have no willing partner to position your boat, try anchoring and cover the shoreline a piece at a time. If the wind is absent or light, set up a drift line a comfortable cast from shore, say 40 to 50 feet, and touch the oars only when necessary to keep your position.

A float tube can be the best device from which to fish a shoreline. Let the breeze ease you slowly along, and use your fins only to correct for distance from shore. Cast at an angle *behind* your direction of travel, so that your progress becomes part of your retrieve.

**Control of the drift.** If you're fishing a streamer, vary your retrieve between modest and fast strips. With wet flies, try a stripping retrieve of modest speed, and occasionally add a staccato twitching of the rod tip to make the fly swim in darts. If you're fishing one or two nymphs, use a slow stripping retrieve at the fastest and a creeping handtwist retrieve if the wind allows such a slow retrieve.

**On the water.** Primarily a means for exploring water to find trout, either by catching them or spotting them rising or cruising, this method often will find you catching a lot of fish by casting to the shoreline and adjacent structure. You've discovered what your explorations are after, so slow down and enjoy life.

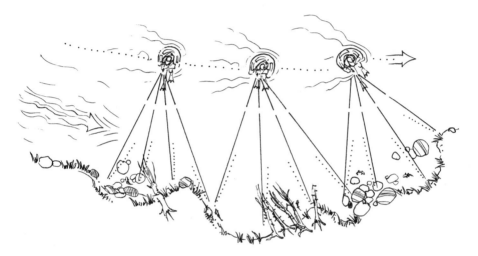

**The trout's point of view.** Trout are not bass; they cruise and feed along shore-lines and around cover more often than they take up ambush positions and wait for prey. If a trout sees your fly—streamer, wet fly, or nymph—moving into its sight lines at an appropriate speed, it will usually put on a burst of speed and gun it down.

**RIG:     FLOATING LINE AND STANDARD
          STILLWATER LEADER**
**Method:  Cast and countdown**

**Situations to solve.** When stillwater trout are not feeding on or near the top, you nearly always will find them on or near the bottom. Sunlight ignites the growth of vegetation where aquatic insects live. The shallower the water, the more sunlight strikes through to the bottom and spurs vegetation growth. In spring, early summer, and fall, when trout are most active, you'll find them feeding on the bottom in water 3 to 15 feet deep, within range of floating lines, weighted flies, and long leaders. In clear water, vegetation and therefore trout can be found as deep as 30 feet, beyond the practical limits of this method.

This floating line method is most effective when trout are less than 10 feet deep, but it has been applied against fish feeding on suspended midge pupae as far as 20 to 25 feet down.

**Tuning the rig.** Start with weighted flies, the more heavily weighted the better. To fish deep or to speed a sinking fly on its way, try pinching a split shot to your leader or molding some putty weight to it 8 to 12 inches from the fly.

The length and diameter of your tippet will determine how far and how fast your weighted flies will sink. If you're fishing in water 3 to 5 feet deep, your tippet should be 3 to 5 feet long. If the water is deeper, lengthen the tippet according to its depth, as much as 25 feet if you're fishing midge pupae to that depth. Tippets that must go deeper than 10 feet are so long that they become difficult to cast. You will find other methods, such as using an indicator, more practical to use when covering such depths.

**Position and presentation.** In all but the shallowest water, you should be anchored, preferably bow and stern. Any swinging of the boat when you're fishing more than 8 to 10 feet deep will interrupt your fishing. Position your boat at least 30 feet from the nearest bit of bottom you want to fish. You will only get your retrieve to about 20 feet from the boat, after which your fly will begin to lift. The farther you can cast, the more bottom your fly will cover on the retrieve. Distance casting is at a premium with this method.

If you're covering a weedbed, anchor your boat away from it, not directly over it. If you're fishing a large cove or broad shoal, you will have no choice but to anchor on it. If you're fishing a drop-off with the floating line and a long leader, then either cast parallel to the drop and fish along its edge, or cast from shallow water toward deep water, let the fly sink to the bottom, and then retrieve up the face of it. Usually anchoring over deep water so that you cast to the shallow side and let the fly drop down the face is impractical, because the floating line hinders the sink too much.

**Control of the drift.** Once your cast is made, drop the rod tip almost to the water and begin your count . . . one-thousand-one, one-thousand-two, one-thousand-three . . . usually in the 5- to 60-second range. Anything beyond that, consider going to a sinking line. Use a slow strip or handtwist retrieve to keep your fly deep as long as possible. A fast retrieve will lift the fly out of the strike zone almost immediately.

If you retrieve weeds, then shorten your count a few seconds and repeat. If you catch trout, keep your count the same. Always retrieve with your rod tip low to the water.

**On the water.** Trout often take a fly on the sink. In reality, you'll rarely know when it happens, but keep a close eye on the leader's point of entry into the water while you count, and you might add more fish to your catch. If the fly unaccountably speeds up, moves right or left, or even hesitates, then set the hook. Most likely, you've found a trout.

**The trout's point of view.** The trout will see a fly creeping slowly through its area of interest just above the bottom, above or alongside a weedbed, along the edge, or on the upslope of a drop-off. Make your fly look like any of the insects that move in those same places, and most likely trout will take it.

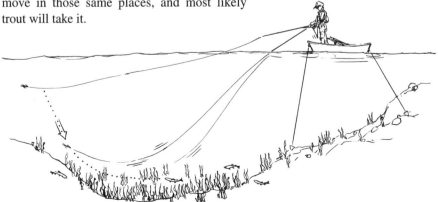

**Situations to solve.** Trout cruising banks and feeding on top can be taken on dry flies, but at least as often, they nose along taking whatever insects or crustaceans they can find at the water's edge. Water boatmen—beetlelike creatures with oarlike middle legs that are perhaps the most abundant insects—must breathe air, so they dash to the surface, take a bubble, and then dart back to the bottom. Trout set up their cruising patterns along the banks, and when they notice water boatmen dashing to the top and back, they rush to take them. If you take up your hidden ambush point, don your Polaroids, and notice trout swimming along in straight lines and then making sudden swift movements forward or to the sides, you can bet they're taking water boatmen.

Many other creatures living along the banks—including mayfly, damselfly, and dragonfly nymphs; midge and caddis larvae and pupae; leeches; and even aquatic beetles—also get eaten by trout. If you observe that any of these creatures are dominant in the water you're fishing, match them, or at least approximate them.

**Tuning the rig.** Use a standard base leader the length of your rod, plus a 3- to 4-foot tippet of 5 to 6X. The fly should be size 16 to 20, weighted just enough to penetrate the surface film and fall slowly toward the bottom. If you tie your own flies for fishing banks, use four to six turns of nonlead weighting wire. If the bottom is weedy and you need to keep your fly from sinking too deep, either dress all but the tippet with fly floatant or line dressing or insert a very tiny yarn or hard indicator at the tippet knot.

**Position and presentation.** Take your ambush position, concealed and unmoving, a rod length or so back from the bank. Try to pattern the movements of a single trout before casting to it. If you spot a trout coming toward you, at least 20 to 30 feet out from your position, cast to it. You must cast 5 to 10 feet ahead of the trout, exactly in its line of travel as it heads almost directly toward you, so that the fly lands in front of the fish with the leader and line extending away from the plip the fly makes when it touches down.

However, it's often best to make your cast when no trout is in sight. Let your fly settle to the bottom, or to a point just above the bottom when it's suspended by the leader or an indicator. Then wait for the trout to arrive before animating the fly.

**Control of the drift.** If you've made your cast to a sighted fish, the fly should be sinking toward the bottom when the trout arrives in sight of it. If you see the trout turn toward it, set the hook when you see another turn or the flash of its mouth—the fly will be taken in and spit back out in an instant. If the trout does not seem to see the fly, then animate it with a few handtwists or a slight lifting of the rod tip when you think the fish is near it. When the fly becomes alive right in front of the trout, the take will often be brutal.

If you've made your cast when no trout is in sight, wait until one appears near the fly; then lift the settled fly off the bottom or animate the suspended fly. Either way, you should have no trouble telling when a trout has taken the fly and it's time to set the hook.

**On the water.** Trout taken while cruising a bank are almost always hooked while they are moving straight toward your position. You will never feel the take; you must see or sense it. This method only works where the water is clear enough and calm enough to spot trout.

**The trout's point of view.** A trout cruising along a shoreline should see your fly either on the sink, as if it is swimming toward the bottom, or suddenly animated, as if it is trying to escape.

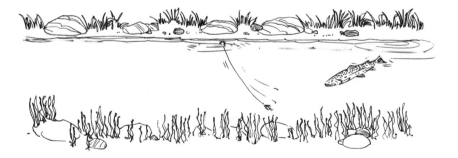

## RIG:          FLOATING LINE AND STRIKE INDICATOR

**Purpose.** This rig is generally thought to be used for reaching far down into the depths, usually to suspend a midge pupa pattern just above the bottom, but it is just as effective for suspending a nymph at any depth from 10 inches beneath the surface to 30 feet down. While most useful with midge patterns, it can also be used to fish with almost any other kind of nymph and is especially effective with a pair of different styles, sizes, or colors when you want to see what the trout might be willing to take.

The indicator rig can be used to fish shallow, to suspend a fly over moderately deep weedbeds, or most often to fish just above the bottom. You also would use it to drop a nymph directly down between stems of rooted aquatic plants, which grow in spaced forests and reach up from the bottom like slender trees. Such loosely constructed weedbeds are full of aquatic insects and thus are prowled heavily by trout. You cannot cast and retrieve through these weedbeeds without getting hung up on the vegetation, but you can simply hang a nymph down there at any depth and wait for a trout to find it.

This rig is also effective for fishing wherever slight currents enter or exit a lake, a little like fishing a very slow run in a river. If there's enough wind to make fishing with any other method difficult, this rig allows you to fish anywhere between the surface and the bottom, if you make your cast upwind and essentially up current. Again, fish the drift as if you were fishing a slow stream.

**History/origins.** Soon after folks began experimenting with strike indicators in moving water in the late 1960s and early 1970s, a few smart stillwater fishermen transferred this knowledge to lakes. Most refinements took place in the Kamloops region of British Columbia, Canada, which is famous for big trout feeding on big midge pupae. The rig pioneered in that region can be transferred to any stillwater, though the fly size should drop from a size 8 and 10 in the north to a size 12 down to 20 in most latitudes favored by trout.

**Knots and notes.** When used with lightly weighted flies alone or with a small amount of putty weight added to the leader, a hinged yarn indicator seems most sensitive to strikes. Tie the indicator to the end of a 4- to 6-foot clubbed leader with an improved clinch knot. The tippet should be tied to the leader with the same knot and slipped against the indicator. Finally, tie the fly to the tippet with a Duncan loop knot.

To fish with heavier flies or more putty weight, you will have to use a somewhat large, hard strike indicator. Kamloops expert Brian Chan uses Thill brand indicators the size of small bobbers, finding the bottom depth with a depth sounder or hemostat clipped to the end of his leader and rigging to fish about 18 inches above it. He holds the indicator in place with a toothpick and ties the fly on with a loop knot. Putty weight is molded 1 to 2 feet above the fly.

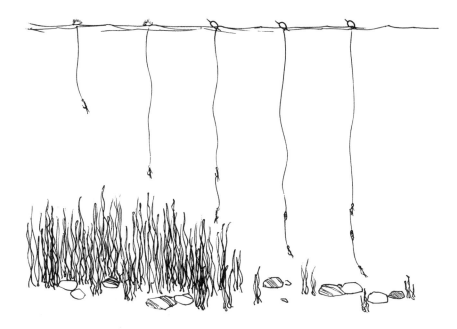

**Adjustments for conditions.** The major adjustment made to this rig is in the length of leader beyond the indicator. You can also adjust the amount of weight on the leader and the weight of the fly itself, choosing among unweighted, lightly weighted, and heavily weighted.

**Rules for the rig.** If you see trout feeding at a specific level, rig to fish at that depth. At times you'll see cruisers working just subsurface. If you own a depth finder, check it to see if trout are suspended at some midrange depth. In the absence of such indications, rig to fish just above the bottom. Determine the depth, and fix your indicator 1 to 2 feet up the leader short of that depth.

**Appropriate flies.** Most flies used with the stillwater strike indicator rig will be based on midge larvae or pupae. Beadheads are excellent. Tungsten beads will help get your fly down to the deepest depths and perhaps negate the need for weight on the leader. Brass beads will add some weight and some flash as well. Flies to be fished in shallow water are effective when tied with glass beads. Most midge patterns are tied too slender to allow additional weight on the hook shank. The most effective colors for flies will be red, brown, black, and olive.

**Situations to solve.** Trout in lakes and ponds spend much of their time cruising and feeding on insects suspended somewhere in the water column, whether it's a few inches deep to a few inches off the bottom or anywhere in between. Unless the water is clear and the sun strikes through it just right, this activity is almost impossible to observe. Sometimes you'll see an occasional rise or bulge at the surface, which indicates that a pod is in the area and actively seeking insects that are not deep. You can almost bet that if you see midge adults emerging on the surface, trout are feeding somewhere below on pupae suspended or slowly rising toward the top. Rig to suspend a pupa pattern, or better yet a pair of them, just above the bottom, and reset your indicator to fish them higher, in 2-foot increments, until you find the level at which the trout are feeding.

This method often succeeds when there are no indications that something else might work better. On many productive waters, your best bet is to start with suspended nymphs, especially if you have been on this particular lake or pond and know where its trout might be located. If midges are not common in the stillwater, use an imitation of whatever food form is most abundant.

**Tuning the rig.** Select an indicator that is big and bright and capable of suspending the amount of weight you'll use. Adjust your tippet for depth, from 1 foot to as much as 30 feet, and base your fly selection on prevalent naturals. If you have no specimens, pick a pair of nymphs in different sizes and colors to help determine what trout want. If you're fishing more than 4 or 5 feet down, separate the flies by 2 feet and pinch a bit of putty weight between them.

**Position and presentation.** The strike indicator method is just as effective from shore as it is from a floating device. On small impounded lakes and ponds, the deepest water is nearly always against the dam, and trout are almost always cruising within an easy cast of it. But you can fish from shore anywhere around the rim of a stillwater, as long as you have room behind you for a backcast, or even a roll cast, and trout water in front of you.

If you're in a boat, especially if you're fishing fairly deep, anchor at both ends. If you're in a pontoon boat and can only anchor at one end, then use your oars to hold a constant position. A float tube will work if the wind is not so strong that you cannot hold the tube in one spot. Wind drifting can be an effective way to fish the indicator rig, but avoid any movement that might lift the fly out of the depth at which you want to suspend it. Most likely, you're over a weedbed, shoal, or drop-off, or in an area where you've spotted trout or suspect their presence, and you want to stay there.

**Control of the drift.** You do not control the drift with this method. The objective is to cast out and let the fly or flies sink to the desired level where they will dangle suspended. A slight wave action may cause your flies to nod up and down, and this movement may help attract trout, but it's not necessary. Trout will take your flies on the sit.

**On the water.** Your indicator will often take a sudden dive, an obvious indication that you've had a hit. Sometimes the indictor will merely bob, send out tiny rings, or even tip its hat in a different direction, all signs that a trout is inspecting the fly by feel. Set the hook before it rejects it. The most difficult part of indicator fishing on a stillwater is keeping your attention from wandering to the nearby scenery. Inattention will cost you fish.

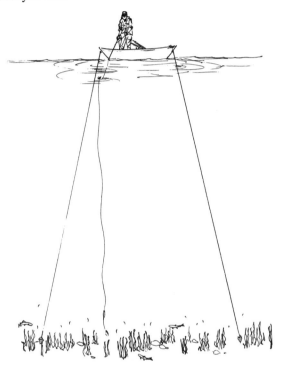

**The trout's point of view.** Trout generally cruise stillwaters somewhat lazily, loafing along and taking whatever naturals they come across, some surprisingly tiny. When one spots your fly, it will turn toward it, perhaps putting on a bit of speed if other trout are nearby, inhale it, and continue on its trip before quickly trying to disengage itself from what is obviously not the living bite it expected.

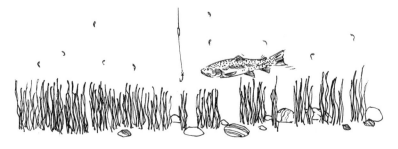

**RIG:          FLOATING LINE AND STRIKE INDICATOR**
**Method:       Wind/current drifting**

**Situations to solve.** A light breeze makes it difficult to fish and hold your fly or flies in one position with the previous suspended nymph method. Lakes and ponds are notoriously windy, but you can make that wind work for you by showing your flies in a slow drift across the bottom and up through the water column. If wind ruffles the surface so that you can't peer into the water to read its features, a wind-drifted nymph, or set of them, can do that exploring for you. Quite often if you fish without a depth finder on lakes, as most of us do, your flies are the only exploratory tool you own.

The slight currents caused by entering and departing streams in the lake are gathering places for trout foods and, therefore, trout. Because these currents work much as a wind might, you'll want to make them work for you, rather than against you.

**Tuning the rig.** Rig the same for this method as for the previous one: Use a supportive and visible indicator, one fly or two flies with a bit of putty weight added to the leader between them, and a tippet the length necessary to reach your desired depth. If you have to make a change, add more weight to keep your flies in the strike zone near the bottom and against the movement of the indicator that tries to lift them out of it.

**Position and presentation.** This method works well from shore, and I often use it when wading shallow shoals in both lakes and ponds. Trout cruise these waters, but in blustery weather they are more susceptible to nymphs than to dry flies. A nymph or two suspended 2 to 4 feet deep can work wonders. If you're in an anchored boat, you can apply the same method. It might be difficult to effectively fish the deepest depths, but you'll have no trouble down to 20 feet.

Fish a wind the same way you fish an inlet or outlet stream current: Cast upwind or upstream from your stationary position, and let the wind or the current nudge your indicator through a slow drift all the way to the downwind or downstream reach of the line that you've cast. Then pick up and cast upwind or up current again. You can extend the drift by feeding line into it, just as you would in a riffle or run.

If you're adrift and want to cover some water, then simply cast out, let your nymph achieve its depth and let the wind ease your craft over the surface while your fly explores the depths down below. This method doesn't work well in a stiff wind, because the line lags behind the boat or tube. But you can throw out a wind anchor to slow you.

**Control of the drift.** Keep your rod pointed straight down the line, with the tip near the water. Use mends, upwind or upstream, to keep your line pointed as straight as possible toward your indicator. If slack forms, draw it out so you are in touch with the indicator and can set the hook. If the indicator reaches the end of its tether and begins to drag so that it might lift the nymph or nymphs off the bottom, feed slack to extend the time they remain on the bottom to tempt trout.

**On the water.** It's difficult to juggle oars and your fly rod. You must have the fly rod in your hand if you're to have much chance of setting the hook at the first sign of a strike. A float tube works very well for wind drifting, because you can control its movement with your feet, thus leaving your hands free. If you're in a pram, pontoon boat, or anything else that requires rowing, you'll have to do your best to control it with a few quick strokes; then let the oars rest and get your rod back into your hands.

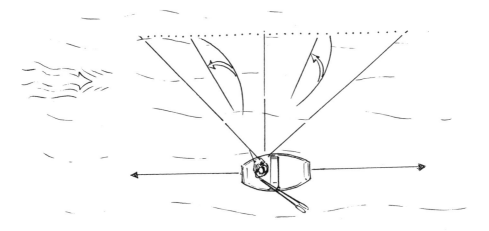

**The trout's point of view.** Wind sets up a current in the water. If you look into this current, you'll see that it is full of living, drifting bits of trout food. When you wind drift, whether from a stationary position or bobbing slowly along, your nymph, or pair of them, will be moving with that slight current and become part of the stew from which traveling trout winnow their meals.

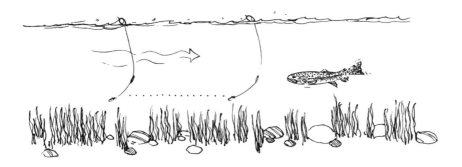

## RIG:    CLEAR INTERMEDIATE OR WET-TIP LINE

**Purpose.** The purpose of the slow-sinking intermediate line and 10-foot sinking-tip line would seem to be to fish sunk flies a few feet deeper than you can reach with a floating line, but the floater, with a long enough tippet and extended countdown time, will fish deep just as well. The better reason to fish these lines is to get your line, leader, and fly just under the surface, beneath the influence of wave action and wind drift. In particular, the clear intermediate line is excellent for fishing just inches to a couple of feet deep when you don't want wind chop or push to get in the way of how you want the fly to fish.

I prefer the clear intermediate when I'm trolling for trout while exploring a pond or small lake, or when I make my mandatory first circuit along the edge of a larger lake. The rig fishes the fly—or pair of them, if I'm pulling a Woolly Bugger followed by a midge pupa pattern—deep enough for trout to find it but still keeps it shallow enough so that I'm not constantly hung up on the same weedbeds that attract the trout.

The wet-tip line is not affected like the longer floating portion at the rear by whatever is happening on the surface. The wet-tip is the better line for casting and retrieving along the shoreline and over the shallows, though when you don't have an intermediate, its deeper missions can be fulfilled almost as well with the wet-tip. Both are better exploratory lines than the floater, unless trout happen to be working the surface.

**History/origins.** The wet-tip was designed in the late 1970s and early '80s before the advent of the indicator-and-shot method to get nymphs deeper in streams. But the wet-tip also found a home as many folks' second line on stillwaters. The intermediate was first used around the same time frame, only for fishing saltwater flats. It, too, quickly found application on stillwaters. One of the two should be spooled on a backup reel and kept handy whenever you fish lakes or ponds.

**Knots and notes.** The rigging used with either type of line is similar to the standard stillwater leader used with the floating line: a tapered base leader down to 3 or 4X and a tippet 2 to 4 feet long and an appropriate diameter to turn over the size flies cast. The same leader will work with the wet-tip line if you're fishing shallow water. If you use the countdown method to get the fly deep, then a shorter leader, 6 to 8 feet, will keep your fly from riding up higher than the line tip. Fluorocarbon leader and tippet are the best for any sunk-fly fishing on stillwaters.

Use the blood knot or surgeon's knot for tapering and tippet sections, the improved clinch for streamers and wet flies, and the Duncan loop for nymphs.

**Adjustments for conditions.** Moving to these lines, instead of the floater or deeper sinking lines, is in itself the primary adjustment you make. Of course, you must adjust the length of your leader to accomplish the goal you're after: Go long and fine with the intermediate to separate the flies from the line, and short and still fine with the wet-tip to get the fly down at the same sink rate as the line.

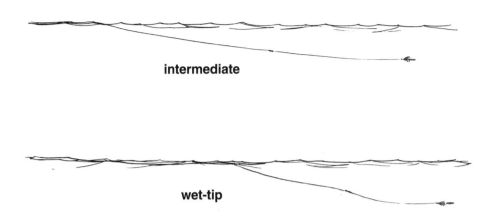

**intermediate**

**wet-tip**

**Rules for the rig.** Use these lines when your goal is either to get your fly just beneath the surface or to get it down quickly in water that is 2 to 5 feet deep. If you want to plumb the depths but don't want to do it with a floating line and either a strike indicator or long count, then you'll be better served with a full-sinking line or the appropriate shooting head.

**Appropriate flies.** You can fish all sorts of sunk flies with the intermediate or wet-tip line. Use streamers and wet flies primarily for trolling or casting to the shoreline and shallows, and employ a modest to fast stripping retrieve. Whenever a specific food form is dominant, either imitate it or choose nymphs that resemble it at least roughly; then use a retrieve that is in keeping with the movements of the natural.

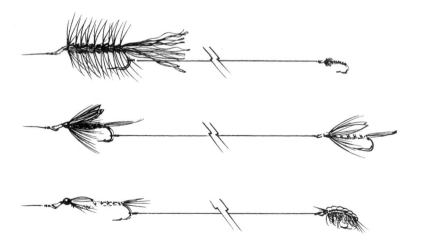

**Situations to solve.** The most common way to use the wet-tip line, and to a lesser extent the clear intermediate, is to position yourself along a shoreline and cast and retrieve to the shore and associated cover and shallows. The wet-tip, perhaps the most useful line for this type of fishing, is employed in the same manner as the floating line, but because it gets the flies down deeper and quicker, it is more effective for casting and retrieving along the shoreline. Because the running portion floats, you can lift the line off the water after a few feet of retrieve and place it at the next bit of bank or cover without having to retrieve it most of the way to the boat, as you would with a full-sink line. Shoreline fishing is one of the best applications for the wet-tip line. For other types of stillwater fishing, the clear intermediate, a full-sink line, or one of your slow-sinking shooting heads will be better.

The clear intermediate also works for fishing the shoreline and nearby cover and shallows, and because many folks find it useful in a wide variety of situations, they have replaced their wet-tip line with one.

**Tuning the rig.** A base leader the length of the rod, tapered to a tippet the correct diameter to turn over the size wet fly, nymph, or streamer you choose, are what you will need for most shoreline and cover situations. If you're fishing in calm conditions, add a 2-to 3-foot tippet appropriate to the size flies you're casting. If you want to fish a two-fly combination, tie a 2-foot tippet to the hook bend of the first fly, and tie the point fly to the other end.

**Position and presentation.** When fishing from shore, look for places where you can navigate the bank and not get tangled in all sorts of briars and brush. Fish the water along the banks in both directions, and then work your casts in a fan to cover all the water you can reach in an arc around you. If the banks are open enough, work your way along them, casting tight to the bank ahead of you as you walk or wade the shallows. If you find any floating logs that are large enough to support your weight without wobbling or sending out waves, first fish around them; then step out onto them and fish from them. Many ponds have tangles of floating logs that let you hop from one to another, fishing pockets between them.

If you're fishing from a float tube, pontoon boat, pram, or power boat, then position yourself a fair but not long cast out from shore. Make each cast precisely to the bank or to a bit of cover, such as near a half-submerged log or under overhanging limbs, and retrieve away from the bank or cover 5 to 15 feet. Use the breeze, or better yet the lack of one, to set up a path parallel to shore at a convenient casting distance, and cover every 3 to 5 feet of shore with separate casts.

**Control of the drift.** With any type of sunk fly, give a short three- to five-second count for the fly or flies to sink. With streamers, initiate a modest to fast stripping retrieve. Use a slow to modest stripping retrieve with wet flies and a slow strip or even slower handtwist retrieve with nymphs.

**On the water.** Most trout will come to the fly within 5 to 10 feet of the shoreline, but trout do not usually tuck themselves tight in against a bank, as bass might. Instead, they set up a cruising circuit near the bank. Be sure to retrieve far enough out so that a trout that has spotted the fly at some distance has a chance to catch up with it before you lift it for the next cast.

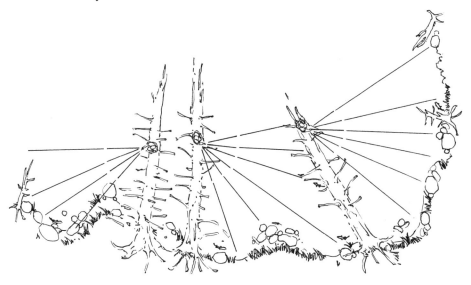

**The trout's point of view.** On its circuit along a shoreline, the trout usually sees your fly at a depth of 1 to 2 feet, creeping, swimming, or dashing according to whether it's a nymph, wet, or streamer. Unless the line has landed on the trout's head, or the fly is unlike anything it has ever seen or eaten, the trout quite likely will move to the fly swiftly and take it.

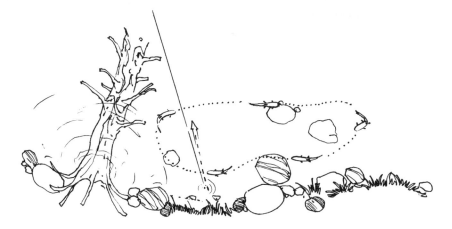

**RIG:          CLEAR INTERMEDIATE OR WET-TIP LINE**
**Method:     Countdown and deep retrieve**

**Situations to solve.** This method is best used with intermediate and wet-tip lines in water 5 to 10 feet deep. Use it when fishing shallows near the shoreline, over weedbeds, above shoals, and over drop-offs that do not plunge into great depths. If you apply the same fly lines to situations deeper than 10 feet, heavily weighted flies and longer counts will be required, and you might be better served by a full-sinking line or shooting head.

Because trout typically are found in relatively shallow water in spring, early summer, and fall, when insects are most active and conditions best for trout, these lines and this method are important components of successful stillwater fly fishing. Other rigs and methods will work better when trout are suspended deep. Try the floating line and strike indicator rig when trout are holding near the bottom and feeding on midges, and employ the full-sinking line or shooting head when they're suspended over a thermocline in midsummer or near the bottom in winter.

**Tuning the rig.** The standard base leader the length of your rod, with a 2- to 4-foot tippet added, works best with this method when flies have substantial weight added. If you want to get unweighted or slightly weighted flies to the bottom, then shorten the leader so that the overall length, tippet included, is between 6 and 8 feet. To get your fly deeper than 4 or 5 feet with the intermediate line, you will have to use a long tippet and weighted fly.

**Position and presentation.** The countdown method is effective when fishing off steeply sloped shorelines, especially when you find a point from which to cast over water that drops off fairly quickly. If you're working such a point from shore, cast to cover one side of it with a full fan of casts, and then move out onto the tip of the point itself and cover that with a fan of casts, before finally covering the last side of the point. One or both sides of the point will often be covered and shallow; your countdown times should reflect that.

If you're afloat and covering any relatively shallow water types down to 10 feet or so, always anchor, at both ends if possible, in a position that places you just a few feet away from the water you want to cover. Be careful not to row or motor up and drop anchor on the heads of the trout you want to catch, or you will drive them off. If you're anchoring over a drop-off, then choose one of two positions: either at the lip of the drop-off, so you can cast and retrieve parallel to it, or a few feet onto the shoal side of it, so you can cast over the drop, let your flies sink, and retrieve them back up the face of it.

**Control of the drift.** Count time and speed of retrieve are the primary ways you can control your fly or flies. Cast long; the farther you can cast, the more bottom you will cover, and the more time your fly will spend down with trout. Try to make your count sufficient enough for your flies to reach bottom—usually from ten to sixty seconds. If it takes much longer than that, consider switching to a faster sinking line. Don't wait patiently for your fly to reach bottom and then immediately lift it back toward the surface with a fast retrieve. Instead, employ a slow stripping retrieve or even slower handtwist.

**On the water.** Always retrieve with your rod tip held low, or even slightly under the water. If you feel a take, even if it's just a tug, lift the rod to set the hook. Don't lift it violently; you don't want to break off a big trout stung by the hook and fleeing the other way. If you feel a tap, release the line and give a count or two for the trout to turn around and take the fly again. Lift the rod to see if a trout is on. If not, drop the rod, let the fly settle, and begin retrieving again.

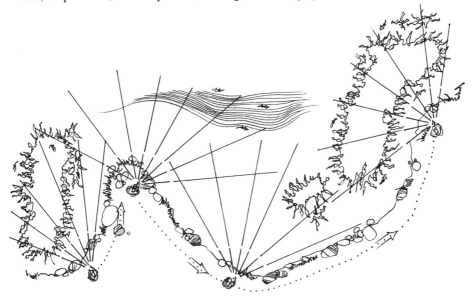

**The trout's point of view.** The trout will see the fly swimming slowly or creeping along, either on the bottom or just above it. Be careful to keep your fly above the weeds, so the hook point doesn't harvest a tendril of them. I've never seen a trout take a fly that trailed even a tiny bit of vegetation.

**RIG:**      CLEAR INTERMEDIATE OR WET-TIP LINE
**Method:**     Trolling to explore relative shallows

**Situations to solve.** When you first encounter any new stillwater, or when you're visiting an old and familiar one but have no clue what might be happening, it's often wise to launch and make a circuit of the shoreline. Begin studying the lake or pond's structure, looking for shoals, weedbeds, drop-offs, and features that attract trout. Watch for signs of visibly feeding trout, either cruising or rising. While you're scouting the stillwater, you can troll a fly, or pair of them, in the hopes of catching fish.

Whenever you find visible trout, you should fish for them. If you find a feature that looks worth sounding out, then fish that. Meanwhile, your fly is your finest exploratory tool: If you hook a fish, at least you've found that one. And in typical stillwater situations, you'll know you have found other trout, because they travel in pods. You'll also know the type of water in which the pods are working.

**Tuning the rig.** My favorite trolling rig for every type of water except the depths is a clear intermediate line; 10-foot, 4X base leader with a size 10 or 12 black or olive Woolly Bugger; and a size 14 or 16 TDC, a black midge pupa pattern, trailing on an 18-inch, 5X tippet. Both flies are modestly weighted. The depth such a rig attains, whether fished on a wet-tip or intermediate line, depends on the speed at which you troll it. Use your own favorite stillwater dressings, as opposed to mine, when you troll.

**Position and presentation.** Once you've moved out to water deep enough to fish with these slow-sinking lines, either make a long cast, 50 to 60 feet over the stern, or peel that much line off the reel, cast just 20 to 30 feet of it, and move off, letting water tension pull the rest of the line through the rod guides. If you're tubing, hold onto your rod while you troll. If you're in a pontoon boat, lock your rod into a holder, and if you're in any other kind of boat, either use a holder or lay the rod over the stern and lock the reel in somehow so that the handle can turn, but the outfit can't jump off the boat. Angle the rod tip down toward the water if possible or straight off the stern if not.

Make your circuit around the shore as close to it as you can get without getting hung up constantly. Use a zigzag pattern to fish both shallow and somewhat deep water: Nose in close to shore; then reverse course, and move 100 or 200 feet out. Not only does this give you a better chance to find trout at different depths, but it also allows you to spot any shoals or drop-offs If you want to make a quick circuit of a small body of water, or you want to move fast on big water, try to vary your course enough to show your fly over different depths, rather than staying off shore the same distance all the way around.

**Control of the drift.** How deep you fish will depend on how fast you travel. By rowing or finning fast, you can keep the flies up near the top, which is effective along the shore and for getting over such obstacles as submerged trees and boulder fields. When you slow down, you let the flies drop 4 to 6 feet deep. If you troll over shallow water and get hung up, speed up. When you move over deeper water, slow down to let the flies sink.

**On the water.** The best speed for trolling is a lot slower than the best speed for exploring. Try to keep your speed down: Kick your fins lazily in a tube, or stroke the oars lightly and infrequently in any sort of boat. It can be difficult to exercise such discipline. If you're moving somewhat faster than you should, and begin getting into trout in an area, slow down and fish it by either casting or slowly trolling.

**The trout's point of view.** The trout, whether it's cruising or simply idling in an area, will see the flies move into view, and will move to take one, if it looks like a natural for the area and if it's in the right location in the water column so that the fish deems it worth the trip up to take it.

## RIG:          FULL-SINK OR SHOOTING HEAD LINES

**Purpose.** The primary purpose of full-sinking lines, or a set of shooting heads, is to fish the deepest stillwater depths, but it might be better to think of them as tools for exploring the entire range of depths in lakes and ponds. You can fish most of these same levels with different line types, even the floater, if you rig with an indicator and weight on the leader or the flies, but you have to be patient in your count and in your retrieve. To get a fly deep with a floater or slow-sinking line, you must count it down forever. And to keep it there, you must refrain from retrieving it at anything but a crawl.

A range of full-sink lines in various sink rates, or a set of shooting heads, will get your fly to the desired depth much faster, anywhere from 5 to 40 feet down, and allow you to keep it there while you retrieve it at a modest clip.

**History/origins.** The largest improvements in full-sinking lines came in the last 10 to 15 years, with density-compensated lines that ensure that the entire length of the line rides at the same level in the water. Previous lines, which were thinner at the tip and had less weight inserted into the line matrix, rode up in the water out toward the fly. Density-compensated lines do not let the fly ride up above the belly of the line.

Shooting heads were first designed in the 1950s by steelhead fishermen who wanted lines that could be cast for distance. Shooting heads still provide excellent distance; you can lift one out of the water, load the rod with one backcast, and with a little practice, shoot up to 100 feet of line with relative ease. Their biggest advantage is that you can buy a set of heads that will sink at different rates but will all load the same rod, so you can switch them quickly.

**Knots and notes.** If you use full-sinking lines, then normal knots will do. Use blood and surgeon's for joining leader and tippet sections, improved clinch or Duncan loop for tying on flies. Shooting heads should have spliced loops at each end. The front of the shooting line and the butt of your leader should have loops as well, so that you can quickly change a head on the water. If you do it outside the rod tip, you won't have to restring the line through the rod guides each time you change heads.

Manufacturers have their own way to designate the sink rates of their lines. One of them uses type I through VI, with I an intermediate, and VI a bomb; another designates its lines as intermediate, slow-sinking, fast-sinking, extra-fast sinking, and high-density. You do not need all of these lines, but you should have a floating line, an intermediate, a fast sinker, and the fastest sinking line you can find. The set of heads that I use encompasses the full range, takes up little room in my boat bag, costs no extra for spare reel spools, and allows me to explore all the fly-fishable depths of any lake.

**Adjustments for conditions.** Four things can be altered on this rig: the weight of your flies, the length of your leader, the sink rate of the line you choose, and the amount of time you count down the line after each cast. If you don't mind counting a couple of minutes, you can fish down to 20 feet or so with less than the fastest sinker, but try to start with a line that might get you too deep, rather than one that

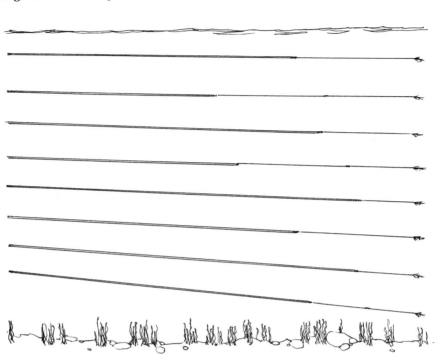

might leave you too shallow. Lines rarely sink as deep or as fast as we think they do. As you go deeper, shorten the leader.

**Rules for the rig.** Choose your line by the depth you'd like to attain and the speed at which you'd like to retrieve. If you use a fast strip, the fly will climb in the water column with all but a depth-charge line. If you're going to use a handtwist, then the flies are going to keep their depth, or sink even farther, as you retrieve them. Use a faster sink rate line for a faster retrieve and a slower sink rate line for a slower retrieve.

**Appropriate flies.** All types of sunk flies are appropriate with this rig. One type to consider that hasn't been mentioned yet for stillwaters is a floating nymph, which is usually tied to imitate portly dragonfly nymphs. Because dragonfly nymphs spend time on the bottom, they are often seen and eaten by bottom-cruising trout. The underbody is layered with closed cell foam before the fly is finished. When retrieved, the fly rides above the bottom, visible to trout, yet immune to snags.

**Situations to solve.** You'll use these sinking lines any time you climb into a float tube, pontoon boat, or anything else that floats and takes you away from shore. But not all folks own tubes or boats, and many times even those who do own them might find themselves wanting to fish a stillwater when what floats is at home. At other times, such as during damselfly and dragonfly nymph emergence migrations, usually in late spring and early summer, you may be better off fishing from shore. Those insects swim toward shore to emerge, and some theorize that a fly fished from a boat will be ignored by trout because it's swimming in the wrong direction. Whether it's true or not, an imitation cast from shore and retrieved back toward it will definitely be going in the right direction.

**Tuning the rig.** Select a sinking line or shooting head with the appropriate sink rate to reach the depths over which you're fishing. If the water slopes off gently to 5 or 10 feet, try a slow-sinking line, though many anglers find their intermediate or wet-tip line works just fine. If the water drops off more steeply toward 10 to 15 feet, then choose between your fast-sinking and extra-fast sinking lines. If you're on a point or along a plunging shoreline and the water drops off sharply toward water that is deeper than 15 feet, go for a high-density sinking line, or a type V or type VI.

The same rules apply to shooting heads: Choose among slow-sinkers, fast-sinkers, extra-fast sinkers, or even lead-core heads, which although common in saltwater fishing are rarely applied to trout fishing, and keep flies deep on the fastest retrieves.

**Position and presentation.** When you have no way to get afloat, your choice of casting positions is almost always defined by the nature of the shoreline. On a brushy lake, you'll be lucky to find any sort of casting position, though surprisingly a roll cast might be sufficient to get your fly to trout, even when using sinking lines. Make one roll to bring the line and fly to the surface; then follow quickly with another that rolls them out. Your distance will be modest, but since trout live in association with the shoreline, you might reach them.

Most often you'll have to choose among an elevated position above the water, which is bad for exposure but good for distance; a shoreline position level with the water, which is good for both exposure and distance; and a wading position that puts your backcast low to the water, which is bad for distance but good for reaching drop offs that you otherwise might not reach.

Whatever position the situation forces onto you, move into it without disturbing any trout in the area. Launch the longest casts you can. Distance is not always attainable, but try to get as much as you can. Cover all the water you can reach with casts fanned in an arc around you.

**Control of the drift.** Your countdown time and retrieve will dictate the depths you fish with the sink rate line you've chosen. Choose among a slow handtwist retrieve, a moderate retrieve with short strips, or a fast retrieve with long strips.

**On the water.** When you fish sinking lines, you're usually looking for the bottom. Use your initial casts to find it, counting each cast down a successively longer time until you either hang up or bring back weeds. Then shorten the count a few seconds and proceed to cover the water. In most places where you cast from shore, the shoreline will be sloped up toward you. Take this into account, perhaps accelerating your retrieve as the fly gets closer or using a floating nymph to let your line bottom out while your fly rides high.

**The trout's point of view.** If your count and retrieve are adjusted correctly for the water over which you're fishing, the trout will see your fly creeping, crawling, or swimming into sight near the bottom, as if heading toward shore for emergence.

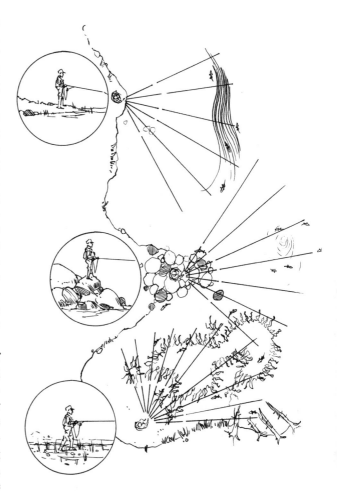

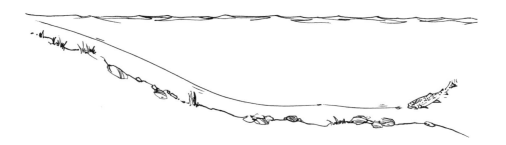

**Situations to solve.** Although mostly considered the best way to explore just the deepest depths, casting a full-sinking line or a sinking shooting head with a well-chosen line also allows you to explore the entire water column, from shallows just 5 to 10 feet deep, through middepths 10 to 20 feet down, to suspended depths of 30 and even 40 feet. In addition, full-sinking and shooting head lines are usually the most efficient way to show your flies to trout along the bottom, whether it's the bottom of the shallows or the bottom of the deeps.

The line type you choose will vary according to the structure you might be fishing, whether shallow shorelines and coves, deeper shoals, weedbeds from 10 to 30 feet deep, or drop-offs at any depth, where trout might be found cruising parallel to the shallow top, the deeper face of the slope, or down the edge, where the water drops into darkness.

**Tuning the rig.** Choose a line with a sink rate suited to the depth of water you're about to fish. If the water is shallow, continue to fish your intermediate or wet-tip line, or switch to a full-sinking or shooting head line with a slow sink rate. If the water is in the middle depths of 10 to 20 feet, use your fast-sinking or extra-fast-sinking line or a similar shooting head. If the water is deeper than 20 feet, use your fastest sinking line or shooting head, and vary your count time to find the depth at which trout hold.

**Position and presentation.** Fishing with full-sinking lines and shooting heads can be awkward from a float tube if it doesn't have an efficient line apron. Any line that is retrieved and allowed to fall in the water, rather than onto the apron, will sink, tangle around your fins, and cause problems that will commonly drive you to shore to solve. A poorly designed pontoon boat will give you the same problems, so try to address them before you launch. Sinking lines are best cast from an anchored craft.

Take your position over or to the side of whatever type of structure you want to fish: weedbed, shoal, drop-off, or suspended depths. Anchor at both ends if possible. Make your cast as long as grace allows, and use your first casts to establish the count needed to reach bottom. Use a faster sinking line than you think you need, and switch to a slower sink rate if necessary.

Once you've made contact with the bottom or with the depth you want to fish—you'll know you have if you catch a fish or feel a tug—then begin covering the water with a fan of casts either on one side of the boat or all around it. The more water you cover and the longer you keep your fly in the strike zone on each cast, the more trout you'll catch.

**Control of the drift.** You control the depth of the fly by the length of your countdown time and by the speed of your retrieve. If you can fish well with a type III line and a handtwist retrieve, you could also most likely use a type IV line and a slow stripping retrieve or a type VI line and a retrieve that is nearly a gallop.

**On the water.** Trout often take flies as they sink. The V-wake where the line penetrates the water should be traveling toward you at an even speed. If it stops, either the line has hit bottom or a fish has hit your fly. If it angles one way or the other, a trout is running with your fly. If that V makes a sudden rush toward you, you know a trout has taken the fly and drawn the line down or away from you. In any of these cases, set the hook with a long pull of your line hand while lifting the rod. You will have to move a lot of line to set the hook.

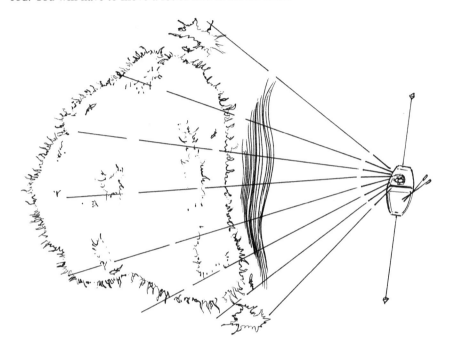

**The trout's point of view.** With normal sunk flies, the trout will see them moving along, from slow to fast depending on your retrieve, through their holding or feeding area. If you are using a floating nymph, trout often will be attracted to the strange but not alarming sight of the line moving along the bottom, perhaps sending up a trail of silt, and then once they notice the fly bobbing along behind, they might take it.

**Situations to solve.** When you arrive at a lake you've never fished before, it's always a good idea to scope the lake first. While you're doing that why not try trolling for trout in the process? Trolling not only gives you a chance at a trout but provides the most likely way to find trout when they're not visible. When you can't see trout, and you lack a depth finder to locate them, your flies are your next best exploring tool.

Trolling is also an excellent way to show your fly, or pair of them, to trout over features that might be dauntingly large—long drop-offs, big shoals, extensive weedbeds, or the length of a submerged stream channel. If you locate trout on any of these features, then you might want to anchor and focus on that specific area. However, you also might want to continue trolling, showing your flies to scattered trout or to trout that are cruising so fast down in the depths that you can't keep up with them while casting and counting flies down.

**Tuning the rig.** Select the proper line to tune the rig for the depth you want to fish. If the lake has much size or any evident depth, then start with a line that sinks faster than you might think necessary. Because it's difficult to keep trolling speed as slow as any retrieve you'd make from an anchored position, your flies are likely to run higher in the water on a given line than they would if you were anchored and casting. The exception is when you troll into a headwind from a float tube; the wind will hold you back, and your flies will drop lower. If you're rowing a pontoon boat or hard boat with a wind, you'll have to sit on your oars to slow yourself down. You can always switch to a slower sinking line if you come onto snags or weeds too often.

**Position and presentation.** Gear your trolling course to any potential water types that you scouted before you launched. Calculate your path to see as much of the lake as possible. Trolling is a method of scouting, so watch the shoreline and shallows for signs of visible trout as you go.

If you see no signs of where to fish, then take up a zigzag course along the shoreline. Choose your inside turning point based on the sink rate of the line you're using: close to shore if you're towing a slow-sinker, 100 feet out from shore if you're trolling with a fast-sinker, and perhaps 200 feet or more from shore if you're using an extra-fast sinking line. Some shorelines drop straight off into such depths that you can troll right along them with a lead core shooting head line. Others remain shallow for so far out that you need to use a slow-sinking line in the middle. Show your trolled fly at a variety of depths until you locate trout.

**Control of the drift.** Once you make your first cast, give the fly, or pair of them, time to sink, and either place your rod low over the stern or hold it in your hands with the tip just above the water if you're tubing. Your speed will adjust the depth at which your fly trolls. If you row vigorously around the rim of a large impoundment even with the fastest sinking line, your flies still might be just 5 to 10 feet down.

**On the water.** Though many believe trolling is not really fly fishing, others, including me, believe that not only is trolling a great way to find fish in a stillwater, but it also provides two of fly fishing's greatest thrills: the great thump of a trout hitting a fly while the rod is held in the hand, and the grand dance of a rod tip lying across the stern of a rowboat. The first will assuredly wake the drowsiest of float tubers, and the second will cause boaters to lose oars in their rush to grab a flailing rod.

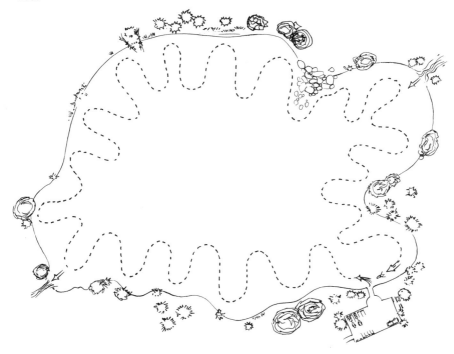

**The trout's point of view.** Who knows what a trout is doing when your trolled fly comes swimming into its view through the depths. The only certain thing is that the trout, first happy at the arrival of what looks like an easy meal and then stung by the hook, will be just as surprised as you are.

# INDEX